Richard William Church

Pascal and Other Sermons

Richard William Church

Pascal and Other Sermons

ISBN/EAN: 9783337160692

Printed in Europe, USA, Canada, Australia, Japan

Cover: Foto ©Lupo / pixelio.de

More available books at **www.hansebooks.com**

PASCAL

AND OTHER SERMONS

BY THE LATE

R. W. CHURCH, M.A., D.C.L.

DEAN OF ST. PAUL'S,
AND HONORARY FELLOW OF ORIEL COLLEGE, OXFORD

London
MACMILLAN AND CO.
AND NEW YORK
1895

NOTICE

ONLY two of these sermons were preached in St. Paul's: and only two before the period of the Dean's residence in London. The rest have been selected from his occasional sermons preached elsewhere than in the Cathedral during his tenure of the Deanery. Mr. Murray has given leave for the reprinting of the sermon on "The *Pensées* of Blaise Pascal," originally published in a volume entitled *Companions for the Devout Life*, and of the lecture on Bishop Andrewes, originally published in a volume entitled *Masters in English Theology*. By a like permission from Messrs. Parker, the sermon entitled "Adam; the Type of Christ" is reprinted from a volume of *Lent Sermons*. The sermon on "Foreign Travel" first appeared in a volume entitled *The Use and Abuse of the World*, and is here reprinted by the permission of the Society for the Promotion of Christian Knowledge. •

CONTENTS

SERMON XI

ASCENSION-TIDE

SERMON XII

EDUCATION

SERMON XIII

PAIN AND REMEDY

SERMON XIV

THE LIFE OF INTELLECTUAL SELF-SUFFICIENCY

SERMON XV

STRONG WORDS

SERMON XVI

THE MINISTRY OF WOMEN

SERMON XVII

FOREIGN TRAVEL

SERMON XVIII

RELIGIOUS DISAPPOINTMENTS

SERMON XIX

A PARTICULAR PROVIDENCE

SERMON XX

THE GREAT RESTORATION

SERMON XXI

THE TIMES AND SEASONS OF GOD'S WORKING

I

THE 'PENSÉES' OF BLAISE PASCAL [1]

"Out of the deep have I called unto Thee, O Lord : Lord, hear my voice."—PSALM CXXX. I.

THE Psalms, which are the records of the purest and loftiest joy of which the human soul is capable, its joy in God, are also the records of its dreariest and bitterest anguish, of the days when all seems dark between itself and God, of its doubts, of its despair. Their music ranges from the richest notes of triumphant rapture to the saddest minor key. The Psalms are the patterns and precursors of that mass of literature embodying the experience of the spiritual life which has grown up during the Christian centuries, and some examples of which are at this time proposed for our special notice. The Psalms contain the germs of it, and, like the Psalms, it varies widely in its scale and tone. It reflects the many sides, the countless moods, of the soul, in its passage through time, confronted with eternity and its overpowering possibilities. It tells of quietness and confidence, of strength and victory and

[1] Preached at St. James's, Piccadilly, 1875, as one in a course of Sermons on "Companions for the Devout Life."

C.S.,P.   B .

peace. It tells, too, of the storm, of the struggle, of the dividing asunder of soul and spirit ; of perplexities which can be relieved only by the certainties of death ; of hope wrestling, indeed, undismayed, unwavering, but wrestling in the dark, and, when beheld for the last time on this side the grave, still obstinate, but still unsolaced. Christian life may be upon the heights and in the sunlight ; the lines fall to it in pleasant places, and " the voices of joy and gladness are in its dwellings." But its lot may be also " in the deeps," where " all God's waves and storms have gone over it " ; where the voices are those of " deep calling unto deep amid the roar of the waterspouts," voices of anxiety and distress, of " majestic pains," of mysterious sorrow.

Such in the main is the voice of that book on which I am to speak to you, the *Thoughts*, as it is called, of Blaise Pascal. It is, as we know, a book of fragments found among Pascal's papers after his death, mainly relating to a projected apology for religion, and variously pieced together, according to the judgment of different editors. This is not the place to speak of its singular literary history, of the strange fortunes which have attended on it, of the fate which has given it so much interest for the soberest and deepest belief, and for the most mocking and most critical unbelief, of France—for Arnauld and Vinet, for Voltaire and Condorcet, for Sainte-Beuve. I shall say nothing of its apologetic value, as an argument in defence of Christianity, nor of its place in French literature ; nor of what it did, with other writings of Pascal, in bringing religious questions from the technical treatment of the schools

into contact with the ideas and language of common
life, to be subjects of keen and serious interest to
the educated and intelligent in all grades of society.
Nor must I dwell on that exquisite purity of
language which in itself makes it one of the most
instructive of moral lessons. In no writer since the
great Greek masterpieces has the "beauty born" of
simplicity and truthfulness "passed" so profusely
into style; a perpetual witness to all who hold a
pen against the dishonesty of conventional and
affected words, warning them of the first duty of
that exact agreement of word and meaning, of that
sincerity of the writer with himself as well as with
his readers, " *ce consentement de vous avec vous-même*,"
out of which, as a principle of composition, Pascal's
excellence grew. My business with it is simply as
a "Companion for the Devout Life"; an office
which it is not the less qualified to discharge that
it makes no formal or direct pretension to do so;
though it is not a book of devotion, nor a guide to
the details of Christian life, nor a body of medita-
tions or counsels, nor intentionally a record of the
history of a religious mind. Nothing was farther
from Pascal's thought than to venture on any such
task; nothing would have shocked him more than
the notion of painting himself. But in spite of
himself he has done so. And if character is
elevated and refined, and our loyalty to the unseen
strengthened, by seeing how one of the keenest of
human minds pierced into the truth of things, and
one of the noblest of human souls thirsted after
holiness, these Remains may profitably go with us
into our chamber, when we are alone with ourselves

and God.   They belong to the last years of Pascal's
short life, into which so much was crowded—years of
sickness and untimely decay.   They are the broken
words of a suffering and dying man, to whom truth
and reality, always precious, have become imperiously
supreme ; whose eye has become preternaturally
clear in discerning the greatness of man's destiny
and hope, the shows and shadows of his present
state ; and who has ceased to live for anything but
God, for the endurance of God's will, and the
imitation of His love, while here.

Pascal's "Apology," if it had been written, would
have been, not a treatise of pure argument, or an
analysis of the grounds of religious belief, but the
passionate expostulation of profound conviction on
the madness and unreason of indifference or loose
thinking on a matter of such importance, and such
high claims, as Christianity. (The religion of Pascal
is the religion of a converted man—of a man, I
mean, who at a definite time of his life had felt
himself touched and overcome by the greatness and
the reasonableness of things unseen, and had consciously turned to God, not from vice, but from
bondage to the interests of time, from the fascination of a merely intellectual life, from the frivolity
which forgets the other world in this.   His eyes had
been opened, and he had been brought "into the
deeps"—"the deeps" far below the mere surface of
custom and transient opinion ; the deeps of truth
about man's condition and God's greatness ; the
deeps of reality about moral good and moral evil,
the relation of eternity to time.   And he writes
"out of the deeps," as one absorbed and awe-struck,

and with every fibre strung, by his vivid consciousness of the strange contrasts, the inevitable alternatives, the mighty interests at stake, amid which
man's course is to be run. His view of religion
rises out of these solemn and unfathomable depths,
the abyss of life and pain and death, the abyss of
sin and ignorance and error, the abyss of redemption and of God's love. Even the mind of Pascal
was not large enough for everything ; these themes
absorb and dominate his imagination and thoughts ;
and, steadied and consoled as he certainly was by
his religion, and capable of the highest transports
of Christian gladness, his book is not one of those
which reflect the joy, the quiet order, the peace and
exultation of Christian life.

The book is a stern one—stern with the severity
of the awful vision of truth which had filled the
writer's mind, and before which he had.trembled ;
and its effort is to be strongly, lucidly, plainly *true*
about the real state of the case—true before the
judgment of the common sense of men of the world.
Pascal showed to the full that passion for simple,
unaffected, solid reality which was the characteristic
of the early days of Port Royal, of that mighty
but short-lived school, the greatest religious birth of
the French Church, before whose heroic and sublime
singleness of mind, and thoroughness of purpose, and
hatred of pretence and display, even the majesty of
Bossuet, and the grace of Fénelon, and the sweetness and tenderness of St. François de Sales, and
the grand erudition of the Benedictines, fall into a
second place. Pascal looks upon the world in which
he finds himself, and two things meet him. On the

one hand, the certainty of the moral law, the certainty
to conscience of its supremacy, the certainty of its
excellence beyond comparison over everything else
known to man ; and, on the other hand, the certain
facts of man's actual condition and nature, the
anomalies, the disorder, the contradictions, the
discords of his present state, the blinding and
oppressive mystery which hangs about all that we
are, and what we are meant for.   The old age of
the world, after all its long experience, finds
strengthening in it still the invincible consciousness
that there is nothing greater, nothing surer, than
right and duty, nothing more sacred than justice,
nothing more beautiful than love.   And yet this
divine idea of duty and right, man's distinctive
prerogative in nature, seems thrown for no purpose
into a world which is for ever contradicting it ; it is
reflected only in broken distortion on the troubled
surface of human society.   Pascal had felt as keenly,
perhaps, as men ever felt them, the triumphs of pure
intellect, in its clearness, its versatility, and its
strength.   He felt the immeasurable distance of
mind and genius above all the greatness of outward
and material things, above the pomp and glories of
riches and power, above all physical perfection.
Archimedes, he says, needed nothing of the grandeur
of " kings and captains and great men according to
the flesh " ; he won no victories, he wore no crown ;
but he was great in his own great order of intellect ;
the mathematician's enthusiasm kindles at his name—
" O how glorious was he to the intellectual eye "—
" *O qu'il a éclaté aux esprits.*"   But there is an order
of greatness higher than that of intellect.   " The

interval, which is infinite," writes Pascal, " between
body and mind, represents the infinitely more infinite distance between intellect and charity. "[1]   This
superiority in kind of moral goodness is Pascal's
fundamental axiom, and he, of all men, had a right
to lay it down.   The strong and nimble mind which
played with difficulties, and to whose force all
resistance yielded, the soaring imagination, the ambition of the explorer on the traces of unthought-of
knowledge, all that made and marked the matchless intellect of his time, the great geometer, the
great physicist, the great mechanist, master, too, of
the keenest satire and the most unapproachable
felicity of language—he and all that he is, bows
down before the unearthly greatness of charity, and
confesses the sovereign and paramount excellence of
moral perfections, the supreme claims of the moral
law of goodness.

And then, with this conviction as to the true law
of man's nature, what does he see round him ?   He
sees a world "out of joint," presenting the most
contradictory appearances, distracted by the most
opposite tendencies, with no remedy for its disorder,
no key to its riddles.   He pursues through all its
forms the contrast between man's greatness and his
littleness.   Read man in one way, and he seems
made for God and truth.   Read him in another, and

---

1   " La distance infinie des corps aux esprits figure la distance infiniment plus infinie des esprits à la charité, car elle est surnaturelle.
Tout l'éclat des grandeurs n'a point de lustre pour les gens qui sont
dans les recherches de l'esprit.   La grandeur des gens d'esprit est
invisible aux riches, aux rois, aux capitaines, à tous ces grands de chair.
La grandeur de la sagesse, qui est nulle part sinon en Dieu, est
invisible aux charnels et aux gens d'esprit.   Ce sont trois ordres
différents en genres."

nothing can express the interval which separates him from all that is holy, perfect, eternal ; his blind stumbling through an existence which has come from chance, the unmeaningness, the vanity of his life. How is it that he knows so much and can think so powerfully, and yet, after all, knows so little and so imperfectly ; why should his knowledge, just where it is most important, find an impassable barrier, and truth elude and betray him just where he most wants it ? To look at his great endowments, his wonderful achievements, his never-ceasing progress, he seems indeed the crown and glory and perfection of God's creation. But look at him again, in comparison with what his very powers enable him to see, the immensity, the inscrutableness of the universe, and he sinks into an insignificance which he has not the imagination to measure or the words to express. Lost in this little corner of creation, in this little breathing-time called life ; lost between the infinities of space, the infinities of time before and after, the infinities of greatness, the infinities of littleness ; lost "in the abyss of that boundless immensity of which he knows nothing," in those "terrible spaces of the universe which encompass him," [1]—what can he think of himself,

---

[1] " En voyant l'aveuglement et la misère de l'homme, en regardant tout l'univers muet, et l'homme sans lumière, abandonné à lui-même, et comme égaré dans ce recoin de l'univers, sans savoir qui l'y a mis, ce qu'il y est venu faire, ce qu'il deviendra en mourant, incapable de toute connaissance, j'entre en effroi comme un homme qu'on aurait porté endormi dans une île deserte et effroyable, et qui s'éveillerait sans connaître où il est, et sans moyen d'en sortir."

" Abîmé dans l'infinie immensité des espaces que j'ignore et que tu ignores." . . . " Je suis dans une ignorance terrible de toutes choses. . . . Je vois ces effroyables espaces de l'univers qui m'enferment . . ."

what can he think that he is worth?—"What is man that Thou art mindful of him, or the son of man that Thou visitest him?" Look at the things which he does *not* know, and his vaunts of knowledge seem childish. Look at the things which enchant him, the prejudices which enslave him, the basenesses to which he. can descend, and is the contempt of the cynic undeserved for so poor a creature? Look at the inevitable fact of death, of the decay which precedes it, or else the untimeliness of its blow, and is it possible to exaggerate the idle fruitlessness of such a lot, except as a link in an eternal and unfeeling chain of fate? So aspiring, so defeated, so undiscouraged ; with the strongest impulses to hope, but ever haunted by arguments of despair, he reveals, by fits and starts, his greater and better nature, in the originality of grand deeds and lofty characters ; but practically, and in the long run, he leads a .life which he might lead without God and conscience, guided by calculation of what is pleasant and prudent, calculating rightly in the main, often miscalculating, miserably and fatally. There he is, this marvellously compounded creature, strong even unto death, and yet unstable as water, crossing and contradicting himself through life ; the slave of nature, which yet bows to the spell of his power ; the slave of habits, yet their creator ; the slave of imagination, of which yet he knows the illusions ; the slave of opinions, for which he is yet responsible, and which he has contributed to accredit ; seeking and finding, and seeking afresh ; so ingenious yet so stupid ; so wise and yet so incredibly foolish ; able to do so right yet constantly doing so wrong ; balancing between good

and evil, sin and repentance, till the wavering is cut
short by death. And that, multiplied by the numbers
of mankind, is the broad aspect of human life.
The mass of mankind look at all this under the
sway of custom and habit, as a matter of course,
familiar as the routine of every day ; and they
take it all as it comes, they feel no surprise ; they
acquiesce and are content. But when they try
to look below the surface, then come the perplexities
and the enigmas. Then come the baffling problems,
and the contradictions which defy explanation. Our
instruments of knowledge fail us or play us false.
We are born with the instinct and idea of certainty,
and imply it in every act and argument; yet certainty
flies from our analysis and our verifying tests. If
we venture to search deeply, then come difficulties
following difficulties, till reason is giddy. Truth is
impossible without freedom of thought ; yet no
sooner is thought free than it eats away all certainty,
historical, moral, religious, scientific, till at last it
turns upon itself, and surrenders its own consciousness
of existence and freedom a prey and sacrifice to a
theory. We are distracted between rival claims on
our allegiance ; [1] between nature and broad common
sense and irresistible convictions—irresistible in spite
of all objections, and " reasons of the heart superior
to those of the intellect " ; [2] and on the other hand,

---

[1] "Qui démêlera cet embrouillement ? La nature confond les
pyrrhoniens, et la raison confond les dogmatiques. . . . Humiliez-
vous, raison impuissante : taisez-vous, nature imbécile : apprenez que
l'homme passe infiniment l'homme, et entendez de votre maître votre
condition véritable que vous ignorez. Écoutez Dieu."

[2] ("Le cœur a ses raisons que la raison ne connaît pas) on le sait en
mille choses. . . . Est-ce par raison que vous aimez ? "

the keen, subtle, finished conclusions of the reasoning faculty, apparently so faultless and impregnable in form, often so formidable and ghastly in their consequences.

What account is to be given of all this? In a well-known passage,[1] Pascal puts side by side the high and the low view of human life, apart from Christianity, in the persons of two eminent representatives respectively of those two views, Epictetus and Montaigne. One set of thinkers, like Epictetus, look only on the lofty side : they insist on man's greatness, and freedom, and moral power; they see in his moral nature the proof of his kinship with the Divine, the image and likeness of God. Another set, like Montaigne, can only smile and doubt, and mock at man's efforts after truth, at his pretensions to rise above the level of mortality; they catalogue his uncertainties, his mistakes, his failures ; they paint vividly his weakness, his ignorance, his shame. Both are right and both are wrong; right in the truth which they assert, wrong as to the truth which they overlook ; but both want the key which unlocks the puzzle, the central truth which reconciles the contradiction. Pascal will explain away nothing, will disguise and ignore nothing. He will put his standard and idea of life as high as Epictetus ; but he sees as clearly as Montaigne, the tricks that custom and imagination play; the treacheries of self-interest, the inconsistencies of goodness, the strange mixture in real life of the ridiculous and the pathetic, the gaps in our logic, the short-comings of our proofs ; he employs the

[1] The conversation with De Sacy.

exaggerations of Montaigne for the purpose of startling men from the trance and spell of mere habit, to realise the strangeness of what is most familiar, the precariousness of much that they take for granted. What is the explanation of these anomalies of man's condition, of the perplexities of his life—anomalies and perplexities which to those who see them are certain and crushing? Why is it that, as has been said, " Life is such a comedy to those who think, such a tragedy to those who feel?"[1] Pascal can see but one explanation to it. Man's greatness is greatness fallen ; it is royal great- ness, but the greatness, as he expresses it, of a king dethroned, dispossessed, disinherited, banished.[2]   A writer of our own time, as subtle and deep as Pascal, has, without thinking of Pascal, expressed Pascal's thought :—

" To consider the world in its length and breadth, its various history, the many races of men, their starts, their fortunes, their mutual alienation, their conflicts ; and then their ways, habits, governments, forms of worship ; their enterprises, their aimless courses, their random achievements and acquirements, the impotent conclusion of long-standing facts, the tokens, so faint and broken, of a superintending design, the blind evolution of what turn out to be great powers and truths, the progress of things, as if from unreasoning elements, not towards final

---

[1] Quoted in Greg's *Enigmas of Life*, p. 192.
[2] " La grandeur de l'homme est grande en ce qu'il se connaît misérable.   Un arbre ne se connaît pas misérable. . . . Toutes ces misères-là même prouvent sa grandeur.   Ce sont misères de grand seigneur, misères d'un roi dépossédé."   " Car qui se trouve malheureux de n'être pas roi, sinon un roi dépossédé ?"

causes, the greatness and littleness of man, his far-reaching aims, his short duration, the curtain hung over his futurity, the disappointments of life, the defeat of good, the success of evil, physical pain, mental anguish, the prevalence and intensity of sin, the pervading idolatries, the corruptions, the dreary, hopeless irreligion, that condition of the whole race, so fearfully yet so exactly described in the Apostle's words, ' having no hope and without God in the world,'—all this is a vision to dizzy and appal, and inflicts on the mind a sense of a profound mystery, which is absolutely beyond human solution.

"What shall be said to this heart-piercing, reason-bewildering fact? I can only answer, that either there is no Creator, or this living society of men is in a true sense discarded from His presence. Did I see a boy of good make and mind, with the tokens upon him of a refined nature, cast upon the world without provision, unable to say whence he came, his birthplace or family connections, I should conclude that there was some mystery connected with his history, or that he was one of whom, from one cause or another, his parents were ashamed. Thus only should I be able to account for the contrast between the promise and the condition of his being. And so I argue about the world; *if* there be a God—*since* there is a God—the human ·race is implicated in some terrible aboriginal calamity. It is out of joint with the purposes of its Creator. This is a fact—a fact as true as the fact of its existence; and thus the doctrine of what is theologically called original sin, becomes to me almost

as certain as that the world exists, and as the existence of God."[1]

If there is a remedy for this tremendous disloca-
tion, impossible as it must be to anticipate its nature,
it must be one adequate to the greatness of the
disaster.[2] And this disaster is the fundamental
supposition of that religion of which the Bible is
the record, and the Christian Church the creation
and witness. It rests on two great foundations :
a great verity of history, experience, and consciousness, man's double nature, his heights and depths,
his worth and his worthlessness, the inexplicable
fact of sin and all its consequences ;—and a great
disclosure which none could make but God, that
man's delivery and restoration are dear to his
Maker, that for man's sake the Highest was joined
to the lowest, Divine Power and Love to earthly
degradation and pain ; the Cross of Christ was the
Passion and Sacrifice of the Son of God. Christianity satisfies the conditions which it ought to
satisfy, if it is a religion for the world, a religion
to demand the attention of a serious man. It is
not bound to tell us everything ; it need not clear
up all difficulties. It must not be a privilege for
an aristocracy of thinkers. But it must be a full

---

[1] Newman, *Apologia*, p. 377. Compare Pascal : " Le nœud de
notre condition prend ses retours et ses replis dans cet abîme. De
sorte que l'homme est plus inconcevable sans ce mystère, que ce
mystère est inconcevable à l'homme." Faugère, ii. 155. See a
passage in Vinet's *Nouvelles Études Évangéliques*, p. 51 :—" Le
nombre de nos misères, leur gravité, leur perpétuel retour n'ont laissé
de choix aux esprits méditatifs qu'entre deux suppositions terribles :
ou le monde est disputé par un bon et un mauvais génie, ou il doit y
avoir au fond de notre histoire un épouvantable mystère."

[2] " L'incarnation montre à l'homme la grandeur de sa misère, par
la grandeur du remède qu'il a fallu."

counterpart to all those great and grave facts in which all men have a share, which make up our perplexity and our misery, and yet impel us to hope. This to Pascal's mind was the decisive point. He felt that the external appearances of a divine sanction in the case of Christianity were so ample and so strongly proved, relatively to the conditions of all our knowledge, as to satisfy his reason ; and his review of these converging and cumulative proofs, incompletely developed as we have it, shows with what originality and depth he had mastered the argument. But he wanted, and he found, more than this. For him, beyond the satisfaction of his critical reason, the overwhelming certainty of religion arose out of its deep and manifold correspondence with what he knew of himself and man; with what conscience told him of the moral law, and the world showed him of degradation and sin. It was not only that its credentials could bear the strain of inquiry ; what brought religion home to his inward sense of reality was that it had the key to the tormenting contradictions of nature, which he knew so well. And so with the difficulties attending it. The facts of experience, as well as the suppositions of religion, make it part of the disorder of the world that moral obstacles to truth are as great as intellectual ones. If religion is what it claims to be, it cannot but be a trial of hearts, a test of character and affections ; it must be the greatest choice that a man can make or refuse, if the choice is offered him ; it must take its place by right, first and foremost among the great things that belong to our moral life. It is a gift to the unworthy, a gift from Him whose disproportion to man is infinite, a gift of His mercy and remedial loving-kindness to their misery and despair; it is a thing which must be received on its own terms, and with the knowledge that the passions, the worldliness, the indolence of men, are its natural rivals and antagonists. Men complain that the tokens of God are indistinct and equivocal; what is this but an exaggeration of the warning of the Bible itself that its God is a "God that hideth Himself"—"*Deus absconditus*"—"hideth Himself" from idle curiosity and unwilling hearts; a warning to remember that the very starting-point of the Gospel is, that man, who was made for God, has lost God, and that the moral separation between God and man accounts for his not finding a God whom he does not care for, whom he does not love, from whom he shrinks. The danger, the plain but terrible certainty, that met Pascal's eye was, that men, while examining the claims of religion and its reasonableness, forgot the tremendous responsibilities of its judges. He who knew so well what intellect *could* do, knew what it *could not* do; and he knew that the decision in such a matter as religion lay not merely with the intellect alone, but with the whole complex nature of man. He knew the solemn truth that in the will, the affections, the conscience of man lay that which determined his creed, his character, his fate. To Pascal no religion could mean anything, or be anything, but one such as that described in the earliest hymns which welcomed the Gospel; one which "visited" men like "the dayspring from on high, through the

tender mercy of our God, to give light to them
that sit in darkness and in the shadow of death, and
to guide our feet into the way of peace"—one
which can call forth from man the thanksgiving,
" My soul doth magnify the Lord, and my spirit
hath rejoiced in God my Saviour . . . For He that
is mighty hath done to me great things, and holy
is His name." Pascal too, looking at the longings,
the agony of creation, looking at the long roll of
God's " noble works," has his Magnificat : " Therefore I stretch forth my arms to my Deliverer, who,
after having been foretold for four thousand years,
hath come at last to suffer and to die for me, at
the time and with all the circumstances predicted of
Him ; and by His grace I wait for death in peace,
in the hope of being united to Him for ever ; and
I live meanwhile rejoicing, whether in the good
things which it pleaseth Him to give me, or in the
evils which He sends me for my good, and which
He has taught me to endure by His example." [1]

And now, how does such a book, a book of conflict, so suggestive of intellectual perplexities and
troubles, serve as a " Companion for the Devout
Life "? How does it help devotion, the habits and
behaviour of the soul in what it has consciously to
do with its God ?

1. It does so by deepening the grounds of devotion, by elevating the level of religious thought, and
enlarging its horizon. Devotion, to be kept pure,
needs ideas as well as feelings. Its life and energy,
doubtless, are in the affections ; love, reverence, trust,
joy, hope, praise. But, as in a family, love is every-

---

[1] *Pensées*, ed. Faugère, ii. 198.

thing, yet love may run in poor and ill-directed and unworthy channels, and we ought to cultivate worthy and fitting ways for the exercise and training of our family affections, so it is in devotion. God will accept the true devotion of the most slenderly-furnished soul, of the narrowest mind, of the most mistaken sincerity; but affection and thought, feeling and truth, ought to have their just proportion to one another. On our knees we need to remember the deep abysses of judgment and mercy in which the foundations of our prayers are laid. We need to keep our mind in with the sense of what is real, and therefore must be so serious, in the familiar things which come before us in every prayer. There are two dangers to which devotion is exposed : it is in danger of becoming formal and uninterested, a sleepy routine ; it is in danger, too, of becoming artificial, fanciful, petty, of wasting itself in the un-chastened flow of feelings and words, of sinking into effeminacies and subtleties and delicate affectations of sentiment and language. This is no fault of Christian devotion ; it is the fault of the weaknesses of our affections, of the impurities and alloys even of our humility, our tenderness, our love. But there *is* the danger ; and I can imagine nothing better calculated to rebuke and correct all these " shadows of religion " than Pascal's clear, downright seriousness, and the startling boldness with which he faces the real facts of life and religion. It is all the more striking, that the book is not a finished work for the public use, but a collection of fragments which he never expected us to see, in which we surprise him, as it were, in private, putting down his thoughts as

they come, not for others but for himself, to test and
clear and ascertain his own ideas.   The great themes
which we are accustomed to in the consecrated
language of the church or the oratory—man's fall
and redemption, his needs, his strength, his law, his
hope—are here the subject of an appeal to men's
common sense and judgment, by a layman speaking
to laymen.   He wakens us up to see the real import
of our sacred oracles, by translating them into the
language of modern life, and that in one of its most
cultivated and perfect forms.   And, again, the great
commonplaces of human life, which are the property
of the moralist as much as of the preacher, he teaches
us to interweave with our prayers.   Others besides
him have dwelt on the strange contrarieties of human
nature.   Montaigne has done so with all his subtle
observation and irony.   Dryden did so with his
terrible strength of scorn.   Pope, in memorable lines,
almost paraphrased Pascal.[1]   But it is one thing to
make these tremendous antitheses the ornaments of
a brilliant work of art, and quite another to contemplate them before the Cross of Christ.   Pascal writes
of them with the continuous sense of their practical
recoil upon himself; he writes of them in the face of
God and death.   A thread of the deepest devotion
runs through the book; the great reasoner, the
accomplished writer, was the humblest and most
fervent of worshippers, meditating on the agony of
Christ, praying for the right use of pain and sickness,
giving rapturous thanks for having found his peace
in God. Agree with Pascal or not, you cannot help

---

[1] Cf. *Essay on Man*, ii. 1-34, with the passage, "Quelle chimère
est-ce donc que l'homme," etc., ed. Faugère, ii. 103.

learning from him *what it is* to think nobly and adequately of the great questions of religion ; you cannot help feeling with him that there are in them depths hard to sound, disasters and hopes which none can dare to make light of. It is difficult not to feel shame, in turning from these pages—so grand in their largeness and precision of thought, their burning and vivid convictions, their simplicity of expression—to our trite and mean conceptions, our contented apathy of prayer, our stilted and empty pomp of phrase, our thin and childish excitement ; to feel the strength with which he has seized the amazing wonders both of our condition and of God's remedy—" Say what you will," he writes, " there is something in the Christian religion which is astonishing "[1]—and then to come back to the superficial apprehension of them, with which we are, so many of us, satisfied, even in our attempts to lift soul and life out of the common grooves of custom.

2. I think the book has another use. If ever there were days which needed bracing and sobering lessons, they are ours. They need it all the more, because in that civilisation which affects us all, and which in so many of its results is in such contrast with the ultimate certainties of life as well as with the spirit of religion, there is so much to call forth admiration and gratitude, so much that is beneficent, excellent, noble. But many of us it certainly weakens, it certainly spoils, it certainly blinds. We sweep along in constant smoothness and order ; we lose our bearings amid the intoxication of new

---

[1] " On a beau dire, il faut avouer que la religion chrétienne a quelque chose d'étonnant."

knowledge, and the consciousness of new powers. We see but a portion of the field: out of the range of our sight are the miserable and the hopeless, a great army, who cannot understand the philosophy of optimism or the blessings of progress. And we who do, almost resent such eloquence as Pascal's ; it seems to us overcharged and unnatural ; we accuse him of the perverseness of painting life in colours unjustly and falsely dark. His severity is not *all* the truth. Many, happily, have found—I ought to say, have been granted—a sweetness, a liberty, an innocence, a tranquillity in living, or else a generous and pure delight in toil, which Pascal could not discover. But his severe view is a great side of the truth. It is a side which has impressed some of the greatest of mankind. It is an echo of *his* experience who said, " If in this life only we have hope in Christ, we are of all men most miserable." ·It is the tradition of the conflicts and temptations which have befallen those who have thought most deeply and felt most keenly, those who have wrestled most stoutly with the evil of their day. If our devotional life is to be the charm with which we may walk safely through so much that is threatening, if our prayers are not to be unmeaning ones, we need in them the tonic of these stern truths. Pascal's austere thoroughness and masculine plainness of speech is very useful to remind us when on our knees 'that neither life nor religion are the easy and soft things we sometimes take them to be ; that, be appearances what they may, there' are close at hand to us, every day, contingencies too terrible to speak of ; there are, at any rate, in the end, dread certainties which

nothing can avert. With our calm days of order and
peace, and our eager ones of triumph, amid the joys
of companionship and joint effort, the successive
achievements of power, the blessings of our homes,
it will one day be a happy thing for us to have
reminded ourselves of Pascal's solemn and pathetic
words, "The last act is always tragedy."[1] "I shall
die alone"—"*On mourra seul.*"

3. Lastly, no professed master of the spiritual life,
no book of practical piety, ever laid down more
distinctly the true method of seeking religious light.
It is implied in every line of Pascal that truth in
religion is absolutely, and from the very nature of
the case, dependent on moral purity and faithfulness.
"Revelation," as has been said, "was not given to
satisfy doubts, but to make us better men, and it is
as we become better men that it becomes light and
peace to our souls, even though to the end of life
we shall find difficulties in it and in the world around
us."[2]   It is the great warning of Pascal, that if men
would find and know God, they must begin by trying
to do His will; they must act according to the
greatness of the occasion, and to the laws not of one
part only, but of their whole human nature; they
must prepare their souls, habits and tempers and
will, as well as intellect.   God, the only God worth
seeking by man, the God not of scientific demonstration or theory,[3] but the living God of Abraham,
Isaac, and Jacob, the God of Jesus Christ, is revealed
only to the heart, the heart of the sincere, the

---

[1] "Le dernier acte est sanglant, quelque belle que soit la comédie
en tout le reste."
[2] Newman, *Parochial Sermons*, i. Serm. 18.
[3] *Pensées*, ed. Faugère, ii. 113-116.

modest, the patient, the self-governed, the loving. And as children who cannot walk learn to walk by walking, so we learn to feel the meaning and greatness of moral truth by acting under the sense of it, by listening in detail to conscience, by being true to what we hear in great things and small. No one ever insisted more earnestly than Pascal that to know we must obey. No one reminds us more impressively of the silent power of habits as they grow up, unwatched and unfelt; how, when we are trifling with self-discipline and prayer, we are laying the foundations of religious perplexity and trouble, clouding the inward eye, and enfeebling the moral taste, our power of insight and judgment, our power of *keeping* the sight of truth which once was given us.

These are not unfitting lessons to carry with us when we retire to recollect ourselves with God. How great a book that is on which we have been commenting, I need not say. The world is agreed on the marvellous gifts which it discloses. But that clearness and penetration of reason, that easy strength, that height and nobleness of thought which captivate our intelligence, that music of expression which charms our ear, are but foils to what is most essential and characteristic in it. It is a book which none can read, friend or enemy, without having it impressed on him that that which drew up this mighty soul to its full height was the ever-present vision of a God of righteousness and love, the reaching after the light of perfect goodness. That is what is shown in these reflections from its thoughts and feelings, broken and imperfect as they are. They show an enthusiasm, which even in its excess is heroic, for all that had the reality of moral excellence. They show one who was ready to count all things but loss for the sake of that Love, that Cross, which had revealed man's true perfection to man—not riches only, and pleasures, and honour and power, but greater things than these, the magnificent triumphs of intelligence, the joys of the discoverer, the glory and the delights of the pure reason. They show one alive to all greatness and all beauty, moulded for sympathy and for all delicate and all tender affections, to whom all was forgotten in the blaze of the glory of Christ's compassion ; to whom, above all beauty, was the beauty of charity, above all greatness the greatness of charity—that charity which Jesus Christ first made known among men. Such a book is no unsuitable " Companion for the Devout Life."

BISHOP BUTLER[1]

ONE of the famous books of the English language is Bishop Butler's *Analogy ;* according to the full title, which is not always kept in mind—*The Analogy of Religion, Natural and Revealed, to the Constitution and Course of Nature.* This great book, with the sermons which illustrate it, has had perhaps, directly or indirectly, more to do with the shaping of the strongest religious and moral thought in. England, in the generation which is now passing away, than the writings of any one who can be named. " Bishop Butler," wrote a great living statesman, " taught me, forty-five years ago, to suspend my judgment on things I knew I did not understand. Even with his aid I may often have been wrong ; without him I think I should never have been right. And oh ! that this age knew the treasure it possesses in him, and neglects."[2] But the *Analogy* passes for a hard book to ordinary readers. It passes for being difficult, not merely for the abstruse character of its arguments, but also for its rugged and obscure style.

[1] A Lecture delivered in Salisbury Cathedral during Advent 1880.
[2] The Rt. Hon. W. E. Gladstone to Mr. James Knowles, 9th November 1873, in a letter printed in the *Spectator* of 13th December 1873.

The obscurity of its style has, I think, been exaggerated : the writing may be said to be ungraceful,
careless, unattractive ; but it is not often that there
can be any doubt what the words mean, and what
the writer intends to say, though the thing that he
means to say may give some trouble to think about.
The difficulty of the argument generally is another
matter.   He means it to be taken and considered as
a whole ; and as a whole it is a long, connected, and
carefully jointed piece of work, in which one part
depends upon and tells on another, and one part has
to be kept in mind while considering another ; and
all the parts, and their relations to one another, have
to be remembered when judging of the effect as a
whole.   And this, of course, is difficult.   It is the
difficulty of keeping together, as in a vice or frame,
and in their proper order, all the pieces of an
intricate pattern ; it is the difficulty of following out
the parts, and play, and working, of a complicated
machine like a steam-engine ; it is the difficulty of
mastering a mathematical demonstration, or a legal
argument ; it is the difficulty of thinking out, and
keeping before the mind's eye, the effects of moves
of chess, or of cards at whist.   It requires close
attention, and clear head, and a good memory.
Without these, no doubt, the *Analogy* is a difficult
book, though the main difficulty, after all, resolves
itself into the necessity of reading with serious
purpose and care, which is always, to many persons,
a difficult thing.   But even if a person cannot
thoroughly master the argument, its tone and spirit,
·and manner of looking at things, is so remarkable, so
high, so original, so pure, and calmly earnest, that

great interest may be taken in it, and an infinite
amount of good may be learned from the book, even
by those who are baffled by difficult argument.

I do not intend to go into the argument of the
book, into the special reasonings by which Bishop
Butler shows how great and how solid a thing
religion is, and by which he meets the difficulties
and objections which are raised against it. I only
wish to try and illustrate the tone and spirit which
are characteristic of his writing. Christianity may
be written about or may be defended in many
different ways, and with very different tempers and
even objects. There is as much to be learned from
Bishop Butler's tone and manner as there is from
the substance of his reasonings. I will only remind
you of the main idea on which his whole argument
is founded. It is the idea of the unity of religion,
and all that we know of the system of the world,
and what we call nature ; the idea that in its great
features and appearances, in its apparent rules and
methods, in its wonderfulness and unexpectedness,
its perplexities, its difficulties, its seeming breaks
and imperfections, religion, before and after the
Gospel, in that side which it presents to us in this
world, is all of a piece with what we find in this
world—with the wonderful though familiar scene
and system of fact, which is the only thing of which
we yet have experience, or of which we can· form
reasonable conceptions ; that the religion given us
in the Bible, alike in what it has done and does, and
in what it does *not* do, follows, often to our surprise,
the same lines, which are not matters of conjecture
or inference but of certain fact, known and felt of all

men in the experience of life. Religion is not, perhaps, what we might expect, if we were constructing
an Utopian system out of our own imagination.
Religion *is* what we might be quite prepared for, if
we seriously considered what we see and know of the
world into which we are come, and in which we have
our lot. We know how easy but how idle a thing it
is to imagine a world made without the anomalies,
the troubles, the insoluble mysteries, which nothing
can here get rid of in nature and human life. If religion comes to us with apparent contradictions, and
seeming to do only half its work, giving us light
but only to a certain point, relieving our pains and
remedying our sin, but not completely, showing us
something of the next world, but little in comparison
with what it conceals, answering some of our
questions and fulfilling some of our longings, but
leaving much unsatisfied—this is only what we have
been familiar with from our birth, in the world
which, for all that, we believe was given us to dwell
in by God who is just and wise, and who, in the
mercies of grace and redemption, carries on the
same system and acts on the same principles as
those to which we are accustomed in our daily
contact with the laws and realities of nature. This
is what Butler means by the Analogy of Religion,
Natural and Revealed, to the Constitution and
Course of Nature. This is his great idea, the idea
which possesses him, and governs all his thoughts.
I will not pursue this further, but will go on to notice
some of the special features of his way of writing.

1. The first thing that I should say is how *real*
he is. Don't think this a matter of course, or an

easy matter for a writer, especially a writer on difficult subjects. A writer is not always able to master
his own thoughts, and say what he wants to say ;
and he is tempted to say something which comes
next to it or looks like it, but is not the thing itself.
"Think what you mean to say, and say it,"[1] is a very
good rule, but an easier one to praise than to follow.
But at whatever cost of clumsiness or awkwardness,
Butler always says the thing that he means to say—
that thing, and not another. " Everything is what
it is, and not another thing,"[2] is an odd, characteristic
axiom of his, which in various forms he is very fond
of. " Things and actions are what they are, and
the consequences of them will be what they will be ;
why then should we desire to be deceived ? "[3]
" For after all, that which is true must be ad-
mitted, though it should show us the shortness of
our faculties." [4] " As we cannot remove from this
earth, or change our general business on it, so neither
can we alter our real nature. Therefore no exercise
of the mind can be recommended, but only the
exercise of those faculties you are conscious of."[5]
And therefore he lays it down as the first law of a
writer that he is " not to form or accommodate, but
to state things as he finds them."[6] And this
honesty and reality of writing is the outward vesture
and form of the mind within, severely trained to the
strictest truth and honesty of thinking. Open-eyed,
cautious, watchful against the tricks and idols of his
own thoughts, the things that come before him he

---

[1] " Look in thine heart, and write ": Sir P. Sidney, Lloyd's *Life*,
p. 105.   [2] Butler's *Works*, Ed. 1836, ii. Pref. xxiii.
[3] ii. 100.   [4] i. 205.   [5] ii. 205.   [6] ii. Pref. v.

tries to see as they are—to see them, not as they
are talked about, or appraised by temporary or accidental opinion, but in their solid, plain simplicity ;
to see them, not as they are shaped by the action of
the imagination, but according to the exact measure
of our knowledge and evidence, whether more or less
limited ; to see the truth, not one-sided and exaggerated, but balanced and completed by all that
bears on it ; not trusting itself to precarious and
arbitrary *à priori* reasonings, but resting on foundations, however homely and unambitious, of facts
within our reach. We feel in every page and every
word the law that writer and thinker has imposed
on himself, not only to say nothing for show or
effect, but to say nothing that he has not done his
best to make clear to himself, nothing that goes a
shade beyond what he feels and thinks ; he is never
tempted to sacrifice exactness to a flourish or an
epigram. A qualm comes over the ordinary writer
as he reads Butler, when he thinks how often heat
and prejudice, or lazy fear of trouble, or the supposed
necessities of a cause, or conscious incapacity for
thinking out thoroughly a difficult subject, have led
him to say something different from what he felt
authorised to say by his own clear perceptions, and
to veil his deficiencies by fine words, by slurring
over or exaggerating. If only as a lesson in truth—
truth in thought and expression—Butler is worth
studying. He is a writer who, if there is any reason
for it, always *understates* his case ; and he is a writer,
too, from whom we learn the power and force, in an
argument, of understatement, the suggestion which it
carries with it both of truthfulness and care, of

strength in reserve. He never wastes a word in fine writing, but he never spares one when it would make him more intelligible. His writing bears the impress of that severe economy and thriftiness of material which comes from a man having taken great trouble to arrange and prepare his work. With him, with all his abounding wealth of ideas, of penetrating and widely-travelled thought, the question about any particular idea or phrase is, not, as it is with so many of us, whether it is clever, or telling, or brilliant, or a favourite one, but, first and foremost of all, whether it is true, and then, whether it is in place. And so you feel in reading him that he is not writing an essay, or weaving an ingenious and original argument, or constructing a theory on paper, but that he is " in touch," as soldiers call it, in actual contact with the solid realities of our state, our life and our fate.

2. Hence that singular seriousness which is so remarkable a characteristic of his books. ˙ He is as serious, it has been said, "as a gamester"; he is as serious as a physician, with life and death hanging on the clearness of his thoughts and the courage of his resolve; as serious as a general with a terrible and evenly-balanced battle on his hands. Such people are impatient of talk, and ornament, and literary cleverness; and so is he. With him the questions which were bandied about among ingenious and witty reasoners, about the truth and evidences of religion, were no questions of words or speculation, no mere interesting philosophical or historical problems, but of far more immediate and more tremendous earnest than anything else in the world could be. Coming to him from ordinary, even religious, writing on the argu-

ments for Christianity, the objections to it, and the
answers to them, is something like the difference
when, after having read in books and newspapers of
trials in courts of justice, we actually find ourselves
present at a real trial, with living men before us in
deep earnest, and with great issues, perhaps life and
death, depending on the debate. There is a breadth,
a quiet business-like plainness about his way of
dealing with questions, a recognition of their difficulty as well as a sense of their seriousness, which
produces an entirely different effect from mere
subtlety, eloquence, passion, or even strength of
thought. Calm and self-contained as he is, he
nevertheless is "the man whose eyes are open,"
who walks among all these things habitually
all day long, as if he were looking at them from
"the certainties of death," with all their issues and
endless possibilities ; he loses patience, not because
men disbelieve, or doubt, or hesitate—he has a strange
forbearance for them if they are serious—but because
they will not open their eyes to see what is certainly
at their doors—because they trifle and play with
questions, on the face of them so eventful and so
awful, which cannot be put off, and on which men
must take their side.

Mr. Pitt is reported to have said of the *Analogy*,
that it was a book which opened as many questions
and raised as many doubts as it solved. Of course
it does. No one can expect to sound the "great
deeps" of God's judgments, the mysteries of His
Being and Government, without meeting difficulties
which defy human understanding. This would be
true of any discussion, going deeply and sincerely

into a subject in which our only possible knowledge can be but " in part," seeing " through a glass darkly." But Butler's object is not to remove all doubts and difficulties, which in such a matter as religion, with light and faculties like ours, is obviously impossible ; but to put doubts and difficulties in their proper place and proportion to what we do see and know, in a practical scheme of life and truth, and in a practical choice between God and the rejection of Him.

As men are haunted by a permanent sense of the vice of the world, or its disease, or its pain, he was haunted by a sense of the flippant irreligion of his age. The absurdity of a shallowness which affected to see nothing in the claims of Christianity, or to give it up as exploded, was a torment to his love of reasonableness. The insolence which dared to mock at so solid and grave a thing irritated and perplexed him. It weighed on him as if it was a kind of public insanity such as is spoken of in Dean Tucker's anecdote of a conversation with him, when he speculated on the question whether whole communities might not like individuals go mad.[1]

" Reflections of this kind," he says, after showing how terribly, even if unequally, vice is sure to be punished in the natural course of things, " are not without their terrors to serious persons, the most free from enthusiasm, and of the greatest strength of mind ; but it is fit things be stated and considered as they really are. And there is in the present age a certain fearlessness with regard to what may be hereafter

---

[1] Bartlett's *Memoirs of Bishop Butler*, p. 93. Cf. "There really should be lunatic asylums for nations as well as for individuals." Sydney Smith, *Letters on American Debts*, 1844.

under the government of God, which nothing but an
universally acknowledged demonstration on the side
of atheism can justify ; and which makes it quite
necessary that men be reminded, and, if possible,
made to feel, that there is no sort of ground for being
thus presumptuous, even upon the most sceptical
principles." [1]   You notice the continual under-state-
ment, and the undercurrent of suppressed irony that
runs through the passage.   But calm as he is in
appearance, you are made aware what a store of
keen feelings lies hid under this grave demeanour ;
and sometimes it is provoked and bursts forth.
" It is indeed a matter of great patience to reasonable men, to find people arguing in this manner ;
objecting against the credibility of such particular
things revealed in Scripture, that they do not see the
necessity or expediency of them. . . . The presump-
tion of this kind of objections seems almost lost in the
folly of them.   And the folly of them is yet greater
when they are urged, as usually they are, against
things in Christianity analogous or like to those
natural dispensations of Providence which are matter
of experience.   Let reason be kept to ; and if any
part of the Scripture account of the redemption of the
world by Christ can be shown to be really contrary
to it, let the Scripture, in the name of God, be given
up ; but let not such poor creatures as we go on
objecting against an infinite scheme, that we do not
see the necessity or usefulness of all its parts, and
call this reasoning ; and, which still farther heightens
the absurdity in the present case, parts which we
are not actively concerned in." [2]

[1] i. 53.   [2] i. 255.

3. Corresponding to this grasp and feeling of reality, is Butler's ever-present sense of the inexpressible greatness of the universe where we are, of its Maker, and Master, and Ruler, of the present reality and awfulness of its government and laws, of the unexplored, unapproachable, unimagined provinces and distant spaces of that infinite empire, of the wonders and mysteries which compass us about, which are in every breath we draw and every word we speak. It is, of course, obvious to any one, the moment he thinks at all, that the most common things are full of what is inexplicable, and far more marvellous than are the marvellous things which modern science has shown us. — " How or why came I here? What is life? What is death? How does life begin? Why does it end? How am I made, soul and body, waking and sleeping? What is it that I am really looking at when I look at the stars above, or the flowers below, or at the invisible things which only the microscope reveals?"—But everybody does not think of these things, or thinks and forgets. But Butler was always and habitually thinking of them. That was the feature of his mind : that he never lost hold on these thoughts, never let custom or other things close his eyes or raise a mist between him and them. It was his *power*, the greatest power perhaps that he had, that what his reason told him was certain and true, he was able continually to see, and feel, and imagine, to be true and real. He had the power of faith. And in a measure he makes his readers feel it, if they have any serious attention in them. The truth is that when those familiar but most wonderful and most solemn things which

belong to our everyday existence and conduct come to be really seen and felt by an open-eyed observer, who can write them down literally as they literally are, the effect is one of novelty and surprise. There are passages in Butler, when we read between the lines of his words, that at first sight look so dry and commonplace, which seem to open a glimpse of the very foundations of the world and nature.

And with this sense of the greatness of God, and the daily wonders of His government; this consciousness kept up without effort, or affectation, or break, of His presence and eye ; this vivid apprehension of what must be the thoughts about right and wrong " in a mind which sees things as they really are," [1]— there is joined an equally characteristic and equally permanent sense of how very little we can really know of all the vast world about us, the plan on which it is administered, the meaning of its appearances ; how very narrow and confined our knowledge is even of ourselves, and much more of what is outside of us. We hear a great deal in these days of a Philosophy of Ignorance, which says that we know so little, we are so cut off from all knowledge of the unseen world, we get into such puzzles about understanding even right and wrong, that it is no use to try and know anything but what we can see and handle, and submit to experiment, and therefore we may live without God in the world. Butler, if he had lived, would have flamed into wrath and sarcasm against such affectation or perverseness of ignorance; against men who turn away their eyes from what the world is full of, and then complain that they

[1] ii. 226.

cannot see. Any pretence was his abhorrence, and
certainly he would not have spared the pretence of
blindness, the pretended impossibility of seeing any
marks of God.

But when we have carried our knowledge as far
as we can go, and we can carry it relatively very far,
then begins the vast immeasurable domain of what
we *do not*, of what we *cannot* know, while we are
here. Compared with this our knowledge is indeed
—not total ignorance, but the knowledge, as he
says, of children. Its very imperfection should make
it infinitely precious to us ; but it should make us
modest, cautious, slow to rash assertion and bold
denial. It should make us measure our words when
we talk of God and His ways, of what He *ought* to
do, and what He *must* do. If we only realise how
little we can see into His counsels, we shall always
feel that we are on very dangerous ground in such
talking. " There is, as I may speak, such an expense
of power, and wisdom, and goodness in the formation
and government of the world, as is too much for us
to take in or comprehend. Power, and wisdom, and
goodness are manifest to us in all those works of
God which come within our view ; but there are
likewise infinite stores of each poured forth throughout the immensity of the creation ; no part of which
can be thoroughly understood without taking in its
reference and respect to the whole ; and this is 'what
we have not faculties for." " This surely should
convince us that we are much less competent judges
of the very small part which comes under our notice
in this world than we are apt to imagine. 'No
heart can think on these things worthily: and who is

able to conceive His way? It is a tempest which no
man can see; for the most part of His works are
hid.   Who can declare the works of His justice?
for His covenant is afar off, and the trial of all
things is in the end'; *i.e.* the dealings of God
with the children of men are not yet completed,
and cannot be judged of by that part which is
before us."[1]

4. In Butler we find one of the most remarkable
instances of what a modern writer[2] has called "the
enthusiasm which lies under the language of reserve."
Reserved he is, as every one knows.   But under the
mask of that calm, cold, dry reserve of language,
ever on guard against show or excess, ever warning
us against what he calls the "deluding and forward"
faculty of imagination, lies the deep, steadily burning
fire of enthusiastic interest in his great subject and
cause.   His reserve is prosaic ; but his deepest conviction is that only in the affections, purified and
exalted, lies the happiness of man.   He will not be
carried away by appearances.   To the brilliant
declamations with which we are so familiar, on the
wondrous conquests of science, he coldly says, with
a touch of his peculiar irony, "knowledge is not our
proper happiness.   Whoever will in the least attend
to the thing, will see that it is the gaining not the
having it which is the entertainment of the mind.
Indeed, if the proper happiness of man consisted in
knowledge considered as a possession or treasure,
men who are possessed of the largest share would
have a very ill time of it : as they would be infinitely more sensible than others of their poverty

---

[1] ii. 226, 227.   [2] Sir Henry Taylor.

in this respect. . . . Men of deep research and
curious inquiry should just be put in mind not to
mistake what they are doing. If their discoveries
serve the cause of virtue and religion . . . or if they
tend to render life less unhappy, and promote its
satisfactions, then they are most usefully employed :
but bringing things to light, alone and of itself, is of
no manner of use, any otherwise than as an entertainment and diversion. Neither is this at all amiss if it
does not take up the time which should be employed
in better work." [1]

His strict habitual attention to justice and proportion is curiously shown in the way in which he
urges people who will not be good, to be at least
as little bad, to do at least as little evil, as they can.
" Since the generality will not part with their vices, it
were greatly to be wished they would bethink themselves, and do what good they are able, so far only as
is consistent with them. A vicious rich man cannot
pass through life without doing an incredible deal of
mischief, were it only by his example and influence.
. . . Yet still, the fewer of his obligations he neglects,
and the less mischief he does, the less share of the
vices and miseries of his inferiors will lie at his door,
the less will be his guilt and punishment." [2] Without
forgetting the formidable aspect of the doctrine of
justice—"if there be at all any measures of proportion, any sort of regularity and order in · the
administration of things, it is self-evident that ' unto
whomsoever much is given of him shall much be
required,' "[3]—he calmly contemplates justice at the
low end of the scale as well as at the high one, and

---

[1] ii. 233.   [2] ii. 269.   [3] ii. 270.

exhorts men who are rich to employ their wealth in
doing good, that so they "may expect the most
favourable judgment which their case will admit of
at the last day, upon the general, repeated maxim of
the Gospel, that we shall then be treated ourselves as
we now treat others."[1]   He is deeply impressed with
the poorness of everything here : the poorness of
human life, the poorness of our knowledge, the poorness of our acquaintance even with religion, the poorness and unsatisfactoriness of all ways possible to us of
examining and proving it.   All is "poor" which man
has or can do in any sphere.   "Indeed, the epithet
poor may be applied, I fear, as properly to great part
or the whole of human life, as it is to the things
mentioned in the objection.   Is it not a poor thing
for a physician to have so little knowledge in the
cure of diseases as even the most eminent have? to
act upon conjecture and guess where the life of
man is concerned?   Undoubtedly it is ; but not in
comparison of having no skill at all in that useful
art, and being obliged to act wholly in the dark."[2]

This is the gist of his teaching.   Human life is
indeed in itself a poor thing, but it is a practical
thing, because it is a part of something, the greatness
of which no thought can fathom and no words
express.   In his narrow, limited condition—how
narrow, how strange, how limited, it is almost
impossible to overstate—he yet is under the government of God.   He is a real part of that infinite,
incomprehensible kingdom.   Its mystery is reflected
on his life and fate.   He has part in its hopes.   He
really touches it at many points though he is utterly

[1] ii. 360.   [2] i. 333.

unable to comprehend it. As these points incidentally touch Butler's argument, they strike out from its hard texture a flash of feeling. His language takes unconsciously a colour of poetry. Religion is a matter for "awful solicitude," for it is that on which "man's whole interest and being, and the fate of nature depends."[1] Physically, "the earth our habitation has the appearances of being a ruin";[2] morally and politically he looks on the "infinite disorders of the world";[3] he sees "a scene of distraction." Revelation, when it touches its greatest confines, "cannot be supposed to give any account of this wild scene for its own sake."[4] What a picture, with all its various suggestions, is presented in that idea, to which he reverts more than once, of children, and of the poor, being strangers in a world in the possession of others ; "the poor who are settled here, are in a manner strangers to the people among whom they live":[5] children find "grown people settled here in a world where they themselves are strangers."[6] These touches of imagination and feeling come in the midst of austere argument or statement ; they come naturally and unforced ; they give us a momentary glimpse, the more interesting because rare, into the depths of a great mind.

Butler, intellectually, compared with other distinguished philosophical divines, may be said to have thrown himself systematically, throughout the various parts of his argument, as contrasted with more subtle or learned reasonings, on common sense—on that practical and homely sense of truth

---

[1] i. 268.   [2] i. 244.   [3] i. 57.
[4] i. 311.   [5] ii. 344.   [6] ii. 304.

and reality, gained by continued and varied dealing
with the affairs of life. But then it is the common
sense of a man who not only knows, but feels, as he
says, " that what is to come will be present ; that
things are not less real for their not being the objects
of sense." [1] To such common sense the world is very
different from what it is to ordinary people. It is
only common sense, *if* Christianity is what it claims
to be, that a man should bow in awe and adoration,
and be thrilled with exulting hope. It is only common sense, *if* Christ be risen, that St. Paul should
count all things but loss for Him, and live and die
for Him. And no enthusiasm of love and joy could
be too great for the soberest common sense, if all
that we believe of God and our interest in Him is
indeed real : not words or ideas, but solid fact.
And to Butler it is so. If the love of God, he says,
" be indeed at all a subject, it is one of the utmost
importance." [2] In that age of cold decorum in the
pulpit, himself the example and champion of calm
reason, he was deterred by no fashionable sneers at
fanatics and enthusiasts from anticipating, before
Wesley, all that was deepest and truest in the
Methodist appeal to the heart. He threw back a
sarcasm on the fashionable preaching of his age,
which had its sting in truth. " We are got," he
says, " into the contrary extreme to enthusiasm
under the notion of a reasonable religion ; so very
reasonable as to have nothing to do with the heart
and affections, if these words signify anything but
the faculty by which we discern speculative truth." [3]
. When he comes to speak of this side of religion, in

[1] i. 274.   [2] ii. 196.   [3] ii. 194.

his sermons on the Love of God, he is not afraid of
soaring as high as the loftiest flights of contemplative
devotion. Through his restrained and measured
diction, restrained and measured both from temper
and habit, and from the awfulness of the subject,
shines the intense faith of adoring contemplation ;
you see a soul to which is present that vision of
God's goodness and beauty, which transported St.
Theresa, St. Francis, and the poet of the *Paradiso.*
"Consider then : when we shall have put off this
mortal body, when we shall be divested of sensual
appetites, and those possessions which are now the
means of gratification shall be of no avail ; when
this restless scene of business and vain pleasures, which now diverts us from ourselves, shall
be all over,—we, our proper self, shall still remain ;
we shall still continue the same creatures we are,
with wants to be supplied, and capacities of happiness. We must have faculties of perception, though
not sensitive ones, and pleasure or uneasiness from
our perceptions, as now we have. . . .

" Recall what was before observed concerning the
affection to moral characters : which, in how low a
degree soever, yet is plainly natural to man, and
the most excellent part of his nature : suppose this
improved, as it may be improved, to any degree
soever, in the spirits of just men made perfect ; and
then suppose that they had a real view of that righteousness which is an everlasting righteousness ; of the
conformity of the Divine Will to the law of truth, in
which the moral attributes of God consist ; of that
goodness in the Sovereign Mind, which gave birth to
the universe ; add, what will be true of all good men

hereafter, a consciousness of having an interest in what they are contemplating ; suppose them able to say, 'this God is our God for ever and ever': would they be any longer to seek for what was their chief happiness, their final good ?   Could the utmost stretch of their capacities look further ?   Would not infinite, perfect goodness be their very end, the last end and object of their affections, beyond which they could neither have nor desire ; beyond which they could not form a wish or thought ?

"Consider wherein that presence of a friend consists, which has often so strong an effect as wholly to possess the mind, and entirely suspend all other affections and regards ; and which itself affords the highest satisfaction and enjoyment.   He is within reach of the senses.   Now, as our capacities of perception improve, we shall have, perhaps by some faculty entirely new, a perception of God's presence with us in a nearer and stricter way ; since it is certain He is more intimately present with us than anything else can be. . . . What then will be the joy of heart which His presence, and the light of His countenance, who is the Life of the universe, will inspire good men with, when they shall have a sensation that He is the Sustainer of their being, that they exist in Him ; when they shall feel His influence to cheer and enliven and support their frame, in a manner of which we have now no conception ? He will be in a literal sense their strength and their portion for ever.

"When we speak of things so much above our comprehension as the employment and happiness of a future state, doubtless it behoves us to speak with all modesty and distrust of ourselves. But the Scripture represents the happiness of that state under the notion of 'seeing God,' 'seeing Him as He is,' 'knowing as we are known,' and 'seeing face to face.' These words are not general or un-determined, but express a particular, determinate happiness. And I will be bold to say that nothing can account for, or come up to, these expressions, but only this—that God Himself will be an object to our faculties, that He Himself will be our happi-ness ; as distinguished from the enjoyments of the present state, which seem to arise, not immediately from Him, but from the objects He has adapted to give us delight. Let us then suppose a person tired with care and sorrow, and the repetition of vain delights which fill up the round of life. . . . Suppose him to feel that deficiency of human nature before taken notice of, and to be convinced that God alone was the adequate supply to it. What could be more applicable to a good man in this state of mind, or better express his present wants and distant hopes, his passage through this world as a progress towards a state of perfection, than the following passages in the devotions of the Royal Prophet? They are plainly in a higher and more proper sense applicable to this than they could be to anything else. 'I have seen an end of all perfection.'—'Whom have I in heaven but Thee, and there is none upon earth that I desire in comparison of Thee. My flesh and my heart faileth, but God is the strength of my heart, and my portion for ever.'—'Like as the hart desireth the water-brooks, so longeth my soul after Thee, O God. My soul

is athirst for God, yea, even for the living God ;
when shall I come to appear before Him ? '—' How
excellent is Thy loving-kindness, O God ; and the
children of men shall put their trust under the
shadow of Thy wings. They shall be satisfied with
the plenteousness of Thy house ; and Thou shalt
give them drink of Thy pleasures, as out of the
river. For with Thee is the well of life, and in Thy
light shall we see light.' . . . ' Blessed is the people,
O Lord, that can rejoice in Thee : they shall walk
in the light of Thy countenance. . . . For Thou art
the glory of their strength, and in Thy loving-kindness they shall be exalted.'—' As for me, I will
behold Thy presence in righteousness ; and when I
awake up after Thy likeness I shall be satisfied with
it.'—' Thou shalt show me the path of life ; in Thy
presence is the fulness of joy ; and at Thy right
hand there is pleasure for evermore.' " [1]

What is there to tell of Bishop Butler's life ?
Not much. A meagre biographical sketch, a few
fragments of letters, perhaps of sermons, a few
signatures in parish books in a Berkshire parish, and
at Stanhope in Northern Weardale, where he wrote
the *Analogy*, a few faded traditions, a few doubtful
anecdotes, a few portraits, a few articles of domestic
use, are all that remain, all that the interest of
admirers have been able to collect. Born at
Wantage, at school among dissenters at Tewkesbury,
suddenly leaving them to go into Orders, at college at
Oriel, preaching at the Roll's Chapel, buried in retire-
ment at Stanhope, discussing metaphysics in Queen
Caroline's closet—he at last emerges into public office.

[1] ii. 216-222.

Bristol, St. Paul's, Hampstead, Auckland Castle, Bristol Hot Wells, Bath, connect themselves with his later years. But he left scarcely a trace anywhere. They tell at Stanhope that he was an impetuous and fast rider; they tell at Bristol that he used to walk late into the night in his garden discussing deep matters with his chaplain. At St. Paul's, where he was Dean for ten years, no scrap of his handwriting remains in the cathedral books. They have a silver jug of his at Oriel, and a silver coffee-pot at Auckland Castle. The house and church at Stanhope have been rebuilt. The favourite retreat at Hampstead, once the house of Sir Harry Vane, has been modernised, and the painted glass with which it was ornamented dispersed. The palace at Bristol where he lived was burnt by the mob in the great riots in 1831, and remains in ruins. Perhaps a wall, or more doubtfully, some windows and enclosures at Auckland, were his work. When he was dying, he ordered all his sermons, letters, and papers to be burnt. No one knows what became of most of his books; yet he must have had a library, for he was a scholar and a reader, as well as a thinker.

But he passes across the scene of history a spiritual, impersonal influence, and like the author of the *Imitation of Christ* the man is lost in his mind and writings, and in those deep and solemn thoughts, the clear, calm utterance of which it was given him to unfold to us.

The fragments, such as they are, which show him in private intercourse, show him such as we should expect, very real and measured in his views of life, temperate and serious in his views of duty. They show him a man of " plain living and high thinking." He was one who, as is shown in his remarkable sermons on Self-Deceit and the Character of Balaam, was accustomed to take his own measure. He was a man of business, and clear-headed in affairs, who had meditated with his usual carefulness and breadth of thought on riches and power; and he was of a princely spirit in the use of them. His first act on going to Durham was to subscribe £400 a year to the Newcastle Infirmary. It is said that he refused the Primacy. He certainly refused to take Durham under conditions which would have reduced the ancient splendour of the see. " Increase of fortune," he writes to a friend who congratulated him on his preferment to Durham, " is insignificant to one who thought he had enough before; and I foresee many difficulties in the station I am coming into, and no advantage worth thinking of, except some greater power of being serviceable to others ; and whether this be an advantage depends on the use one shall make of it ; I pray God it may be a good one. It would be a melancholy thing in the close of life, to have no reflections to entertain oneself with, but that one had spent the revenues of the bishoprick of Durham in a sumptuous course of living, and enriched one's friends with the promotions of it, instead of having really set oneself to do good, and promote worthy men ; yet this right use of fortune and power is more difficult than the generality of even good people think, and requires both a guard upon oneself, and a strength of mind to withstand solicita-

tions greater—I wish I may not find it—than I am
master of." [1]

There is the same measuring of things as they
are, the same undazzled looking forward to the
future as it is to be, in a letter in which, after describing the interest and beauty of his new home at
Auckland, and his plans for improving it, he goes
on :—" I seem to have laid out a very long life for
myself ; yet, in reality, everything I see puts me in
mind of the shortness and uncertainty of it : the
arms and inscriptions of my predecessors—what
they did and what they neglected, and (from accidental circumstances) the very place itself,[2] and the
rooms I walk through and sit in.   And when I
consider, in one view, the many things of the kind I
have just mentioned, which I have upon my hands, I
feel the burlesque of being employed in this manner
at my time of life.   But in another view, and taking
in all circumstances, these things, as trifling as they
may appear, no less than things of greater importance,
seem to be put upon me to do, or at least to begin ;
whether I am to live to complete any or all of them
is not my concern." [3]

One more glimpse we have of him; it is in a
series of letters, preserved at Lambeth, describing
his last days, written by his chaplain to Archbishop
Secker, his schoolfellow and friend.   They are really
touching, for they tell simply, from day to day, a
story of great weakness and depression, in a strong
and patient soul, borne with resignation and devout

---

[1] Bartlett's *Memoirs of Bishop Butler*, p. 116.
[2] He had, no doubt, been there from Stanhope in Bishop Talbot's
time.
[3] Fragment of a letter to the Duchess of Somerset (1751).

C.S.,P.   E

composure, and of the deep and anxious affection of his friends. But they show him only silent, lying in hopeless but unmurmuring feebleness of body. They preserve no deathbed sayings, or deathbed traits, except the " emotion and kindness " of his farewells. It was his fate, after his death, to be persistently slandered for gloomy superstition and unfaithfulness, even for final apostasy to Rome, by anonymous writers, who, as it turned out at last, were men who, holding preferment in the English Church, claimed to avow and teach Arianism.

Butler's epitaph in Bristol Cathedral has been written by Southey, and it is one of those epitaphs which are worthy of their subject. When applied to, to write it, Southey hesitated. An epitaph, he said, ought to be precise and faultless ; and his own rule in writing had always been to think as much as possible about what he had to say, and as little as possible about the manner of saying it ; however, he would try. He sent it, and it was submitted to the Canon in residence, the great Hebrew scholar of the day, Dr. Samuel Lee, who boldly ventured to criticise and correct Southey's English. Happily there was present on the spot a young Fellow of Butler's College, Mr. C. P. Eden, afterwards a distinguished tutor and preacher at Oxford. He earnestly remonstrated against any attempt to mend what Southey had written. It was a delicate matter for him to interfere, but his interposition was successful ; and we owe it to him that the epitaph was not spoilt. I conclude with that portion of it which speaks of Butler's distinguishing work as a Christian teacher :—

Others had established the Historical and Prophetical grounds
of the Christian Religion,
And that sure Testimony of its Truth,
Which is found in its perfect adaptation to the heart of man.
It was reserved for him to develop
Its analogy to the constitution and course of nature ;
And laying his strong foundations
In the depth of that great argument,
There to construct another and irrefragable Proof ;
Thus rendering Philosophy subservient to Faith ;
And finding in outward and visible things
The type and evidence of those within the veil.

III

BISHOP ANDREWES[1]

BISHOP ANDREWES holds an important place in the line of those English divines who have affected the course of English theology. Only two years younger than Hooker, his life and his influence were prolonged for more than a quarter of a century after Hooker's comparatively early death.[2] He had been Hooker's contemporary, a student and labourer in the same field, perhaps his friend, certainly his admirer, in the later years of Elizabeth; and when Elizabeth's world, and Hooker's, closed with the sixteenth century, Andrewes lived on, and won his fame in the new world which opened with the seventeenth. His mind and character were those of a man who had come to middle age, and passed beyond it, under the last of the Tudors.[3] With this training and experience, the main work of his life coincided nearly with the reign of the first of the Stuarts.[4] Thus, though belonging

---

[1] Delivered at King's College in 1877, being one in a course of Lectures entitled " Masters in English Theology."

[2] Hooker, b. 1553. Andrewes, b. 1555.
Hooker, d. 1600. Andrewes, d. 1626.

[3] Eliz., d. 1603.

[4] James I., d. 1625. Andrewes, d. 1626.

to Hooker's generation, he lived to see Charles I. on the throne, and Laud in his first bishopric, and to be looked up to and studied by the men of Laud's generation as the greatest living theologian of the English Church. He is the connecting link between Hooker and Laud,[1] and after Laud, Cosin and Jeremy Taylor and Hammond, Ken and Bull, Beveridge and Bishop Wilson.[2]

Of Andrewes' long life there is not much to be said. It was the life, during the first part of it, of a severe and resolute student, unsparing of time and labour. His morning hours of study were to the last jealously guarded ; the rare exceptions to his usual

[1] See Hallam, *Const. Hist.*, ii. 62. *Literature*, ii. 308.

[2] The following comparative dates may be convenient :—

Hooker.	Andrewes.	Bacon.	Field.	Donne.	Laud.
b. 1553; M.A., 1577;	b. 1555; M.A., 1578;	b. 1560-1; Gray's Inn, 1577; In Parlmt., 1584;	b. 1561;	b. 1573;	b. 1573;
Temple, 1584; Boscombe, 1591; E.P. i.—iv., 1594; E.P. v., 1597; d. 1600.	St. Paul's, 1589;	1584;		At Linc.'s Inn, 1590;	
	..		Linc.'s Inn, 1594;	With Essex, 1596;	M.A., 1598;
	..	..	..	..	
	Dean of Westmr., 1601; Bp. Chiches., 1605; Bishop Ely, 1609;	.. Sol.-Gen., 1607; ..	... d. 1616.	M. 1603, or 1604; ... Ordained, 1613?	President St. John's, 1611; Dn. Glouc., 1615;
	Bp. Winton., 1619; ..	Chancellor, 1618-19; Sentenced, 1621;	..	.. Dn. St. Paul's, 1621;	Bishop St. David's, 1621; Bp. B. & W., 1626;
	d. Sept., 1626.	d. April, 1626.	..	d. 1631.	Bp. Lond., 1628; Abp. Cant., 1633.

sweetness and gentleness of temper were provoked
by those who disturbed these hours. "They were
no true scholars," he used to say, "who came to
speak with him before noon." He became specially
distinguished as a "Catechetical" teacher, both at
College and in London, and he was "deeply seen in
cases of conscience." At St. Paul's, where he was
Canon, he read the Divinity Lecture three times a
week in term time ; and he is described as walking
about the aisle, ready to give advice and spiritual
counsel to any who sought it. At Westminster,
where he was Dean, he took the greatest interest in
the boys of the school. He would come into school
and teach them himself, during the absence of the
master. Bishop Hacket, a Westminster scholar under
him, records his care about their studies and the books
they read, and describes his walks to Chiswick "with
a brace of his young fry," and his "dexterity in that
wayfaring leisure, to fill these narrow vessels with a
funnel."[1] When he was called into public employment, he lived, as great Church officers did in those
days, through a round of sermons, Court attendances,
and judicial or ecclesiastical business, varied by occasional controversies and sharp encounters, on paper or
face to face, with the numberless foes and detractors
of the English Church and State ;—from great Car-
dinals, like Bellarmine and Duperron, to obscure
sectaries, like Barrow and Mr. Traske, the reviver
of a mongrel Judaism.[2] It was the life of many men
of that period. What is specially to be noticed in

---

[1] Henry Isaacson's *Life*, with Notes, in Mr. Bliss's edition of
Andrewes, vol. vii. pp. vii., viii., xviii., xxxvi.
[2] Bliss's edition, vii. pp. ix., 81.

his case, is the high standard which was recognised both in his learning and his life. " Our oracle of learning " ; " the renowned Bishop of Winchester " ; " the matchless Bishop Andrewes " ; " that oracle of our present times "—these phrases of Bishop Hall express the admiration and reverence of his contemporaries. He was a man in whom scholars like Grotius and Casaubon acknowledged an erudition and an enthusiasm for wide and thorough knowledge akin to their own. Bacon, remembering in his day of trouble his " ancient and private acquaintance " with Andrewes, who survived him by a few months, submitted his writings to his friend's criticism, and took pleasure in unfolding to him the great plan of the *Instauratio.*[1] Andrewes was himself an observer and lover of Nature. " He would often profess that to observe the grass, herbs, corn, trees, cattle, earth, waters, heavens, any of the creatures ; and to contemplate their natures, orders, qualities, virtues, uses, etc., were ever to him the greatest mirth, content, and recreation that could be, and this he held till his dying day."[2] And he was not only an observer, but in some departments an experimentalist. He was one of the few to whose sympathetic interest, as an observer of Nature, Bacon felt he could confidently appeal in his physical investigations, and in his daring attempt to put the knowledge of Nature on a new and sound basis. Andrewes had also, in an eminent degree, what was the characteristic virtue of his time. He was always on the watch to seek out the promise of ability and worth in the poor and friendless, and to

---

[1] *Letters and Life of Bacon*, Spedding, vii. 371-375.
[2] Isaacson, p. vi. ; Spedding, *Bacon*, iv. 24, 63.

encourage by a noble liberality the learning of others.
Loaded with preferment, after the custom of his day,
he turned his revenues to large and public uses.   He
selected poor scholars and helped them.   He was
attentive, in a degree which attracted notice, for it
was not common in the bishops of the time, to the
claims upon his purse of the churches, institutions,
or estates entrusted to his stewardship.   He put his
houses in good repair.   He discharged out of his own
income debts which he found hanging over a school
or a hospital.   He largely increased their permanent
endowments, either by his gifts or his good husbandry.
Bacon's thoughts turned to him as one likely to help
towards the expense of costly researches and experi-
ments.   " He was single," Bacon writes, " and he was
rich."   And he was one of those large givers who
prefer in their lifetime to incur the suspicion of parsi-
mony rather than fall in with the mere conventional
fashion of munificence expected from the wealthy.[1]
In an age of much self-seeking, and many unscrupulous ways of getting rich, he was acknowledged
and honoured as an example of genuine public spirit
in his strict and conscientious method of administration, in his patronage, and in an expenditure which,
when the occasion called, could be princely.

All evidence attests the loveableness of his nature.
The lives of scholars, especially of scholars in the
days of Andrewes, have not usually had much to
attract and interest those who do not share their
aims and employments.   But in the pictures which
have been preserved to us of the relations between
friends, there are few things more charming than

---

[1] Isaacson, p. xiv., *note.*

what is disclosed of the effect produced by Andrewes'
character and converse on the illustrious scholar
who had sought a refuge in England from the
intolerance and persecution, first of Geneva and then
of Paris, Casaubon. The graciousness, considerate-
ness, sympathy, with which Andrewes first welcomed
Casaubon, growing, as the two men came to know
each other better, into an affectionate tenderness, a
delight in one another's company, not only among
their books but in recreation, in visiting sights, in
the enjoyment of the open air, are exhibited in
Casaubon's letters.   Casaubon's able biographer, Mr.
Pattison, no favourable judge of Churchmen, or of
those who spend their lives in the pursuits to which
Andrewes devoted his, is not insensible to the noble
and beautiful friendship between the two men, or to
the attractions and sweetness of Andrewes' character.
"Of all those whose piety was remarkable in that
troubled age," says another discriminating, though
not more lenient or friendly, writer, Mr. Gardiner,[1]
"there was none who could bear comparison for
spotlessness and purity of character with the good and
gentle Andrewes. Going in and out as he did
amongst the frivolous and grasping courtiers who
gathered round the King, he seemed to live in a
peculiar atmosphere of holiness, which prevented him
from seeing the true nature of the evil times in which
his lot had fallen." Perhaps in this he was not
singular. It may be doubted whether any of us
fully understand the true nature of either the good
or the evil of the times in which our lot is cast.
We, looking back to the past, can see much evil and

[1] *History of England*, 1603-1616, ii. 33.

much good that the men of the past could not
distinguish or recognise when it was near them and
round them. But it would be well for the men of
any age if they loved the good and hated the evil
which they do recognise, with the sincerity and
single-mindedness of Andrewes.

But the best men are under the prejudices and
delusions of their time, and Andrewes was no exception. He was under the prejudices and delusions which surrounded the thrones and the persons
of the Tudors and the Stuarts, as all were who
served them. He is said to have been one of the
bishops who sanctioned the burning of the Arian
Leggat.[1] To us this is rightly and naturally
shocking. It was not shocking, but necessary and
right, to the whole religious world of the day—to
Archbishop Abbot, who pressed it on and canvassed
the judges who ordered it ; to the great Puritan party.
It was not shocking to the Church historian, Fuller ;
it was not shocking to Neal, the historian of the
persecutions of the Puritans.[2] It is almost a greater
surprise and disappointment to find Andrewes one of
the majority in pronouncing for a divorce in the
shameful Essex case, in which the harsh and narrow-
minded Abbot, to his lasting honour, took the side
of right and truth, though with the feeblest reasons,
against wickedness and folly in high places.[3] What
blinded the eyes of Andrewes in a case which to us
seems so clear, we cannot tell, for his reasons for his
opinion are not preserved. Yet he was not one

[1] Pattison, *Life of Casaubon*, 331 ; and Gardiner, ii. 43-45.
[2] Hook, *Life of Abbot*, pp. 267-70.
[3] Gardiner, ii. 92-96 ; Hook, *Life of Abbot*, p. 272.

who feared the face of man, even of the King. But in those troubled days, when men were reaping the penalties of the sin of many generations, and when the rebound from superstitious submission to the Pope had created the superstitious faith in the Divine Right of Kings as the only counterpoise to it, there seemed to be a fate which, in the course of a Churchman's life, exacted, at one time or other, the tribute of some unworthy compliance with the caprice or the passions of power ; and the superstition must have been a strong one which could exact it from such a man as Andrewes to such a man as James.

But Andrewes was an important person not so much by what he did—by a policy and an administration—and not so much even by what he wrote, as by what he was known to be, and by what he was known to think and hold on the questions of his day. Unlike Hooker, who was a writer, and a man little seen in the great world, Andrewes was by calling a preacher, and one who moved much in society, and left his mark on it by the qualities which tell on society—quickness and brightness of parts, a ready and perfect command over large stores of knowledge, the strength of an original and well-furnished mind acting through rapid comprehension, play, and nimbleness of wit, and with this a sharpness and force of expression which made words remembered. It was this power which gave him his influence· with James ; and it is seen in his Sermons, of which the outward form is in curious contrast with the substance. In matter, no sermons like them had yet been preached in the English Church. If the stupendous facts of the Christian Creeds are true, no attention,

no thought is too great for them ; and their greatness, their connections, their harmony, their infinite
relations to the system of God's government and
discipline of mankind, and to the hopes and certainties of human life, are here set forth with a breadth,
a subtlety, a firmness of touch, a sense of their reality,
a fervour and reverence of conviction, which have
made the Sermons worthy and fruitful subjects of
study to English theologians.   They bear the marks
of what we know they had, the most careful meditation, the most unsparing pains in arrangement and
working out.[1]   But to us of this day, it no doubt
does surprise us to be told that—as was certainly the
case—they were the most popular and admired
sermons of the time.   We hardly know how far in
their present shape they are skeletons, which were
filled up and illustrated in actual delivery.   But a
hearer of our day would be at once overwhelmed
by the profusion and rush of ideas, and disconcerted
by the sparseness of expansion and development.
The majestic and connected eloquence which made
Hooker's style so remarkable is absolutely wanting.
There is depth of thought and depth of feeling,
fertility, energy ; there are passages which disclose
the imaginative and poetic side of a rich and
beautiful mind ; but the style is like the notes of
the unceremonious discourse of a very animated and
varied talker rather than the composition of a preacher.
In its quaintness, its perpetual and unexpected
allusions, its oddly-treated quotations, its abrupt and
rapid transitions, its fashion of tossing about single
·words, it is of the same kind as the style of much of

[1] Isaacson, pp. xxv., xxxvi.

Bacon's writings, especially his speeches.   It belongs,
in point of literary character, to the age before
Hooker.   It abounds in those quips and puns which
are the almost invariable resource of early humour,
playful or grave ; in passages, too, of powerful irony,
though the form of it sometimes raises a smile.
Bacon, indeed, used to send his writings to Andrewes,
" to mark whatsoever should seem to him either not
current in the style, or harsh to credit and opinion, or
inconvenient for the person of the writer." [1]   Such a
style satisfied and pleased the day, though it does not
satisfy or please us ; and we wonder, perhaps, that,
after a different standard had been set by Hooker, it
could be endured.   But students of English thought
and literature are not deterred by the harsh fashions
of Bacon's writings, and students of English theology
will find, under the quaint form of Andrewes' Sermons,
enough to justify his reputation as a divine, both in
his own day and since.

I am glad to recall some comments on Bishop
Andrewes' style, made long ago by a writer who has
since become famous, and whose remarkable gifts
the world learned in their full extent only at the
moment when illness has disabled for the time one
of the deepest and most original minds of our time.
" Andrewes," wrote   Dr.   Mozley in   1842,[2] " has
peculiarities of style, partly belonging to his age
and partly his own, which considerably prejudice us
against him at first, and to which, accustomed as we
are to so much more flowing and regular a way of
writing, we can never quite reconcile ourselves ; but

[1] Spedding, *Bacon*, iv. 141.
[2] *British Critic*, Jan. 1842, pp. 173-175.

with these peculiarities of his own, he has also
felicities of his own, which are displaying themselves
at every step.   His theological explanations show
the connection of one great doctrine with another,
the bearing of one great fact of Christianity upon
another, with admirable decision and completeness.
He is so quick and varied, so dexterous and rich in
his combinations ; he brings facts, types, prophecies,
and doctrines together with such rapidity ; groups,
arranges, systematises, sets and resets them with
such readiness of movement, that he seems to have
a kind of ubiquity, and to be everywhere and in
every part of the system at the same time. . . . He
has everything in his head at once ; not in the sense
in which a puzzle-headed person may be said to
have, who has *every idea confused* in his mind because he has *no one idea clear*, but like a man who
is at once clear-headed and *manifold*—if we may be
allowed the word—in his ideas, who can do more
than apprehend one point clearly or many dimly—
can apprehend, that is to say, many keenly.   And
this peculiarity has a good deal to do with the
peculiarity of his style : it is obviously a natural
one, and expresses the working of his own mind.
He is never longer in stating a thing than he can
possibly help, because his mind being always, as
it were, two or three steps ahead of his pen, he
lays down the point in passing on his way to something else, and therefore does not apply himself
more to it than is necessary in the way of business ;
what he is going to say, occupies him ; what he
is saying, he only says, and no more. . . . His
sermons, in fact, have both the advantages and

disadvantages, whatever these may be, of being
more like very copious and connected notes for discourses than discourses themselves.   They have
the terseness, freshness, and condensation of ideas
first put together, together with their want of form
and polish ; though we gather from Andrewes' contemporaries, that the delivery made up considerably for this deficiency."   And the critic notices
especially two points :   1. Andrewes' method of
hammering the same idea into his hearers again
and again.   " He is never tired of using the
same word.   The idea, ever thus renewed, and
recreated, as it were, gains strength and power by
the mere act of repetition, and each successive blow
comes down with increased effect."   And 2. The
animation of his discourse.   " Whatever faults he
may have, he never sleeps : he is always on the
move in one direction or another.   Incessant aim
and activity is the pervading characteristic of his
sermons ; his shortnesses, quaintnesses, his multiplied
divisions ; his texts wielded with such dexterity, and
ever at hand—ever, as it were, on service—all keep
up the stirring and business-like character of the
scene ; all are at work fulfilling their various tasks
and parts in the construction of the discourse, and
occupying themselves like bees in their hive :—

Et munire favos et dædala fingere tecta." [1]

Merely, however, as a preacher, as a master, in
those early days, of the language and rhetoric of the
pulpit, Andrewes would claim less interest than
Donne ; for in Donne there is not only the matter,

[1] *British Critic*, Jan. 1842, pp. 193, 202.

but the not unsuccessful effort after form and art which Andrewes entirely neglected. But Andrewes was primarily a theologian ; and his theology has permanently influenced the range and character of theological thought in the English Church.

Andrewes' theological opinions were formed about the same time, and under the same circumstances, as Hooker's. The two men had much in common, both in their strong recoil from the popular traditions and systems which, under Elizabeth, had more and more loudly claimed to interpret and represent exclusively the English Reformation ; and also in the positive ground which each was disposed to take, as the true and authentic basis of the teaching of the English Church. Both, too, had in common that devotional temper, those keen and deep emotions of awe, reverence, and delight, which arise when the objects of theological thought and interest are adequately realised, according to their greatness, by the imagination and the heart. Hooker made the first, at any rate the most conspicuous, venture to cut across the grain of public prejudice. But Hooker, great as he was—and the Englishmen of Shakespeare and Bacon's age could not fail to recognise his greatness—was yet but an obscure country parson, who may be said to have failed in London, and who certainly was not much seen in the houses of the great. Andrewes not only followed for a quarter of a century after Hooker's death in the path which Hooker had opened, but Andrewes was the companion and trusted counsellor of the holders of power. He was one of the greatest and most considered men in England, rising to the high places, one after another, of the Church; in the opinion of some of the wisest observers, the only fit man for the highest.

In Andrewes, as in Hooker, we come on a wide divergence from the language of the early theologians of Elizabeth, and from the way in which they presented the relative importance and proportion of different parts of the doctrinal system of the Church. Before it is said that this was a departure from the spirit of the Reformation, it ought to be brought to mind what the Reformation was. It was not a thing in all its parts done, finished, completed for good. Part of it was final—the independence of the National Church, the repudiation of superstition and corruption; part could not be accomplished at once. It started as a progressive and tentative effort to mend things which had been long and deeply injured, to put straight things which the custom of centuries and the ignorance of the day had turned awry; but it looked on this as a gradual process, which it was too much to hope to see done at a stroke, and which was to exercise the wisdom and patience of years to come. It cannot be sufficiently remembered that in James I.'s time, and in Charles II.'s time in 1662, the Reformation was still going on as truly as it was in the days of Edward VI. and Elizabeth. The English Reformation was, theologically speaking, one of the most adventurous, and audacious—bravely audacious—of enterprises. Its object was to revolutionise the practical system of the English Church without breaking with history and the past; to give the Crown and the State vast and new powers of correction and control, without

C.S., P.   F

trenching on the inherited prerogatives of the spiritualty ; and to do this without the advantage of a clear, solid, well-tested, consistent theory, or else, as in Luther's case, of a strong exaggerated cry and watchword. Smarting under the sting of monstrous practical abuses, and quite conscious of the impossibility of making sudden changes to be deep ones, the English reformers adopted what their enemies might well call a hand-to-mouth policy of experiment in finding what they still hoped might be a growing, improving, yet permanent settlement. The Roman theory of the Church, and of Church reform as pursued at Trent, was compact and complete ; the Calvinist theory of Church reform and Church reconstruction was equally logical and complete ; in each case all was linked together, consistent, impregnable, till you came to the final question of the authority on which all rested, and till you came to square the theory with certain and important facts. With a kind of gallant contempt for the protection of a theory, we in England shaped our measures as well as we could, to suit the emergencies which at the moment most compelled the attention of the steersman at the helm. The English Reformation ventured on its tremendous undertaking—the attempt to make the Church theologically, politically, socially different, while keeping it historically and essentially the same—with what seems the most slender outfit of appliances. Principles it had ; but they were very partially explored, applied, followed out to consequences, harmonised, limited. It sprung from an idea, a great and solid one, even though dimly comprehended, but not from a theory or a system, such as that unfolded in Calvin's *Institutes*. Its public and avowed purpose —I do not say that of all its promoters—but its public purpose was, taking the actual historical Church of Augustine and Ethelbert, of Becket and Wolsey, of Warham and Pole, the existing historical representative and descendant of that supernatural Society which is traceable through all the ages to Apostolic days, to assert its rights, to release it from usurpation, to purge away the evils which this usurpation had created and fostered ; and accepting the Bible as the Primitive Church had accepted it, and trying to test everything by Scripture and history, to meet the immediate necessities of a crisis which called not only for abolition, but for reconstruction and replacement. What was done bore the marks of a clear and definite purpose ; but it also bore the unmistakable marks of haste and pressure, as well as violence. Laws,—all but the most indispensable ones,—canons, synods, tribunals, the adjustment of the differing elements of its constitution, were adjourned to a more convenient season, which, in fact, has never arrived. It began with arrangements avowedly provisional. On the great dogmatic controversies of the moment it defined cautiously, its critics said, imperfectly : it hardly had made up its own mind. For the systematic confessions of the Continent, it provided a makeshift in the Thirty-nine Articles, put to a use for which they were not originally designed. But it did four things :—1: It maintained the Episcopate and the Ordinal ; 2. It put the English Bible into the hands of the people ; 3. It gave them the

English Book of Common Prayer ; and 4. To bind all together with the necessary bond of authority, it substituted boldly and confidently, in place of the rejected authority of the Pope, the authority, equally undefined, of the Crown, presumed to be loyally Christian and profoundly religious, and always acting in concert with the Church and its representatives. It has been called a *via media*, a compromise. It is more true to fact to say that what was in the thought of those who guided it under Henry VIII. and Elizabeth was an attempt, genuine though rude and rough and not always successful, to look all round the subject ; to embrace in one compass as many advantages as they could—perhaps incompatible and inconsistent ones—without much regard to producible and harmonising theories : antiquity and novelty, control and freedom, ecclesiastical and civil authority, the staid order of a Church as old as the nation and the vigour of a modern revolution of the age of the Renaissance, a very strong public government with an equally strong private fervour and enthusiasm ; to stimulate conscience and the sense of individual responsibility, and yet to keep them from bursting all bounds ; to overthrow a vast ancient power, strong in its very abuses and intrenched behind the prejudices as well as the great deeds of centuries, and yet to save the sensitive, delicate instincts of loyalty, reverence, and obedience ; to make room in the same system of teaching for the venerable language of ancient Fathers, and also for the new learning of famous modern authorities.

· The task was a difficult one, as it was unique among the various projects opposed to it, or likened

to it, going on at the same time in Western Christendom. Abroad, the idea of the English Reformation
appeared, as it still appears abroad, an illogical
and incomprehensible attempt to unite incompatible
principles and elements. That government should
interfere with religion, should change it, should
impose it, was perfectly understood both by Protest-
ants and Catholics. But that reformers in England,
having broken with the Pope, should not make a
clear sweep of the whole of the inherited system and
begin afresh; that they should embarrass themselves
by maintaining the continuity and identity of the
existing Church with the historical Church of the
past; that they should be so bold, yet so guarded
and reticent,—this was unintelligible, both at Rome,
Paris and Madrid, and at Wittenberg, Jena, Basle
and Geneva. It must have seemed to many—not
merely to the worshippers of absolute hypotheses,
but to cool and practical judges of the probabilities of
human affairs—a very unpromising, if not forlorn
and desperate venture. So daring a disregard of
obvious inconsequence and anomaly; so delicate a
balancing of conflicting tendencies; so apparently
artificial and arbitrary restraints on their natural
development; all, too, depending on the chances of a
single life, and the personal influence of a character,
did not wear the look of permanence. It might have
been plausibly foretold that the English reformed
Church must soon choose its side; must soon either
go backwards or forwards; backwards to its old
allegiance; forwards to the clear, definite position of
the great Swiss and French reformers. But that it
should go on strengthening itself in spite of its

double openness to attack, unfolding and developing
the energies of life in spite of its logical incompleteness ; that it should long escape the dangers from
internal quarrels and outward hostility, might well
have seemed one of the most unlikely of suppositions. The hopes and forecasts of the prophets of
evil may be seen in the controversial literature of
the Roman advocates, in the pamphlet literature of
the Puritan champions of the " Discipline."

The experience of three centuries has shown that
the apparently loose, ill-jointed, halting polity which
they so contemptuously criticised, had both a firmness
and an elasticity which more showy systems failed
in. It has borne the brunt of time and change. It
has never lost its original informing, animating idea.
It has shown a wonderful power of obstinate tenacity
against jars and shocks, a force of continuous growth,
and of vigorous recovery after disaster and stagna-
tion. It has certainly vindicated its claim to life and
reality. But at starting, the dangers were indeed formidable. In the first place, the principle of authority
had been most rudely shaken ; yet it was necessary
to invoke it at every turn. It is not easy for us to
realise the effect of the shattering, in an ignorant,
yet eager and excited age, of the religious authority
of the Pope. It seemed to leave a void in the
public control of belief and conscience which every
one might fill as he pleased. Yet the world had
been accustomed to authority, and the void could
not be left unoccupied. The Crown, its ministers
and its council ; the Bishops, its trusted advisers ; in
those days in a less prominent, but still important,
degree, the Parliament and the Synod, slipped into

the vacant place.   But though authority maintained
itself, it did not maintain itself easily.   The subtle,
intangible, yet deep and mighty force of moral
authority which had existed of old, and which the
Popes had strained till it broke, had not been, could
not be, replaced.   As a substitute for it, came in an
exaggerated idea of the divine and personal rights
of the Crown.   It was partly a very real and natural
idea at the time ;   it was partly a factitious and
scholastic one ;   it partly expressed, vaguely and
imperfectly, the claims of public law.   But it served
to consecrate the force which was judged necessary
to maintain what had been settled as the order of
the Church ;   and the temptation to appeal to it,
whenever its countenance could be hoped for, became
on all hands irresistible, where, as it seemed, time
and patience and argument, and the growth of
reasonable and sober opinion, could not be waited
for or relied upon.   The result was the unquestionable harshness of the Tudor and Stuart ecclesiastical
government, and the ever-renewed exasperation and
bitterness of its unruly subjects, whom we see to
have been self-willed and unreasonable, but who then
thought, not unnaturally, that its authority had no
claim to their respect nor binding force on their
consciences.

And with this impaired sense of authority at
home the English Reformation had to confront the
mightiest, the most imperious and exacting authority
outside, which ever claimed and bore a universal
sway over human conscience.   It had to confront
the Roman authority, now turned into the most implacable and aggressive of deadly enemies ; and this,

not simply on the ground of argument and influence,
but in the field of political action. The struggle
between England and Rome under Elizabeth, and in
the first years of James, was a struggle of life and
death.   It was a struggle, begun in its desperate
and murderous fierceness by the Popes, in which no
scruples were felt, no terms kept on either side.
Controversy, never silent, and always truculent and
unsparing, was but a light matter compared with
the terrible hostilities carried on, not by word, but
by deed ; war and conspiracy and massacre, the
fanaticism of assassination and treason, met by san-
guinary legislation, by cold and determined "execution of justice." We may well be aghast at the
horrors of that struggle. The deep hatreds and
deep injuries of the political conflict gave to the
theological controversy—the necessary theological
controversy—an unfairness and a virulence from
which it has never recovered, and which have been
a disgrace to Christendom, and fatal, not merely to
unity, but in many ways to truth. But there was
something more on the Roman side than the cruel
intrigues of Popes and Jesuits and the brutality
of pamphleteers.   Since the age of Julius II. and
Leo X.. and the first sittings of the Council of Trent,
Roman controversy had become intellectually much
more formidable. The stress of the Reformation had
forced it to look narrowly into its own case and its
grounds.   Against the learning of Erasmus and the
genius and thought of Calvin, it felt the necessity
of something more than the stock arguments and
quotations of its earlier defenders, Eck and Caietan.
And the result was remarkable.   The order of the

Jesuits arose to place, not merely enthusiasm and political unscrupulousness at the service of the Pope, but learning, the spirit of research, intellectual activity and literary skill. Vast scientific systems of theology, like the great work of Suarez, unfolded and established with philosophic calmness and strength the Roman doctrine. To match such works as these there was nothing—I do not say in England, but even in Germany and Switzerland. There was nothing to match the subtlety and comprehensiveness of the *Controversies* of Bellarmine. There was nothing to match the imposing historical picture presented in the annals of Baronius. Rome had much more to say for itself than had appeared to Cranmer or even to Jewell.

There was a third danger. The foreign Reformation, in its most vigorous and intellectual representatives, undoubtedly the French and Swiss reformers, started with an imposing breadth and simplicity of principle, absolute and sweeping, to which the English laid no claim. Calvin and Zwingli, both in what they destroyed and what they built up, had no occasion for the qualifications, the hesitations, the revisions and amendments and corrections, which abound in the course pursued in England. But, as is according to the nature of Englishmen, many Englishmen who were brought into close contact with the keen and powerful minds who swayed the Reformation abroad, were deeply impressed and attracted by them. Through them the opinions of the foreigners, recommended by their extreme and uncompromising logic, found a footing in England. Geneva and Zurich became

rival centres of influence to Rome ; and a school
was founded, strong from the first, and always,
either in the government or in opposition to it,
energetic and determined, whose object was to carry
change in the English Church, both in doctrine,
usages, and discipline, to a point where all likeness
was lost, not only to the unreformed but to the
ancient Church.   It became their steady, persevering
policy to impose the Calvinistic theology in its
severest form as regards the Divine decrees as well
as the doctrines of grace, both as an authoritative and
as a popular system of teaching, on the documents
and on the organs of the English Church ; and to
disparage and intimidate with the note of disloyalty
and treason any departure from the definitions and
phraseology of the great foreign divines, who in
those days were supposed to be in exclusive and
certain possession of the interpretation of revealed
truth.   Calvinism, transplanted into the serious and
earnest   nature   of   Englishmen   and   Scotchmen,
flourished with a vigour of life which it rapidly lost
in its native seats.   How nearly it succeeded in
making itself master in the English Church is seen
in the history and language of Hooker's books, and
in Whitgift's " Lambeth Articles " of 1595.   And
with the imperious and exclusive demand of the
Calvinistic theology had also come other claims.
That early fraternisation with the foreign reformers
in the first stage of our own Reformation, natural,
inevitable, excusable as under the difficulties of the
time it may have been—that wholesale acceptance
of their authority, and that deference to the judgment
of their disciples, which gave even to John Knox a

part in the theological language of Edward's second Prayer-Book [1]—furnished a ground for claiming that the English Reformed Church should go on to full conformity with the ecclesiastical doctrines of the great foreign masters. The only safeguard for their theology was the full acceptance of their Church " platform " : the one was as much of Divine authority as the other. We have no right to wonder that this party aimed high. They aimed at nothing less than what they afterwards carried—not a mere change in this or that point, but a substitution of an entirely new polity and constitution for the existing one—of an entirely new idea of the Church for that on which the Reformation in England had been based. Toleration was then on all sides not merely unacknowledged but condemned. The demand of the Puritan was that nothing should be allowed but Puritanism.

Through these trials the English Reformation had to make its way. In Bishop Andrewes, as in Hooker, we see the pass to which things had come : —the pressure of the hostile forces ; the vulnerable points on which they bore heavily ; the awakening in the Church of wider knowledge, of freedom and independence of thought, of calmer and steadier judgment ; and the effort of reviving intellectual power, after the haste and hurried confusion of the early practical struggles for reformation, not, indeed, to construct a theory for it, but to put what it had done, and what it aimed at doing, on a reasonable and tenable ground. The later years of Elizabeth, which, in spite of their troubles, were

[1] See Dr. Lorimer's *John Knox and the Church of England*, chap. iii.

settled and quiet compared with the beginning of
the century, cleared up much that had been confused
and uncertain.   The larger and richer and more
powerful minds had time to think, to learn, to
balance, to weigh and analyse arguments, to follow
out consequences.   The English Church, at its
Reformation, had taken up its ground on the
Scriptures and the Primitive Church.   It had
avowed its object to be a return, as far as was
possible, to what the teaching of the Apostles and
their disciples had made the Primitive Church to be.
At the outset, all that was much insisted upon was
that the Primitive Church was certainly *not* like the
modern unreformed Latin Church.   By the end of
Elizabeth's reign, men had found leisure to inquire
carefully and honestly, with less prejudice and heat,
what that model *was* like, which the English Church
had declared its wish to copy in all things essential.
Arms were still needed, as much as ever, against the
never-ceasing hostility of Rome : but something
more was clearly necessary than the mere negations
of earlier controversy and invectives against Roman
corruption and pretensions ; some more positive
ground on which to rest the claim that England was
better and more primitive than Rome.   Such a
ground it was not easy to find in that narrow
Calvinism which the Puritans were trying to force
on the Government, and to make the popular religion
of the country.   Something was wanted broader,
more intelligible, and more refined than their mode
of presenting the ideas of justification and God's
predestinating and electing grace, and their fashion
of summing up loyalty to Christ and truth in petty

scruples about innocent and natural usages and
ceremonies. Something was wanted, as fervent, but
more true, more noble, more Catholic, than their
devotion and self-discipline. The higher spirits of
the time wanted to breathe more freely, and in a
purer air. They found what they wanted in the
language, the ideas, the tone and temper of the
best early Christian literature. That turned their
thoughts from words to a Person. It raised them
from the disputes of local cliques to the ideas which
have made the Universal Church. It recalled them
from arguments that revolved round a certain
number of traditional formulæ about justification,
free-will, and faith, to a truer and worthier idea both
of man and God, to the overwhelming revelation of
the Word Incarnate, and the result of it on the
moral standard and behaviour of real and living
men. It led them from a theology which ended in
cross-grained and perverse conscientiousness, to a
theology which ended in adoration, self-surrender,
and blessing, and in the awe and joy of welcoming
the Presence of the Eternal Beauty, the Eternal
Sanctity, and the Eternal Love, the Sacrifice and
Reconciliation of the world.

Andrewes, by nature and choice an indefatigable
student, a ready and accomplished teacher, a devout
and self-disciplined seeker after a life with God, was
only by necessity a polemic. There was abundance in
the world of his time to disquiet and offend him—to
offend his large knowledge, his idea of religion, his
convictions of the sacredness of morality, his balanced
reason ; to disquiet him, as to the result of the mischievous elements working round English religion.

But only in one direction did he throw himself avowedly into controversy. He threw himself into it as an Englishman, as a servant of his country and King, as well as a Churchman. The great Roman rally, which dated from the institution of the Company of Jesus, and which had been growing in strength and uncompromising aggression through the sixteenth century, had given a pressing and menacing importance to the Roman controversy in England. For the Roman claims called in question not simply the foundations of the English Church, but the foundations of the English State and society. The prominence given to the revived doctrine of the deposing power had received meaning not only from what had been attempted in England, but by what had been accomplished, avowed, celebrated in France. We sometimes speak as if the crimes of the Roman party culminated in the massacre of St. Bartholomew and the cruelties of Alva. But besides that these, unhappily, had a terrible balance on the other side, they were not the worst. It is in the French wars of the League, in the principles invented by their ecclesiastical leaders, proclaimed in the pulpits of Paris, spread abroad by a thousand emissaries, put in practice by the assassins of Henry III. and Henry IV., that we see the real character of theories put forth by great and popular champions of Rome, and their fatal bearing on the primary conditions of human society. The murder of Henry IV. drove the calm and impartial Casaubon to say, "that he thought it now part of his religion · to make public profession of his belief in the Royal Supremacy." The sense of these dangers, indignation

at the atrocious wickedness and profanations which
marked the policy now so highly in favour at Rome,
the wrath of a man of learning at the gross abuse of
learning for the support of sophistry, which in the
cause of reckless ambition ended in perjury and
murder, forced Andrewes reluctantly, but very reso-
lutely, into this barren and dreary field.   James
claimed the aid of his learning and keen wit against
the foremost leaders of the Roman claims, Bellarmine
and Duperron.   The gossips of the Court record that
controversy was neither to his liking nor according
to his supposed aptitudes ; but they also record with
what power he accomplished his task.[1]   He met his
opponents on ground new to them.   He met them as
a man at least as deeply learned in ecclesiastical
history and literature as themselves.   One of the
triumphant devices of the later Roman argument
had been to take the English Church at her word,
as a Church which avowedly aimed at making the
ancient Church her standard, and to contrast this
with the dogmas and the "platform" too hastily
adopted from Geneva by some of her divines in the
reaction against the intolerable abuses of the days
of Leo X.   Andrewes gave a new turn to the controversy.   He was not afraid of what was genuine
early language and early usage.   When Cardinal
Duperron drew a detailed comparison between the
Church of St. Augustine and of the four first
Councils, and the Churches of his day, Roman and
Reformed, and asked which of the latter bore the
greater resemblance .to the earlier type, Andrewes
fearlessly met the challenge, on behalf of the Church

[1] *Vide* Note in Bliss's ed. of Andrewes, vii. pp. ix., x.

of England. The challenge was, indeed, a fallacious one, from the vast changes which had passed over the world, and from the enormous differences between the fifth and the seventeenth centuries, which one side as much as the other had to take account of. Yet there were times, doubtless, in the history of the Reformation when it would have been hazardous to have met such a challenge before those acquainted with history. But Andrewes wrote with the advantage which enlarged knowledge and experience had thrown on the aims and language of both sides in the struggle ; and he did not shrink from claiming for his Church as large and essential a conformity with antiquity, even in outward things, as could be pretended by Rome, and a far deeper agreement in spirit.

With the Puritans he did not enter so much into direct controversy as Hooker had done. With the exception of some partial and incidental disputes with individuals—such as his correspondence with Du Moulin—or a passing touch of rebuke, protest, or humorous satire in his preaching, his resistance to Puritanism was an indirect one. He looked for producing his effect on the tone and course of religious thought in England, not by arguing, but by presenting uncontroversially the reasonableness and the attractions of a larger, freer, nobler, more generous, may I say, more imaginative, system of teaching. His administrative weight as a Bishop was, of course, thrown on the side which resisted the tyrannous narrowness of Puritanism, and aimed at greater expansiveness and proportion in doctrine, and dignity and solemnity in worship. But he did not trust to administration and power as Laud did. The weapon by which he attacked Puritanism, the instrument by which he endeavoured to enlarge the sympathies and refine the religious ideas of his day, was his Sermons. In those sermons—belonging as they do in style and manner to their time— there is a clear and strong contrast with the way in which Christianity had usually been presented in the preaching of the previous generation. This preaching professed to represent the original creed of Calvinism—stern, hard, positive, but thoroughly earnest and very mighty—and with a gloomy and savage grandeur and nobility, in its passionate loyal assertions of the irresistible Sovereignty of God, against the claims, the worthlessness, and the insignificance of man. But this stern creed, for a short moment a living one, had, as was sure to be the case, degenerated into a dry, unreal, stereotyped, scholasticism, to which the mediæval scholasticism was fruitful and interesting. In Andrewes you feel as if he had broken bounds. You see at once a wider horizon, objects of faith and contemplation at once more real, more personal, more august; you become aware of your relation to a vaster and more diversified world, a world full of mystery, yet touching you on every side. Doctrine you have, dogmatic teaching as precise and emphatic as anywhere : but it is doctrine as wide as the Scripture in its comprehensiveness and variety, reflecting at every turn the unutterable and overwhelming wonders which rise before us when we think of what we mean by the Creeds ; corresponding in its dignity, in its versatile application, to the real history of man,

C.S.,P.   G

to the deep and manifold wants of the soul, its
aspirations, its terrible sins, its cruel fears, its capacities for hope and delight, the strange fortunes of the
race, and of the story of each individual life. He is
not a mere moralist, not simply a preacher of high
duties and elevated views of human nature and prospects.[1]   He is, first and foremost, a theologian, whose
deepest belief is the importance of his theology,
and who profoundly reverences its truth. But his
theology is very different from that so long in vogue.
It approached man on his many sides. It was instinct with the awful consciousness of our immense
and hopeless ignorance of the ways and counsels of
God—with that shrinking from speculation on the
secret things of the Most High which he shared with
Hooker, and which as a professed law of divinity
was something new in the theological world of the
day. " For these sixteen years, since I was ordained
priest," he says, in his judgment on the " Lambeth
Articles," " I have never publicly or privately dis-
puted or preached on these mysteries of predestina-

---

[1] " Since the Revolution of 1688 our Church has been chilled and
starved too generally by preachers and reasoners, Stoic or Epicurean :
first, a sort of pagan morality was substituted for righteousness by
faith ; and latterly prudence, or Paleyanism, has been substituted even
for morality.   A Christian preacher ought to preach Christ alone, and
all things in Him and by Him.   If he find a dearth in this, if it seem
to him a circumscription, he does not know Christ as the *pleroma*, the
fulness.   It is not possible that there should be aught true, or seemly,
or beautiful, in thought, will, or deed, speculative or practical, which
may not, and which ought not, to be evolved out of Christ and the
faith in Christ ; no folly, no error, no evil to be exposed, or warned
against, which may not, and should not, be convicted and denounced for
its contrariancy and enmity to Christ.   To the Christian preacher, Christ
should be in all things, and all things in Christ : he should abjure every
argument which is not a link in the chain, of which Christ is the staple
and staple-ring." (Coleridge, *Notes on English Divines: Donne*, i. 86.)

tion "—on which every one else was disputing ;
"and now I would much rather hear than speak of
them."[1]   His aim was to give accuracy and breadth
to dogma, and to put life in its expression, as St.
Augustine, St. Chrysostom, and the great Greek
Fathers had done : not to plunge into the abysses
of the unknown, and of that which it is impossible
to know, but to fix thought on the certainties and
realities, passing all wonder, that we believe *are*
known, and to accompany their contemplation with
that encompassing train of Christian affections and
graces, without which they have been revealed in
vain—faith, and reverence, and high hope, and the
desire after holiness, and humble patience, and the
joy of God's love.   The power of Puritanism was
now no longer in its scheme of doctrine, but in its
fierce Judaical hatreds, which, natural at one time
against intolerable superstitions, had passed into a
superstition as intolerable and mischievous.   How
best to fight against the blind powers of ignorance
and prejudice, when they have been unloosened, and
aspire to govern churches and direct religion, is
always an anxious question.   Andrewes conceived
that the most hopeful way was to spend his life and
gifts in presenting continually in the pulpit the
counter-attraction of a purer and nobler pattern of
faith : a religion with vaster prospects and wider
sympathies ; which claimed kindred with all that
was ancient, and all that was universal in Christianity ; which looked above the controversies and
misunderstandings of the hour, to the larger thought,
and livelier faith, and sanctified genius of those in

[1] Andrewes, *Minor Works*, 294.

whom the Church of Christ has recognised her most
venerated teachers.

His efforts failed at the time. Probably they
would have failed equally, in spite of Clarendon's
opinion the other way, if he had been called to
succeed Abbot at Canterbury.[1] That unqualified
idea of Royal power, the ruin of Spain and France,
in which Churchmen of that day put their trust, and
to which their opponents would equally have trusted
if they could have got it on their side, was a doomed
one in England, and must have brought defeat for
the time on all who had identified themselves with
it. Puritanism failing, first under Elizabeth and
then under James, to get hold of the government, as
it once hoped to do, had thrown itself into the
struggle for English liberty, and for the moment it
was to reap the reward of its courage. And it
must, I fear, be added that Andrewes or any one
else would have been greatly hampered by the bad-
ness of his own party. There were sycophants
and corrupt trucklers to power among the bishops :
there was ignorance and there was sordid greed
among the clergy. " Quis custodiet ipsos custodes ? "
he asks, in his stern and menacing Latin Sermon at
St. Paul's, before the Convocation of 1593. The
rulers of the Church did not come with clean hands
to repress the extravagances of Puritan prophecy-
ings and consistories, and the insolence of Puritan
pamphleteers. What Andrewes did was less for his
own generation than for those that came after. In
the course of a long and active life, he broke the
yoke of prejudice, and unloosed the tongue of

[1] Clarendon, *Hist. of the Rebellion*, i. 157.

English theologians. Without departing from the position or the lines of the original Reformation, he greatly enlarged its field of teaching. In the outskirts and fringes of its system, where it had been characteristically reticent, he was not afraid to supply from the authorities, to which it had all along appealed, what was wanting to complete the harmony and fulness of its doctrine. Thus with respect to the idea of the Christian Sacrifice in the Eucharist, on which the language of the ancient Church was so clear and strong, and on which, from the superstitions and errors of the Mediæval Church, the English Prayer Book was so reserved, Andrewes, without hesitation and as of full right, recurred, both in controversy and in teaching, to the language of the Liturgies, familiar to the early writers from Irenæus to Augustine. So again, in respect of those forms and offices for special occasions not provided for in the general office-book of the Church, he threw himself, as an ancient Bishop would have done, on his inherent episcopal authority to supply the want. It is mainly according to the model used by him that our churches are even to this day consecrated Full of discrimination for what really had the authority of the ancient Church, he was the most fearless of English divines, when he had that authority. English theology would be in danger of being much less Catholic, much more disconnected with that of the earlier ages, much more arbitrarily limited in all directions, except towards Geneva or else towards simple latitude, but that a man of Andrewes' character and weight had dared to break through the prescription which the Puritans were trying to establish against the doctrinal language, at once more accurate and more free, of the ancient Church. Without him and his school, we might perhaps have had Hales of Eton, and Chillingworth and Tillotson, great and weighty names ; and on the other hand, John Newton and Toplady and Thomas Scott ; but we could not have had Jeremy Taylor and Bull, and hardly Waterland.

But Bishop Andrewes has left behind him something which, even more than his preaching, explains his influence, it is the evidence of that power of character which has so strong, though so indirect and subtle, a hold on men. He is one of those who like St. Augustine have left us, besides their writings, their very secret selves, as they placed themselves in the presence of their God and Saviour. In Bishop Andrewes' case this was certainly without intending it. After his death was found the book in which he had consigned the words selected by him to express the usual attitude of his soul in private, his usual feelings and emotions, his usual desires, when upon his knees. The book has been long familiar as Bishop Andrewes' _Greek and Latin Devotions._ It has received in our own times one of those rare translations which make an old book new.[1] It seems to me that the key to the influence which Andrewes had in his own day, and which recommended his theology, is to be found in his _Devotions._ For they show what was the true meaning and reach of his theology, how unspeakably real and deep he felt its language to be, and how naturally it allied itself and was interwoven with the highest

---

[1] By Dr. Newman, in 1840.

frames of thought and feeling in a mind of wide
range, and a soul of the keenest self-knowledge and
the strongest sympathies.   There are books which
go deeper into the struggles, the questionings, the
temptations, the discipline, the strange spiritual
mysteries of the devout spirit.   There are books
which perhaps rise higher in the elevations of
devotion.   But nowhere do we see more, so original
and spontaneous a result of a man's habits of
devotion ; nowhere, that I know of, does the whole
mind of the student, the divine, and the preacher,
reflect itself in his prayers so simply and easily and
harmoniously as in this book.   His knowledge, his
tastes, his systematic and methodical theology, the
order and articles of his creed, translate themselves
into the realities of worship.   All his interests, all
his customary views of God, of man, of nature, of
his relations to his place and time—all that he has
been reading about or employed upon, suggest
themselves when he places himself in God's presence, and find their natural and fit expression in
the beautifully applied words of Psalm or ancient
Liturgy.   Nothing can be more comprehensive and
more complete in their proportions than his devotions
for each day ; nothing more tender and solemn ;
nothing more compressed and nervous than their
language.   The full order of prayer and all its parts
is always there : the introductory contemplation, to
sober, to elevate, to kindle ; the confession, the
profession of faith, the intercession, the praise and
thanksgiving.   There is equally there the consciousness of individual singleness, and the sense of great
and wide corporate relations.   His confessions show

in severely restrained and precise language the
infinite acknowledgment of unworthiness and want,
and the infinite hope in God's mercy and love, in
one who searched and judged himself with keen and
unflinching truth. But he did not stop at himself, his
sins and hopes. He also felt himself, even in private
prayer, one of the great body of God's creation
and God's Church. He reminded himself of it, as
he did of the Object of his worship, in the profession of his faith. He acted on it in his detailed and
minute intercessions. And then he surrendered himself to the impulses of exulting wonder and rejoicing
at the greatness of his Christian lot. The poetical and
imaginative side of his nature shows itself in the vivid
pictures which he calls up, with a few condensed and
powerful touches, of the glories of Nature, and the
wonders of God's kingdom, its history, its manifold
organisation. Thus, " the connection of every day,"
says a writer before quoted, Dr. Mozley,[1] " with the
great works which each day saw in the work of creation, converts the several days of the week into beautiful mementos of the fact that we and all that we see
are God's creatures, as well as of the sanctity of the
week itself as a division of time ; and it evidences that
character of mind in the writer which realises the
facts of Scripture, sees mysteries in common things,
and feels itself still living amid visible traces of
a Divine dispensation. It is obvious how such a
method gives the beauty of natural objects a place
in his religion." The Apostles' Creed is no dry
recital, but expands day after day into petitions and
·desires founded on its awful facts. And so again,

---

[1] *British Critic*, Jan. 1845, pp. 189-192.

" man, human society, his country, as an object of
prayer, is not the mere human mass—a number of
individuals, but man and man in certain relations to
each other, high and low, rich and poor, king and
subject, noble and dependant, all living together in
the system of God's ordinance " . . . " actual trades
and states of life," definitely enumerated, as Homer
enumerates names of men and places ; not only " king
and queen, parliament and judicature, army and
police, commons and their leaders," but " farmers,
graziers, fishers, merchants, traders, and mechanics,
down to mean workmen and the poor." There is
no class of men, no condition, no relation of life,
no necessity or emergency of it, which does not at
one time or another rise up before his memory, and
claim his intercession : none for which he does not
see a place in the order of God's world, and find a
refuge under the shadow of His wing.

Into such devotions I think it would be impossible
to translate the Puritan theology of the time. It is too
narrow, too suspicious, too much enslaved to technical
forms and language. The piercing and rapid energy
of Andrewes' devotions, their ordinary severe concise-
ness, their nobleness and manliness, their felicitous
adaptations, their free and varied range, the way in
which they call up before the mind the whole of the
living realities of God's creation and God's revelations,
and, in the portion devoted to praise, their rhythmical
flow and music, incorporating bursts of adoration and
Eucharistic triumph from the Liturgies of St. James or
St. Chrysostom, recalling the most ancient Greek
hymns of the Church, the *Gloria in Excelsis*, and
the Evening Hymn preserved at the end of the

Alexandrian manuscript of the New Testament,[1]—
all this is in the strongest contrast to anything that
I know of in the private devotions of the time.   It
was the reflection, in private prayer, of the tone and
language of the public Book of Common Prayer, its
Psalms, and its Offices : it supplemented the public
book, and carried on its spirit from the Church to the
closet.   And this was the counterpart of what Andrewes
taught in the pulpit.   To us it shows how real and
deeply held his theology was ; and it also explains
that persuasiveness of conviction, which has as much
to do as intellectual force and breadth, in making
men listen to their teachers and accept their words.
The reformed English Church had had its martyrs,
statesmen, doctors, champions ; in Andrewes it had a
saint—not called so, not canonised, but one in whom
men felt the irresistible charm of real holiness.   It
had some one in high place not only to admire, but
to love.   And churches need saints, as much as
theologians and statesmen, and even martyrs.

In these ways, Andrewes marks a period and a
step in the unfolding of the theology of the Reformed
Church of England and in the practical course of the
Reformation.   Hooker had vindicated on its behalf
the rights of Christian and religious *reason*, that
reason which is a reflection of the mind of God.
Andrewes vindicated on its behalf the rights of Christian *history*.   Hooker had maintained the claims of
reason, against a slavish bondage to narrow and
arbitrary interpretations of the letter of Scripture.
Andrewes claimed for the English Church its full

---

[1] φῶς ἱλαρόν ; translated in the *Lyra Apostolica*, No. 62.   See
Bingham, vol. iv. p. 411.

interest and membership in the Church universal,
from which Puritan and Romanist alike would cut off
the island Church by a gulf as deep as the sea.   The
spirit of historical investigation had awoke in England as in the rest of Europe, against the passion
for abstract and metaphysical argument which had
marked and governed the earlier stages of the
Reformation.   It had converted Casaubon from Calvinism, and at the same time made him the most
formidable critic of the magnificent but unhistorical
picture presented in the annals of Baronius.   Widened
knowledge had done as much for Andrewes and the
men of his school, Field and Donne and Overall, may
I not add, in this matter, Andrewes' close friend,
Lord Bacon?   History had enlarged their ideas of
the Church universal.   Its facts and concrete lessons
and actual words had overborne the traditions and
general assumptions in which the necessities of an
age of religious war had educated them.   They
opened their eyes and saw that the prerogatives
which the Puritans confined to an invisible Church,
and which Rome confined to the obedience of the
Pope, belonged to the universal historical Church,
lasting on with varied fortunes through all the
centuries from the days of Pentecost ; on earth " the
habitation of God through the Spirit."   Maintaining
jealously and stoutly the inherent and indefeasible
rights of the national Church of England, •and
resisting with uncompromising determination the
tyranny which absorbed in a single hand the powers
of the Catholic Church, they refused to forget, even
in England, what God's Spirit had done in other
portions of Christendom, perhaps far removed, per-

haps for the time bitterly hostile. They learned to pray, as Andrewes did, " for the Catholic Church, its establishment and increase ; for the Eastern, its deliverance and union ; for the Western, its adjustment and peace ; for the British, the supply of what is wanting in it, the strengthening of that which remains in it." They recognised the authority of its great and unquestionable decisions. They were willing to appeal to its authority, if it could be expressed legitimately. They introduced, even into controversy, at least to some extent, the habits of discrimination and respect. Their teaching shows how, after the first fever and excitement of the revolt against Roman usurpation had passed, the leaders of the English Church felt that much natural misstatement and exaggeration had to be qualified and corrected ; it shows how anxious they were, in accordance with the declared policy of the Reformation, to keep hold on the undivided and less corrupted Church of the early centuries as their standard and guide ; it shows how much they found, in their increased acquaintance with it, to enrich, to enlarge, to invigorate, to give beauty, proportion, and force to their theology.

Still, as I said before, in this unique example of Church polity—unique in its constitution, unique in its strong permanence and its fruitfulness—they hardly attempted a complete, consistent, systematic theory. There was none agreed upon. There was none put forward, as in the vast elaborate systems in fashion on the Continent, where, in folio after folio, everything is rigorously deduced from its principles, and everything is in order and in its place. To the views and positions of Andrewes and his school,

broadly stated, there were obvious objections which
they did not care to probe, and to which an answer
might not have been easy.   And their appeal to the
idea of Church authority grew into shape, and the
ecclesiastical administration based on it was carried on
and enforced, under the shield of James I.'s interpretation of the Royal Supremacy, which meant a
right to meddle with everything, and settle everything by his personal wisdom.   But I suppose the
truth was, though they felt it only in a partial way
and without putting it into words, that they saw that
though the English Church, according to the current
theories, was an anomaly, it was only an anomaly
among anomalies—amid universal anomaly.   The
sins, the crimes, the misrule of centuries had brought
their inevitable, their irremediable consequences, and
made claims and rules inapplicable and impossible
which belonged to times when these evils were yet
in the future.   It was a saying of a wise observer,[1]
that "whoever enters on the study of Church history must be prepared for many surprises."   And
certainly the course of Church history has not run,
either for good or for evil, in the course which
theories would have prescribed to it.   Stern and
terrible facts stand up in it, not to be disguised by
the most pretentious of theories.   And, happily, on
the other hand, mischiefs which seemed inevitable
have found unthought-of compensations or remedies.
I doubt whether Andrewes cared much for that
intellectual completeness of theory which we make
much of.   He knew that Rome in his day was
unprimitive, tyrannical, aggressive, unscrupulous :

[1] Charles Marriott of Oriel.

he knew that Puritanism was narrow, uncatholic, cruelly intolerant ; and he would not be cheated out of the facts which he saw, for want of a convenient theory. He fought both Romanist and Puritan with such weapons as he found in his hand. But his governing rule was a noble one—that expressed in the ancient saying, Σπάρταν ἔλαχες, ταύταν κόσμει, "Sparta is your portion, do your best for Sparta " :—noble, I say, because so honest, and so unpretending ; for in religion, which means man's blindness and weakness as well as his hope, it does not do to be ambitious, or to claim great things for men or for systems. England might have faults, mistakes, shortcomings, inconsistencies ; let him do his best to bear their discredit, or to mend their evils. But England and its Church had lived on before he was born, and would live on after he had done his part and passed away. The feeling with which he laboured in his work of life is, I conceive, expressed in the following passage from Archbishop Bramhall : [1]—

" No man can justly blame me for honouring my spiritual mother, the Church of England, in whose womb I was conceived, at whose breasts I was nourished, and in whose bosom I hope to die. Bees by the instinct of nature do love their hives, and birds their nests. But God is my witness that I, according to my uttermost talent and poor understanding, have endeavoured to set down the naked truth impartially, without either favour or prejudice, the two capital enemies of right judgment. . . My desire hath been to have Truth for my chiefest

---

[1] Quoted in Newman's *Prophetical Office of the Church*, p. vi.

friend, and no enemy but error. If I have had any bias, it hath been desire of peace, which our common Saviour hath left as a legacy to His Church, that I might live to see the reunion of Christendom, for which I shall always bow the knees of my heart to the Father of our Lord Jesus Christ. . . .

" Howsoever it be, I submit myself and my poor endeavours, first to the judgment of the Catholic Œcumenical essential Church, which, if some of late days have endeavoured to hiss out of the school, I cannot help it. From the beginning it was not so. And if I should mistake the right Catholic Church out of human frailty, or ignorance (which, for my part, I have no reason in the world to suspect ; yet it is not impossible, when the Romanists themselves are divided into five or six several opinions, what this Catholic Church, or what their Infallible Judge is), I do implicitly, and in the preparation of my mind, submit myself to the True Catholic Church, the Spouse of Christ, the Mother of the Saints, the Pillar of Truth. And seeing my adherence is firmer to the Infallible Rule of Faith, *i.e.* the Holy Scriptures interpreted by the Catholic Church, than to mine own private judgment and opinions, although I should unwittingly fall into an error, yet this cordial submission is an implicit retractation thereof, and I am confident will be so accepted by the Father of Mercies, both from me and from all others who seriously and sincerely do seek after peace and truth.

" Likewise I submit myself to the Representative Church, that is, to a free General Council, or so General as can be procured ; and until then to the

Church of England, wherein I was baptized, or to a National English Synod. To the determination of all which, and of each of them respectively, according to the distinct degree of their authority, I yield a *conformity* and *compliance*, or at the least, and to the lowest of them, an *acquiescence*."

For principles and convictions such as these, Andrewes, pre-eminently among our Divines, made a home in the Reformed Church of England. It was these principles and convictions which taught English Churchmen of the next generation, amid the direst ruin that ever fell on an institution, in exile abroad among mocking or pitying strangers, in utter overthrow at home, not to despair of the Church of England.

IV

THE PLACE OF THE EPISCOPATE IN CHRISTIAN HISTORY [1]

"And who is sufficient for these things?"—2 COR. ii. 16.

Καὶ πρὸς ταῦτα τίς ἱκανός.

THE disproportion between the professed ends of religion, and what we see of its means—between the hopes which it avows, and their likelihood, as it appears on the face of things here—is a thought which is familiar to us in the Bible, as it is too obvious for any one to have overlooked who has reflected at all. The disproportion, I mean, not between those ends and hopes, and what we believe to have been provided by Almighty God for their fulfilment, for no one can think that means fall short of ends in a redemption of which the Incarnation and the Cross were the conditions and price, and the gift of the Spirit is the continuing stay ; but the disproportion now, between all that goes on before our eyes, or is done by us directly for the ends of religion, and what those ends are when we really

[1] Preached in Westminster Abbey at the Consecration of Dr. Moberly as Bishop of Salisbury, St. Simon and St. Jude's Day, 1869.

C.S.,P. II

think of them. The sense of disproportion arises, when that divine work of saving and restoring— begun so awfully in " the might of signs and wonders, in the might of the Spirit of God "—is continued in the world of every day, as it has fallen back into its old customary paths. The early days felt it as much as we do. They saw a cause, which claimed everything and promised itself boundless victory, start on its career in the utmost obscurity and help- lessness. " The foolishness of preaching "; "the weakness of God "; "a treasure in earthen vessels "; "we walk by faith and not by sight ";—these are some of the frequent and often startling expressions met with in St. Paul, all telling the same thing, the hourly contrast between what an Apostle had to do and meant to do, and what appeared to be his equipment here for doing it. And it is this thought which, in the text, seems to strike St. Paul with sudden and almost oppressive force, coming home to him with that shock of surprise with which familiar truths sometimes startle us, when in an hour of unexpected insight they open upon us with a cer- tainty and vividness which make them seem like new ones. " To the one, the savour of death unto death ; and to the other, the savour of life unto life. And who is sufficient for these things? "

This sense of disproportion, which must be pre- sent to every thinking man in all steps affecting the interests of the kingdom of God, cannot but be one among the crowd of thoughts and feelings which accompany an occasion like the present. A great commission is to be given. The burden of a great trust is to be imposed. A famous chair of Christian teaching and government is again to be occupied. A seat is to be filled which, we may almost say, has never been unfilled while there has been English history.   A place is to be supplied in that ancient company of teachers which stretches back without a break through such wonderful changes of time to the first days of the Gospel.   It is one of those occasions which bring before us in strange and touching harmony the hopes of the living and the memory of the dead.   Who can be insensible to the solemnity of what we are about?   And yet what is all that we are doing, compared with the ends, in order to which it is all done?   What is this high and special ministry, to the mass of evils which it is appointed to keep down and heal?   What is it to those purposes of another world, which are the reason why it exists?   What is this great machinery, this great office, great as indeed the ideal of it is, when we think of what it aspires to, and put side by side what we aim at and what is our sufficiency?   If such thoughts did not come to us of themselves, there are those who are quite ready to remind us, from their point of view, of that disproportion which so struck St. Paul.   Here, all is to us overwhelmingly real and sacred : a man can look forward to no more serious account than for such a charge as is conferred to-day.   But outside, we should be met by those who regard it as the transaction of a decent or impressive conventional form, or as the filling up, by the customary process, varied according to the associations of the office, of a gap in one of the great establishments of an ancient State ; while to others it is simply an idle nothing, a vain fashion remaining

from what once was a social power and meant something ; for men thought so then, and that gives
meaning and power ; but their thoughts are changed,
and it means nothing now.   Why should we be surprised ?   They do but impress upon us, in their own
way, the force of the great contrast—what all that
we do must look like, in the eyes of those who
judge but from what they see here.   What does
it mean, but that St. Paul is right : that nothing that
we can show, no ministry that man can bear, no
function that man discharges, can possibly appear
adequate to ends and issues which belong to the
next world.   And what, after all, can any one now
say more than Jewish Rabbis, and Greek thinkers,
and Roman statesmen might have said of the chances
of a preacher like St. Paul changing the course of
belief and life in the Empire, and when the Empire
had perished, in a new world after it ?

Disproportionate every religious service of man
must seem to any one who has imagination enough
to put it side by side with those things behind the
veil, to which it professes to minister ; but disproportionate does not mean either unreal or ineffectual.
St. Paul's *" who is sufficient ? "* finds its answer a few
verses on, in an experience which left him not in
doubt of the power which was at work behind his
own insufficiency : " Our sufficiency is of God, who
hath made us able ministers of the New Testament."
The Apostle's instruments were feeble, but " mighty
to God," to the " casting down of strongholds."
They were foolish, yet they did what wisdom could
· not do ; they were obscure, yet they were felt even
then to be moving the world, and beginning the

greatest of its changes. He looks on and beholds the weak things of the world, which God had chosen, confounding the mighty ; the base and despised things, yea, and things that are not, bringing to nought things that are. We, who hope that we are continuing his work, who in this great function and ministry believe that we hold his Master's promise and gift, have we any corresponding experience to appeal to ? We, like him, are men in the flesh, with an enterprise beyond the grave, and a work which passes on into heaven for its consummation. Earth is very far from heaven, and human life incommensurable with what is to come. We cannot know yet, nor imagine what the end shall be ; but have we anything in the working of this great institution, in its known results and proved utilities, to set against the consciousness not only of personal insufficiency, but of disproportion, inherent in all things entrusted to human hands, in the office itself ? In what we believe and hold about it, we do not depend on- results, but on the word of Christ ; but His word is not in vain, and cannot be fruitless. We have a promise ; have we an answering history ? We believe that we have. The ideal of our Ordinal has not failed. History is, indeed, but too full of many a grim irony about it. It tells of great errors and great crimes, as well as of great achievements. But there has been ample to justify the obstinate hold which the institution of Episcopacy has kept on the Church. It has been very long in the world, and has worked on a great scale, and under the most varying conditions. It offers itself for a wide and comprehensive estimate, in which we can afford to

put aside local or temporary appearances—partial
mischiefs, incidental benefits, personal successes—
and watch its natural action in its broad results.
And we need not be afraid of the review. We do
not need the scene to close, in order to know what
the Church owes to it. When we are oppressed
with what we see too near and too partially, vexed
by the comparison of what has to be done with what
we can do, we may find, in a severe and honest
survey of the past, a countercharm to the disappointments, the continually exaggerated disappointments,
of the present, an encouragement to work and hope
for what is to come.

I will venture to dwell on this for a few moments :
the place which the Episcopate has, as a matter of
fact, filled in Christian history. I am not speaking
of questions which our Services take as settled, as to
its origin, authority, and grace ; but only of some
more obvious aspects of its influence, as we seem to
trace them in the long run. Everywhere we see
these lines of consecrated persons descending with
the lapse of the centuries, radiating as conversion
extends the Church to people after people. They
start from times where our keenest inquiries cannot
pierce the unknown. They come down, in great
Churches of Christendom, in some of the foremost of
modern nations, practically without a break, to this
day. What is before us is a succession of single
persons, singly in themselves the recognised deposi-
taries of public authority in things spiritual, the visible
representatives in their day of the original commission,
keeping up the idea of personal charge and responsibility and appointed leadership ; not merged in a

body of equal teachers, but standing out singly, chief after chief, to take the consequences, each man of his own administration, for praise or blame, to carry on, or else to debase and turn aside the great office of feeding the flock of God.   We see further that these lines are continued, on a definite basis and according to fixed rules, by the transmission of authority and place from hand to hand ; nowhere is the function a new thing, at least it does not allow itself to be such ; nowhere, since the first days, do we see it starting as from a fresh and independent origin.   It is always something given, not self-assumed ; passed on, not made for the occasion ; an ancient inheritance taken with all chances of advantage and inconvenience, not a recent change and reform, the growth of experience and necessity, consequent on altered conditions and increasing wants, and greater knowledge of both.

In looking back on what on the whole has come of all this in the history of religion, the first thing that strikes us is the part which the Episcopate has had in keeping up the continuity and identity of the Christian society ; the idea in it, and not only the idea, of its perpetuity—that from first to last it is one.   I do not think we always sufficiently appreciate what to me seems the astonishing fact, merely as a fact, of this continuous lasting on, through so many ages, and such trying ones, of the Christian body.   A shrewd man in the first centuries might well have doubted, according to all experience, whether such a body would be able to keep together for any length of time ; whether the first feeling of unity could continue amid the vicissitudes of time and the activity of the human mind ; he might have

further doubted whether, if it could, an institution
like Episcopacy was the way to secure it ; he might
have thought this but a slender and precarious provision to trust to, for the government of a society
like the Church. We have, indeed, nothing to boast
of in the matter of unity ; yet what we have, measuring by the great and constant forces against it, seems
to me remarkable enough ; the article of the Holy
Catholic Church has not dropped out of our creeds ;
the thrill is a real one which is called forth by the
great name of Christendom ; the inextinguishable
conviction that after all this unity is greater than it
seems—the longing, if it were but possible, to see it
come nearer in visible fact to its idea—are what the
best men feel, and have always felt, in their best
times.   And that which has kept on from age to age
this sense of the oneness of the continuous Christian
body is, I cannot doubt, as far as anything outward
has done it, the unfailing presence of the Episcopate.
There were other influences, doubtless, out of sight
and deeper ; but this one was immediate and direct.
If, in spite of all our differences, we all of us feel
ourselves one with the first ages, one with the Church
Universal of all times, instead of an entirely different
body growing out of it and coming into its place, it
is along these threads and networks of the Episcopate
that the secret agencies have travelled, which have
kept alive the sentiment of identity, amid so much
that seemed to contradict and defy it.   Along these
lines the main history of the Church has run ; about
them its main organisation has gathered age after
age.   A chain of men, transmitting the place which
they fill—with the memory of many predecessors,

and not doubting that they will have successors—
definitely connected with places which their presence
has made illustrious and filled with great recollections,
and which show, in works of grandeur and beauty,
the marks of their hands in many different epochs—
appeals, as the immemorial and hereditary always
do, to the imagination of society ; but here associations, rich in all that makes things venerable and
august in this world, are joined with others, full of
the majesty of interests beyond this world.   The
Episcopate has these two things : it has a history
inextricably associated with that of Christianity ;
and next, it is a public sign of community of origin
and purpose, and an assertion, never faltering, of
confidence in a continuing future.   Other organisa-
tions have with more or less success kept up
Christianity; but they date from particular times,
and belong to particular places, and are the growth
of special circumstances.   Only this has been everywhere, where Christianity has been ; only this belongs peculiarly to Christianity, as a whole.   A Bishop
is a representative person, and he represents much
more than the authority and claims of anything
present or local ; his functions and commission are
of the most ancient derivation, and of the widest
recognition ; he is an organ of a great movement,
the officer of a great kingdom, which has been going
on since the beginning of Christianity, and allows
itself no bounds but the world ; of that power which,
as a matter of fact, presented Christian truth to mankind, and has rooted it among them.   The witness
and memorial of a great past, of widely-extended
relations, of a great company of others like him,

most remote in time and space, he recalls, even now, the almost obliterated image of a once embodied and visible communion of Christians, still able to be one. His office is a thing of public and common interest, a trust for Christianity as such, which no party or school can venture to claim for its own, in creation or in use. Even to those who do not accept it, his ministration, conspicuous in all Christian history, is a memorial of that in which all Christians are concerned ; it is the sign not only of the appeal, but of the force, the spread, the duration, the rooted hold of their common faith ; he is one who could not be where he is, but for the long preceding efforts and victory of Christianity. The institution has borne the changes and the rough usage of time ; often abused, often disbelieved in, sometimes sunk in desperate scandals, it has the power of recovery, of preserving and returning to its type ; and it is impossible to imagine it stopping, come what may, as it is impossible to think of Christianity coming to an end. These ancient lines of bishops—representing an authority whose first steps are lost, not springing from the State, though, it may be, in every possible degree affected and controlled by it, not springing from the congregation, not springing from private theories, or reforms, or needs—carry home to the public mind, as a matter of manifest fact, even to those who hang loose to all religious forms, that we are living, and have been for ages, with a great public religious society round us, distinct from all mere associations of men ; as impersonal as the only thing like it on earth, the State ; which may at times reflect an individual mind or the tendencies of a period, but which is on the whole, and in the long run, too vast, too open, too manifold, to be the reflection, any more than the work, of any man, or any party, or any age.

The Episcopate represents the Christianity of history; it represents, further, the Christianity of the general Church, as distinguished from the special opinions and views of doctrine which assert their claims in it. Its long lines tie together the Christian body in time; they are scarcely less a bond, connecting the infinite moral and religious differences which must always be in the body of the Church. The Bishop's office embodies and protects the large public idea of religion, the common belief and understanding; that which all more or less respond to, and recognise as neither of this party nor of that, and allow a place to, even if not personally satisfied with it. For here, as in morality, as in politics, there is always, around what is personal and individual, and wider than all special schools and doctrines, a larger atmosphere in which all alike live — a *communis sensus* of simpler, more elementary, accepted truths, vague, perhaps, homely, apparently commonplace— "those mean despised truths that every one thinks he is sufficiently seen in";[1] of inferior interest compared to each man's favourite views, yet the condition and basis of them all. Within this there is sure to be much divergence; how can there fail to be, when the soul has free play, and opens into real life, on the tremendous and absorbing objects of religion? Who, too, can doubt the vast part which belongs to this independent action of individuals?—the vast

[1] Abp. Leighton, in Coleridge's *Aids to Reflection*, p. 103.

part, in all great things, of personal influence—the incalculable service rendered by individual desire of excellence, and hatred of evil, by the devotion, the charity, the spirit of reform, the love of truth, in private men ; often, no doubt, disturbing and embarrassing, fruitful of fresh difficulties while remedying old ones, threatening unwelcome change; but, well or ill, with mistakes or with good success, not letting the talent lie buried ; forcing us to remember, if but partially fulfilling, the great but often dreaded law of continually attempted improvement, without which all good would perish.   Every one who is himself in earnest, must of course see much to condemn, in what many others are in earnest about.   But I don't know why that should keep us from seeing, in great movements of the individual and private spirit, in efforts after reform and perfection, which perhaps we most thoroughly dislike from our several points of view—say, in Monasticism, in the theology of the Schoolmen, in the mendicant orders, in Puritanism, in the many phases of nonconformity, in the Company of Jesus, in the noble but vain revolt of Jansenism—much which the world could ill afford to be without.   Certainly, as I read history, it is difficult to say how much we all owe to every one of these many opposite movements, in which men, obstinately and devotedly, counting no cost and reserving no retreat, have given themselves to fulfil some high purpose which their own hearts and thoughts had shown them, and about which no one at first thought and felt like them.

But there is one thing these great movements cannot do : they cannot fill the great compass of man's nature, and aims, and needs. They are one-sided; they must leave much untouched; and, further, they would, if they were strong enough, destroy all that they cannot assimilate or subdue. The two greatest uprisings of the private religious spirit and temper against what was common and customary were, I suppose, Monasticism and Puritanism; but Monasticism and Puritanism, outwardly so different, yet with so many deep affinities both in their good and their evil, if they could have had their way unchecked, would have broken up the Church in the attempt to cleanse it. And there was something greater than both of them : there was an ideal of Christian life, a tone of Christian sentiment, a reach of Christian thought, a Christian harmony of gifts and powers, a free and living Christian morality, a great simple Christian faith, which, with all their high efforts and intensity of purpose, they failed to comprehend, they knew not how to reproduce. And of this wider, more generous, and yet humbler and more self-distrusting religion—often, doubtless, imperfect and inconsistent, yet perhaps not oftener so than these narrower and sterner rules of religion fell short of their standard—the Episcopate was the natural head, and bond, and visible symbol. The Bishop was the mouthpiece of a theology which was not peculiar to an order or a school. The religion of which he was the natural exponent was one which individuals might in various ways think not enough for them, but in which, so far as it went, they could meet on a common ground. Its language was the possession and inheritance of all Christian people, not a dialect moulded by the history of particular

opinions. The great Creed, so simple in words, so
overwhelming in meaning, of which he was the
guardian, was one which belonged at once to cate-
chumens and divines, to the child's bedside prayer
and to the most solemn worship. Whatever he
might be personally, in his office he was not his
own ; he belonged to the public : that office was an
expression of public thought, public belief, public
sentiment, within which private opinions might have
their field of debate ; and private opinion, when it
became ambitious and aggressive, whether in earlier
Monasticism or in later Puritanism, met in his place
and authority its natural check. The worship over
which he presided was marked by two special
features : it was old, and it was for all men. It was
venerable with the majesty of long and wide use : it
had the power which belongs to that which is a
common and public thing, open to all, of no private
devising, and of which no one thinks of the origin
and beginning. Its piety was expressed in collects
and offices and liturgical and sacramental forms,
which have been in the Church for ages, and of
which, for the most part, no man knows the author.
And it had that depth and force which belongs to
what all of us can respond to and join in, as men :
it could express the devotion of the aspiring and the
homely, the reserved and the eager alike ; it could
be the comfort and shelter of those who love what is
old, and quiet, and unpretending, and it could render
thoughts and feelings for those stirring and deep
minds in their most solemn moods, under whose
activity old things become new. A certain tone and
temper of religious feeling has sprung from all this ;

in its seriousness and balance, all, whether with
approval or not, see a contrast to the fervour and
vehemence of particular phases of the devotional
spirit ; and yet it alone has a key of sympathy, to
understand even what goes beyond it, and to respond
to what is not its own.   Again, the Bishop's special
functions were ministrations of wide reach and
concern, belonging to all, affecting all.   To this one
man, in his laying on of hands, young and old looked
in that solemn time when he committed each
generation of children to God's keeping in the world ;
from this one man, and from his laying on of hands,
a whole body of clergy drew their authority, and
learned and unlearned gained or suffered by the
pastors whom he commissioned and governed.   In
all that he was and did, in his administration and
official speaking, the idea was ever present of what
was of common import to all, of what bound all
together, of what belonged not to to-day or yesterday,
but was born with man, or was coeval with the
Gospel.   Others might have newer, perhaps deeper,
perhaps more eventful things to say.   He was there
to remind Christians of that vast, wide, spiritual
society which was meant to embrace us all ; of the
force and value of what is common, and public, and
continuous, and customary.   He was there to bind
together in each age the old and the new, the weak
and the strong ; to witness, amid the vicissitudes. of
individual thought and energy, for something which,
with less show, wears better and lasts longer ; for a
common inheritance of faith and religion, which
needs indeed to be filled up in its outlines by private
conviction and activity, but without which everything

private risks becoming one-sided in ideas, and cramped in sympathy, and, at last, poor in heart.

Such an institution can bear the test of history. Its broad results are before the world ; the world can see and judge whether it has been in vain, and whether it is not doing still what it was doing centuries ago. If only it had done what it has done, in keeping the Church together, and in guarding at once Catholic faith and Christian freedom, it would have justified its place. And yet this alone does not satisfy what the Church conceives of the office. If this were all, we might speak of a successful and salutary organisation ; but there would be no need for an Apostle to cry out, and for those after him to echo his cry, " Who is sufficient for these things ? " The great men of this world do not so shrink under their burden. But men may well say so, if they think as St. Paul thought of what they are charged with, of the risk of going wrong. If it is an institution and organ of Christ's Gospel and Kingdom, it must have aspects which are beyond the domain of history. It is on pain of degrading our conception of it that we lose sight, in the stress we lay on its practical bearings now, of functions which are in order to the unseen and the future. It is a great ministry of religion ; and when we name religion, we name something beside which all experience here is soon at fault, all faculties of thought at last find their term, all creations of imagination are pale and tame. We believe that this office serves the Gospel of Jesus Christ ; and the Gospel of Him who came to seek the lost, to save sinners, to abolish death, to judge mankind, runs up, by the very force of the terms we use, into that which utterly leaves behind all that "eye hath seen or ear heard." We cannot grasp it, no, not in its most reduced and attenuated form, without coming upon what is in the sharpest contrast to all that we have to do with now. Call this mystical, intangible, transcendental: so it is, but Christianity starts with the assumption of the incomprehensible greatness of what is out of sight, and presupposes a world of mystery; and so, in reality, view it as we will, does human nature. If St. Paul's ministry had its most matter-of-fact prosaic side, of business and drudgery, of daily trouble and stiff opposition and frequent disappointment, it also took into view another side, which in the incredible vastness of its claims, its responsibilities, its stakes, its prospects, must seem to the judgment of mere experience, as it did to Festus, the extravagance of a dream. And if there is a ministry on earth which in any sense inherits from the Apostles of the New Testament, it, too, must not shrink from the thought, that in some of its chief parts it has to work, and trust, and wait, but not to see; that it belongs to that world above our reach, of which the Psalms are the echo, and which is the unchanging background of St. Paul; and that while now it binds the Church with society, linking on earth past with present, and preparing the present for what is to come, its highest functions look to things "not seen," its issues reach to that time when all will be over here, the judgment on it has to pass before "no assize of man,"[1] its success and its reward

[1] Andrewes' *Sermons*, v. 117 (translation of 1 Cor. iv. 3, ὑπὸ ἀνθρωπίνης ἡμέρας).

are for that unknown hour when the Master and His
servants shall meet for their last account, and when
the last test shall decide on the secrets and on the
ventures of us all.

The day that is passing, and that " kingdom where
space and time are not,"[1] are both our Master's, and
to both His servants owe their debt. *Here*, they
have to meet the realities of the moment, to face
actual difficulties, to choose their course, to keep
their balance, undazzled and undismayed ; here, they
need courage, patience, forbearance, soberness. *There*,
they need to live with the thought that they are
ministers of something much greater than anything
that men can be themselves ; that they are charged
with words which are not their own ; that powers
and blessings of the other world come with them, to
help and comfort souls—judgments inscrutable, and
ways past finding out, and a love which is beyond
understanding, the love of Christ. *There*, they have
to believe, and to hope, to pray, to adore, to bless.
Their great trust calls, indeed, for the best of that
without which no man can do nobly here—public
spirit, large-hearted sympathy, manliness, straightforward wisdom, steady judgment, humbleness of
soul ; " plain living, and high thinking," and true
work. Man, in his strength and honesty, is sufficient
for these things. But there is something further, for
which, by himself, he is not sufficient : to take up
for his own day the burden borne in theirs by
Patriarchs, Prophets, Apostles ; to be the chosen and
special servant of a dispensation not of this world,
most awful, eternal, infinite ; to have, as the end and

---

[1] Wordsworth, *Excursion*, p. 118.

business of life, to be a foremost witness of the will
of God and the hopes of man, and to bear on high,
in a world of sense and time, always passing away,
the Everlasting and Most Holy Name ; to be charged,
above all other men, with understanding the purposes,
guarding the truth, distributing the graces, of the
Unseen and the Most High ; to fulfil functions such
as are described in the words of Scripture—" over-
seers of the Church of God," " stewards of God's
mysteries," " ambassadors for Christ," " workers together with God," " to whom He hath committed the
ministry of the reconciliation of the world."   " For
these things, who is sufficient ? "   Who, indeed—
without that Spirit of counsel and might, that Spirit
of power and love and soberness, with which the
great Master once strengthened His messengers.
May He grant it indeed to all who are in any way
responsible for the interests of the kingdom of God.
To Him, having done their best, may they be able,
with prayer and faith, and deepest humbleness of
trust and will, to commit their way.   And then they
must leave their work in those Strong Hands which
uphold the world, which have so wonderfully preserved His Church, and in whose keeping are the
hopes and the life of all things that He has made.

V

THE GIFT OF THE SPIRIT [1]

" And as they ministered to the Lord, and fasted, the Holy Ghost
said, Separate Me Barnabas and Saul for the work whereunto I
have called them."—ACTS xiii. 2.

THIS is the account of the first Ordination in the
Church, since the full purpose of God as to the character of the Christian Church had been declared by the
conversion of Cornelius.   That great surprise—" then
hath God also to the Gentiles granted repentance
unto life "—had brought home to the minds even of
Apostles how imperfectly they had as yet understood their high commission.   It had reversed their
undoubting suppositions as to their field of action,
and what they were meant to do.   In place of a
completed and renewed Judaism, completed by the
coming of its King and renewed to fresh life by His
Spirit, and drawing by a new attraction throngs of
heathen proselytes into the fold of Israel—in place
of this great change, magnificent as it might seem
in God's own land and city, among the multitude
of Jewish communities dispersed throughout the
world—in place of this there was substituted as the

1 An Ordination Sermon, preached in Wells Cathedral, 19th
December 1880.

destined scene of their labours, with all its difficulties, with all its openings, with all its hopes, *the
world itself.* All the multitudes of mankind, unre-
claimed, astray, godless, "aliens from the commonwealth of Israel and strangers to the covenants of
promise," Gentile society, east and west, mighty,
organised, deeply corrupted, with all its fringes of
surrounding barbarism, "the publicans and sinners"
of humanity, despised by Jews, shunned, hated,
because so steeped in vice, and so utterly unintelligible
and uncongenial—these and not Jews prepared by a
Divine discipline of a thousand years, these were the
materials out of which the Apostles were, after all,
to build up the Church of God. As this great and
novel conception of the work before them gradually
grew into distinctness, and they became accustomed
to it, it naturally took possession of all their thoughts.
It pointed to new efforts, a new departure, new
functions. The result we read in the text. Apostles
of the Gentiles were called to extend and perfect
what had been begun and was not given up by the
Apostles of the circumcision. As they waited at
Antioch, and pondered and prayed, and wondered at
what was to be, the call came. "Separate me
Barnabas and Saul for the work to which I have
called them"; and the building up of the Church
Universal began. It was the first Ordination of the
Catholic Church, in which there was no 'longer
"Jew nor Gentile, bond nor free, but all were one in
Christ Jesus."

It was no human agency which pronounced this
call, which sent forth Barnabas and Saul on their
eventful mission. If there is anything on which

stress is laid in the New Testament, it is that He
who sends forth the ministers of the Gospel of
Christ, who calls them, who equips them for their
task, who is the promised source to them of light and
strength and influence, is God the Holy Ghost. He
who sanctified the Baptist from his mother's womb,
He from whom the Son Himself received the seal
and anointing of His earthly ministry on the banks
of Jordan, He who was the special gift from their
departing Master to the Twelve, He whose presence
with them was the special qualification of the Seven,
the first Deacons, " men full of the Holy Ghost and
of wisdom "—He, too, again gives the word when
Barnabas and Saul are sent forth from Antioch to
head " the great company of the preachers " to the
end of time.   And never from that day to this has
the Church forgotten that it is from His co-operation,
and sanction, and gracious blessing that all that is
real in her Ordinations comes.   Forms vary and
customs alter, and one language dies and gives
place to another, and sacred words are spoken in
differing tongues as far from one another as the east
is from the west.   But the central belief is never
lost, is never changed—that from God the Holy
Ghost the Church in England receives power and
authority to commission the ministers of each generation, that He is with her and her representatives and
chief pastors in the exercise of this office ; that from
Him comes to each one in Ordination, comes individu-
ally and personally, the awful gift of His consecrating
presence, to be prized, and cherished, and faithfully
served, or to be despised and rejected —but, in any
case, never to be recalled.   On whom the Holy

Ghost has set His seal, the seal must remain either for blessing or for judgment.

It will not, I hope, be thought disrespectful to the congregation here assembled, if on an occasion like this, I take leave to address the few words I have to say, exclusively to one part of it. For to some of you a time is come which, to any one seriously believing in the reality of things unseen, is in simple truth inexpressibly solemn. Even in this world's point of view it is a solemn thing to feel ourselves standing on the verge of a new career— to have left and put off the old, to have begun for the future what is new and strange. How much more when that new career is the Christian ministry —the ministry of the Crucified, the ministry of the Holy Ghost. On this occasion, then, the first step in a new, lifelong course, I will venture to ask your leave to try, in the few minutes allotted to me, to refresh in you thoughts which no doubt have been present to all of you.

What is the foundation of this new condition of your life which is impending over you? In what does this change begin? You are about to pass solemnly from the layman to the clergyman. I am not speaking of all that is implied in this; but I will ask you to think, What does this new life before you rest upon? What must be at the bottom of it? What above everything is its root and ·spring, feeding it, moulding it, giving it its true character and colour? It must be—if it is to be what your Master wants for you, if it is to be in truth what it claims to be, if it is to answer its purpose and not wander into alien paths and employment for which

it was not meant—it must be the work of the Holy
Ghost in and with your spirit. From Him it must
spring ; by Him it must be sustained. It is with
Him you have to do. It is He who sends you on
your road. It is with Him that you will have to do
your work. It is to Him that you will have to give
account.

This must be at the bottom of everything ; this
must be foremost and paramount, if we are to think
and feel truly and fittingly of what we are called to,
in being clergymen. There are countless things
which press into notice and hide it from our thoughts ;
countless things which seem incongruous with it ;
countless things which in the name of their immediate
importance claim to come first in the interest of
practical men. It is easy to forget in this our
energetic and exacting society that a clergyman has
to do with the silent powers of the world to come,
with the secret but real gifts and purposes of God
the Holy Ghost. You have forgotten it, perhaps,
sometimes, in the labour and effort of your preparation, in the anxiety and trial of your examination.
You will forget it, perhaps, in time to come, in the
inevitable routine and vicissitudes of necessary
business, in the worries, and weariness, and excitement, and disappointment of clerical work. You
will forget it, perhaps, when you are hard driven by
calls, which you find it hard to meet, on your
strength, on your resources, on your powers of
thought and teaching ; when you are perplexed by
questions which you cannot answer, and difficulties
out of which you do not see your way. But, behind
all the dust and hurry and turmoil of your business,

the great truth remains. The clergyman is the
minister of Christ, the unseen, the real Christ ; and
the clergyman's teacher and appointed guide and
strengthener, the giver of His gifts, to whom he
must turn for help and light, who alone can enable
him to do his duty, is, very really, very specially,
that invisible but mighty Comforter of us all, God
the Holy Ghost.

1. You will have first to do with yourself. You
have to know yourself, to learn more about yourself
than perhaps you have yet learnt ; to be master over
yourself, to govern and direct your purposes so as to
suit yourself to your new calling and way of life.
And what is the first thing to be ever remembered ?
Is it not that, in this your life and profession, it is
God the Holy Ghost who in His providence and good
pleasure has chosen and called and picked you out
from among your brethren for what you have to do?
In the immediate forefront of all our lives, the front
place of what we see, there are all the human
purposes and influences and reasons which have
determined a man's line of life ; but, behind all that,
the apparent accident, the motives of duty or con-
venience or inclination, the secular ties and constraints
which have had much—perhaps too much—to do with
his choice, there is the sovereign election of God who
finally places us where we are.

And He has finally willed to place you here.
He who chose Saul and David for their respective
trials, He who destined Prophet and Apostle for
their tasks, He who " ordained " Jeremiah to be " a
prophet to the nations," and separated Paul from
his mother's womb, and called him by His grace,

He has led each one of us, each one of you, through
all the changes, and what we call the chances of
life, to the front where we stand now. In the unfathomable purposes of His eternal election He
knew each one of you, and appointed this to be your
business in the world, and ordered your circumstances
to meet and suit your own plans and wishes and
choice, accepting your offered service—if offered of
good will ; if otherwise, taking you at your word.
And now the Holy Ghost, who chose you and sealed
you at your Baptism, who came to you with His
proffered benefits at your Confirmation, who, if you
have ever had a good thought or desire, has been
speaking in your heart, comes to you the third time,
the third solemn time, in Ordination. Can we help
recalling the sacred words, the thrice repeated
question—the sacred words rise of themselves to
our thoughts—" Simon, son of Jonas, lovest thou
Me—lovest thou Me—lovest thou Me, more than
these ? " He singles you out for a charge which
all your brethren have not. He promises you gifts
and a commission specially meant for you. He
chooses you, not for higher honours, not for higher
prerogatives over your brethren, but for more defined
and more exacting service, for the alternatives of a
severer trial of your whole-heartedness and self-
devotion, in which your distant crown of victory
may be brighter, but also your failure more disas-
trous. Indeed there is nothing to puff you up or
exalt you, in the highest estimate we can form of
the Holy Spirit's calling and gifts in Ordination.
They are the measure of our never-ceasing responsibilities. They are the ground of hope and strength

when human hope fails and human strength sinks.
But God save us from our miserable downfall if we
build on these the fabric of self-conceit and self-
consequence, or ever allow the thought to rest in
our minds that we are better men and more faithful
than laymen—God's favourites, for being clergymen.

2. And next, you have to do with others ; and
it is for others that you are chosen for your place
and work.   Remember, then, that in what you have
to do *with* them and *for* them, your true, your only
adequate relation to them is as the steward and
minister of the Holy Ghost ; His servant and
minister in the work which He carries on in the
Church, and in the souls and characters and consciences of men.

The calls upon a clergyman are many.   The
ways in which he may be useful are manifold, even
opposite.   The work and necessities of .the Church
and society increase in mass and in diversity as time
goes on, and in them all the clergyman has his part.
But he forgets himself, forgets what he was called
to, forgets the reason and purpose of his Ordination,
if he ever lets himself forget that he is, first and
foremost, the servant of that Divine Person who
rules the Church, and commissioned him for his
work in it.   The fountain and regulating principle
of your influence must be a constant recollection of
His high service, and true-hearted loyalty to 'it.   It
is not enough for a clergyman to do good and useful
work, to be a profound and accomplished scholar.
It is not enough˜ to be a successful parish priest,
a great and instructive preacher, a statesmanlike
organiser, an active manager of some religious in-

stitution, a conscientious teacher, a powerful advocate
of truth against gainsayers.   He must be more than
all these.   He must live in the consciousness—a
consciousness which rules his heart, and shapes his
aims, and inspires his devotion—that he belongs
essentially to God's divine and heavenly ministry
of grace and reconciliation and restoration ; that his
office is, in the last resort, in its truest meaning, a
spiritual one ; that be his employment what it may,
he is in his heart of hearts the servant of a Power
whose mystery none can fathom, and whom no
conquest can satisfy but the wills and characters
of men won back to His obedience and peace.

Think of your calling and work in this way, as
having to do nothing merely temporal or earthly,
but the work of the Holy Ghost, the Divine hope
of light and goodness for men, and you will never
be tempted to rest content and self-complacent with
some cheap appearance of success, some short cut to
popular influence, some temporary and superficial
stirring up of interest, or feeling, or zeal.   Think of
your work in this way, as doing what the Holy
Spirit in your Ordination has laid upon you to do,
and doing it with Him as the witness of your soul ;
and then, come what may, you will have a spring
of strength and comfort within you which success
alone cannot give.   You may seem to fail, as many
of God's truest servants have seemed to fail, while
men of shallower and more alloyed religion have
seemed so useful.   You may be baffled by your
own disqualifications, by obstacles which are too
strong for you.   You may spend your labour, and,
what is more, your prayers, your tears, your heart,

and not see any good for it. Such things are no
uncommon incidents of a clergyman's career. But
if you are not working for your own glory and ends,
but for that invisible Spirit who gave you your
charge, and is with you while you fulfil it ; if you
nourish and cherish in your soul the recollection
that to work under Him and with Him is now the
real end of your life ; if you try to keep before your
mind that in His dealings with you your life as a
clergyman began, and only by continued communion
with Him, and by His help and guidance it can
safely end, you will learn to bear discouragement as
nothing but faith and sincerity can bear it. You
will come to see that there are worse and emptier
things in the world than disappointment, where it
is disappointment in honest service. A true man,
a man who believes in the presence, and wisdom,
and guidance of the Holy Ghost, would rather have
it than the deceptions and unrealities of a hollow
and selfish success. The work is not yours but
your Master's. There may be ends to be answered
in your failure greater than there could have been
gained by your success. So that you have not
forgotten in whose hands you are, a chequered, un-
popular, or a rejected ministry need not mean to
to you the failure of your life.

    Yes, my brethren, the ministry you seek, if it is a
real thing, is a thing of heaven, with all that there
must be of mystery and strangeness, when the things
of heaven come down to the life of time. It has
been said, with some justice I think, that often we
do not appreciate in our popular teaching the place
which the office of the Holy Ghost fills in the teaching

of the New Testament. It is difficult, no doubt, to speak of it wisely and well : of so Divine a thing we can but speak with dim ideas and imperfect words. But it certainly does come before us, interwoven with the very texture of the New Testament, not merely in the mysterious sublimities of the Epistles to the Romans and the Ephesians, but in every dogmatic and every practical lesson. And neither our life nor our teaching can be in harmony with the New Testament if we let it drop out of our minds.

I doubt not that you are men who will take trouble with yourselves to keep up your thoughts and convictions to the point from which you start at Ordination. Set it then as a definite object in your self-discipline, to keep before you, deep and strong and keen, the remembrance of that awful and gracious Person with whom you will have to work, and who sends you forth. In your continued devotions, without which your service will be worse than vain, make it a definite subject of prayer that you may know Him, as far as man can know Him, more and more ; that you may receive the Divine Blessing in the way and order which Scripture reveals to us, that as you turn to the Father for mercy, and to the Incarnate Son for sympathy, so you may turn to the Spirit for light and strength ; that in the special functions of your ministry, in teaching and counsel and warning and consolation, in the administration of Christ's Sacraments, you may look for help to the special source where Scripture bids you seek it, in the manifold and promised gifts of the Holy Ghost. Pray definitely that you may never forget Him, never lose sight of Him, ever have Him with you. Pray definitely that He will ever kindle and purify your affections, as well as guide your thoughts. Pray that He will give you warmth of soul, without which religion withers ; and soberness and seriousness of judgment, without which truth is wrecked and reason lost. Pray to Him, and for His gifts, in the spirit of the Collects of this season : let them become your constant companions. Pray to Him in the spirit of the first preparatory Collect in the Communion Service. Pray to Him in the *Veni Creator* Hymn ; and may He hear all our prayers for the light and strength and purity we so much need.

O God the Holy Ghost, who hast called us to this place in Thy service, as Thou hast begun Thy work, so also continue and finish it in us. Save us from our besetting sins, from pride, and bitterness, and faintness of heart, from sloth and self-deceit, and the curse of an unsubdued will ; and grant us to know and to follow, to do and to suffer Thy will, Who with the Father and the Son livest and reignest one God, for ever.

VI

ADAM, THE TYPE OF CHRIST[1]

" Who is the figure of Him that was to come."—ROMANS v. 14.

ὅς ἐστι τύπος τοῦ μέλλοντος.

" Qui est forma futuri."

I ASSUME that there can be no doubt as to the meaning of the words which we render, " Him that was to come"; and that the ambiguity to which the Latin version, *Qui est forma futuri*,[2] might have possibly lent itself, can have no place in the original. In Adam, the Apostle's phrase leads us to see, not the likeness of *what was to be*, but the Figure of *Him that was to come*. Doubtless, we may read in Adam the foreshadowing of what was to happen in the world, of the future of his race; but here, the Apostle speaks of the First Man as the Type of a Person, the First Type of Jesus Christ the Lord.

We are accustomed to this way of speaking, and often it hardly arrests our thought. And yet it might; for between Type and Antitype, in this case, the relation appears at first sight that of the extremest opposition of condition and character, and

---

[1] Preached in St. Mary's, Oxford, during Lent, 1870.
[2] *Vide* Aug. *Epist.* clvii. 20; *De Pecc. Mer.*, i. 13, iii. 9.

resulting work and consequences. "As in Adam all
die, even so in Christ shall all be made alive." "The
first man is of the earth, earthy; the second man is
the Lord from Heaven." What opposition can be
greater? Yet Adam is the Type of Christ. He, in
whom we see the whole history of our sin and the
true image of our falling short, is the figure of Him in
whom is summed up all our hope of righteousness
and the whole promise of our completeness. He who
stands at the head of the history of this world—a
history so strange, so dark, so short—is the figure
of the Father of the everlasting Age to come. He
of whom, in the utter dimness of the beginning
of time, we in vain attempt to form a conception,
stands as the type of that Brother and Friend whose
words and ways and mind are ever open to us, and
whom we can know and love as we can none other,
who has been among us and has gone from us. He
who had a great trust and betrayed it so lightly is
the type of Him who came to do His Father's will,
and was obedient, even unto death. By what
common likeness can we join together him in whom
we behold the Fall, with Him in whom we receive
the great and eternal Restoration? How can the
great failure be the type of the great victory? the
great transgression, of the great forgiveness? the
great disaster, of the great recovery? fatal defeat and
fault, of fulfilment and perfection? Every figure
must in some respects be a contrast; and con-
versely, every contrast implies a parallel and correspondence; but here, the contrast seems to ex-
tinguish the likeness. How is darkness to be the
figure of light? sin, of righteousness? death, of life?

C.S.,P..   K

How should the beginning of the downward road of evil reflect the beginning of the new creation of righteousness? how should the Creature, in his first misery and weakness, suggest and represent the Creator, Holy and Strong—"the Lord from Heaven," dwelling among us in His awful Power and Love, to reverse our doom?

But high and low lie very near to one another, in that order in which the First Man and the Second are made by St. Paul to be answering counterparts. It is in a world where things are less real, where our thoughts are swayed by opinion and half knowledge and custom, that we shrink from putting them together, except as opposites. But the wisdom of God, which sees all things from end to end in the infinite vastness of the dispensation of grace, has no such restraint. In the first man, in the depth of his fall, it traces the lineaments of that Holy One who was in the fulness of time to bear his flesh and blood. He who made man was not ashamed of him. He who made man did not disdain to share the necessities of his humiliation, He accepted the community of his loss and shame. He bore man's likeness; He grudged not that man should bear His own; that man, in the very moment of his overthrow, should be the prophecy of his Deliverer. He was not ashamed that we should see, in him in whom the world was lost, reflections of His own peculiar glory, the image and the promise of what He was Himself to make perfect. In the very beginning of human history and destiny, we find the figure of its fulfilment, which yet was to be so different.

We see in the great type of the Apostle two
things. He to whom, step by step, our blood goes
back, he in whom were the germs of all that we are,
is set before us as the eternal memorial, at once of
what man was meant for, and of what man has
become. In him are seen together, the intention
and the swerving, the purpose and the disappointment. He stands not alone in this melancholy
significance. The Bible has many such types of
good made frustrate, and the actual world is full of
them. But in Adam it is the fortunes of mankind
that we see summed up. He stands for us all ; for
all living souls, who from generation to generation
receive and hand on the breath of human life. In
him is the image of all his seed. His is no mere
personal calling, no mere personal fall, like those of
Saul and Judas. Meant for what he was, even
man's perfection, yet in his mortality and pain,
though brought upon him by himself, he makes his
mute but undoubting appeal for restoration ; he
witnesses that all has not been in vain, that he was
not made for nought. Where the glimpse that is
given us is of the destinies of mankind, there, where
the purpose and the failure come together, they seem
to demand the remedy, and to announce it. So
those, whose thoughts are moulded by the Spirit of
the God of Hope, instinctively gather ; so the Bible,
from first to last the comforter and upholder of
human hope, bids them believe that their thoughts
are true. He in whom we fell is the Figure of Him
that was to come, because he faintly shadows forth
the unimaginable perfection reserved for human
nature in its true Head ; and because, in the depths

of his own ruin and failure, he cries out and stretches
forth his hands for the fulfilment of what he has
missed ; and by those cries and yearnings to the
Father who made him, is the warrant and promise
of it.   The type of our lost estate, to all experience
irrecoverable, the type of our common disaster which
once seemed as if it might have alleviations, but no
reversal, is transfigured, while we gaze upon an
image, faint yet surrounded with titles of awful
honour, of One in whom the obstinate longings of
man were to be more than made good ; One by
whom the "creature," long "subject to vanity,
should be delivered from the bondage of corruption
into the glorious liberty of the children of God."
For the First man stands at the head of the
genealogy of the Second, as "Adam, which was the
Son of God."   The First man has that awful thing
said of him which is said of the Second, in however
more ineffable a meaning—"In the image of God,
created He man ;"—the Son, "Who is the image of
the invisible God," "the express image of His
person."

In Adam we have announced to us the archetype
of man ; what was the design of his being, what was
the end and original law of his nature :—"Let us
make man in our image, after our likeness" ; "So
God created man in His own image : in the image
of God created He him."   In Adam, we are told
at the very opening of the Bible of the unity and
brotherhood of mankind, that last discovery, long
fought against and hardly recognised, of the widening thought of ages, of the conspiring feelings and
reason of civilised man.   In Adam, we have that

position of man as the crown of all that we know, which is so absolutely unique and overwhelmingly mysterious—as the bondsman and victim of nature, yet its lord ; in all its infinite spaces, the one thing free ;[1] free to choose, free to obey, free to rise ; endowed, he alone of things here, with the wonderful power of self-conquest, self-correction, self-improvement ; with capacities infinite of drawing nearer and nearer for ever to the Father, in whose Image he was made; the one thing able to know God, and to know what to God is good,—the one among creatures here whose perfection lay in the perfection of his *will*, in owning the sway of those strange, awful words, *ought* and *ought not.*

And that was the prerogative and calling which was cast away. That was the purpose which was made void. That was the place in the order of God's creation, which from that time to this the race has

---

[1] " The first appearance of man in nature was the appearance of a new being in nature. . . . The sun had risen, and the sun descended, the stars looked down upon the earth, the mountains climbed to heaven, the cliffs stood upon the shore, the same as now, countless ages before a single being existed who saw it. The counterpart of this whole scene was wanting,—the understanding mind : that mirror in which the whole was to be reflected ; and when this arose, it was a new birth for creation itself, that it became *known*—an image in the mind of a conscious being. But even consciousness and knowledge were a less strange and miraculous introduction into the world than *conscience*. . . . Mysterious in his entrance into this scene, man is *now* an insulation in it. . . . What can be more incomprehensible, more heterogeneous, a more ghostly resident in nature, than the sense of right and wrong ? What is it ? Whence is it ? The obligation of man to sacrifice himself for right is a truth which springs out of an abyss, the mere attempt to look down into which confuses the reason. Man is alone, then, in nature ; he alone of all the creatures communes with a Being out of nature ; and he divides himself from all other physical life by prophesying, in the face of universal visible decay, his own immortality."—Mozley, *Bampton Lectures*, iii. pp. 88, 89.

not fulfilled. In this image of what man was made for begins the terrible record of what man has been; the unfolding of that terrible and almost infinite variety of failure and sin which crowds the pages of human history, and is its first and deepest impression. "In Adam all die": nothing remains unspoilt; no promise reaches its true fulfilment, no good abides without decay and degeneracy: all wears out—evil, happily, too, or the world would perish—but also good. "In Adam all die": we see it in man's greatest types as in his lowest; we see it in his refinement and in his degradation; we see it in his polities and in his Churches, as well as in those monstrous aggregations of unorganised men, without law, without country, without home, which crowd the outskirts of our great cities. Even in all those great doings of his, so elevating, so hopeful, of which the world is full, yet there lurks the taint of the heart not whole and the will infirm; and on them all waits death, breaking off the great labour of good, beating down the great triumphs over evil and folly. And what are these great labourers, great conquerors, whose work, too, has to begin afresh when they go, —what are these few among the so many, who " as soon as they are born, begin to draw to their end, and have no sign of virtue to show"? Take the men and women, as we meet them in the streets; take the huge multitudes of the average; leave out the extremes on both sides—extremes are rare in all orders of things, though they are less rare on the low side than on the high—and what a spectacle rises before our mind, of falling short of standards, of things marred, of misuse, of emptiness, of decay. Think

only, in all generations of time, in all countries of
mankind, of the *waste of life;* of what to us, at least,
can only seem the waste of life ; the waste of life
wantonly cut short, the waste of life, *itself wasted* in
the having; the wastes of savage idleness; the wastes
of barbarian wars and destructions :—life wasted in
the artificial vices and wants of the highest social
state ; the waste of life, in *men,* for war, and, it must
be said, for much that we call industry ; the waste
of life, in *women,* who live for man's sin, and by it.
These, we know, are things on a great scale ; they
are things accepted, as what cannot be helped, as
what in the nature of things must be.   Do they not
reveal to us a world in which—who can tell how much
—life is wasted ; wasted by men for themselves, wasted
by what others do with them.   "One day telleth
another, and one night certifieth another"; and the
tale they repeat is the same dreary story, of to-day
fruitless as yesterday, of to-morrow sure to be thrown
away as to-day ; of irremediable, continuing *waste.*
In such things as these we see, in its true measure,
what is meant by the Fall.

Is not so manifest a purpose, and so manifest a
falling short, the very ground and prophecy of hope ?
I do not suppose that we can always argue from
tendency to effect ; that every unfulfilled promise,
and capacity, and aspiration, implies at last its fulfilment.   But there are failures which are final, and
there are failures which, in the very moment of their
ill-success—by what they *might* do, by what they
do—carry with them the promise of being at last
repaired.   The fall of Sodom was not like the fall
of Israel, or the going astray of Greece and Rome.

And here, in Adam and the race he stands for—
amid ruin, amid incredible debasement, amid the
very mysteries of iniquity and apostasy around him,
amid horrors not to be exaggerated, not to be told,
of his history—still are to be discerned the outlines
of the image of God. Can that image stay with
men, and not be to them the pledge of remedy?
Can that image strike its print so deep—can the
dream of nature, contradicted everywhere, yet be
always and obstinately of goodness, of what is
noblest, and purest, and most divine—and not lift
mankind to the looking-for of deliverance, of that
day when the old shall pass, and all things be made
new? Can man feel, as he must feel, that sin is not
his fate, that evil is not his natural law—and not
find in the power within him, of correcting what is
amiss, of repentance, of improvement, the irresistible
argument of hope? Surely, from Adam's Creation
and Adam's Fall, from such a purpose and such an
overthrow, did not the cry go up, prophetic of the
grace that listened to it, for retrieval, for a new
beginning? " In Adam all die,"—Adam, who was
made in the image and likeness of God. Is it
not reason, indeed, that from that time till now,
" the whole creation," in him made subject to vanity,
" groaneth and travaileth in pain together," crying
out to be redeemed ; not accepting as its fate " the
" bondage of corruption " ; earnestly expecting the
accomplishment of a destiny too great to fail at
last ? Is not this the expostulation and plea of our
nature— in its deep humiliation, in its unconquerable
consciousness of what it was meant for and in *whose*
hand it lives,—

O remember what my substance is ;
The work of Thine hands ;
The likeness of Thy countenance.
Despise not Thou the work of Thine own hands :
Hast Thou made for nought Thine own image and likeness ?
For nought, if Thou destroy it.[1]

Human nature—in what it is and in what it is not ; in what it would be and cannot be ; in its aims and its incompleteness ; in its stateliness and its deformity ; in its charm and its repulsiveness ; in its power and its failure—sends up the cry for restoration. Man, but a link in the chain of nature, may stretch forth hands in vain to laws which cannot hear and cannot change. But can man, *the Spirit*, cry to the God who made him, the Father of Spirits, the Living, the All-compassionate, the True, without the prayer for help and redemption being itself the pledge of its fulfilment ?

And thus, in his double character of greatness and of misery—of the greatness of his end and the misery of his state ; in his longings and their disappointment, in his wish for good and inability to resist the present, in the eternal conflict of conscience and passion, in the strange humiliation of a real *will*, ever defeated and defeating itself ; in all the astonishing and deep contradictions of his condition, his desires, his history, he foreshadows and foretells the deliverance which corresponds at once to the awful, height of what he was meant for, and the depth, beyond our measuring, to which he had sunk. For his Deliverer was one like himself ; yet with all the difference that there is between the Creature and the

---

[1] Bishop Andrewes' *Devotions*, Day I.

Creator. He who " took hold " of him was He who
made him,—after whose Image he was made, whose
Likeness he was meant to attain to : greater none
could be, to stamp and make certain the greatness
of his nature. But who can tell the depth of the
humiliation of the Second Adam ? " The Lord
from heaven," the " quickening Spirit " by whom
the dead are made alive, the " Word made flesh " ;
what was He but the likeness of His creature, in the
wretchedness in which he had gone forth from
Paradise ; in the " form of a servant," in " the likeness
of sinful flesh " ; seeking the lost in the company of
the lowest of the lost ; the friend of publicans and
sinners, accepting the reproach of their companionship ; tempted and scorned, a man of sorrows and
acquainted with grief; bearing in the eyes of the
world all the marks of ignominious and unsuccessful
sin ; judged, in the name of the Highest, as a deceiver
and a blasphemer ; made sin for us, made a curse
for us ; forsaken of God, a worm and no man, the
very scorn of men, and outcast of the people ? What
has man done of worst evil, of which the apparent
shadow did not rest on his Deliverer ? What
unrest, what pain, what privation, troubles his lot,
which his Deliverer did not share ? what is there
in the sinner's doom at the Fall—shame, sorrow,
death—which the Sinless does not accept, in order,
in accepting it, to reverse it ? Face to face with
the amazing contrarieties of the Fall are the amazing
contrarieties of the Incarnation. Face to face with
the greatness and the misery of the First man are
the greatness and the misery of the Second.

And so, at the point where the Fall leaves man,

Redemption meets him : and the meeting-point is at
the lowest depths. The Fall left him a being of
mysterious and surmised greatness, but at most real
and visible distance from all that he seemed made
for ; struggling with corruption and sin, or sinking
under them ; struggling with disaster, struggling with
pain, struggling vainly with death ; ever haunted by
dreams of perfection, by dreams of bliss, and by the
waking certainty of wretchedness and vanity. Whatever else may be true about him, what is palpable
is his humiliation. And then, at the very point of
deepest ignominy and disorder, starting from all its
disadvantages, traversing its paths, surrounded by
all its badges, reflecting its dreary colours, not refusing the semblances of its more real evil ; amid
that mortal confusion and degradation of conscience,
in which good is taken for evil, and evil for good,
and in which the Holiest was thought the vilest of
sinners—the Restorer of man begins His new and
strange work, His new creation. In Adam we see
what Christ was to meet with, and to begin with ;
where Adam had descended to, Christ descended
to meet him : in sorrow, in infirmity, in defeat, in the
humiliations of mortality, in all but the evil of our
treacherous *will*, man's partner : his partner in such
anguish as is described in the Psalms ; in daily
company with his distresses and all that train of unknown and nameless suffering which surrounds the
Son of Man in the Gospels. The work of heaven,
it begins on earth, amid the too well known conditions of our state,-the too well known and familiar
realities of what we are and what we have to go
through. From that which seems to be but the

continuation of the doom of the Fall, from that which
seems to be its aggravation in the person of the
innocent, from the darkness and dreary gloom with
which Adam's history closes, issues forth the power
which is to repair the wreck, the light which is to
make it no longer hopeless, the Life which is to
quicken the dead. The figure is fulfilled ; its conflicting aspects are reconciled in the transcendent
Antitype. " In Adam all die . . . in Christ shall all
be made alive " ; but not before the death of the First
man is repeated in the Second ; not before God
had " made Him to be sin for us who knew no sin,
that we might be made the righteousness of God in
Him " ; not before the Captain of man's salvation
should by the grace of God taste death for every
man ; should be made perfect through sufferings.

Adam is " the Figure of Him that was to come,"
the figure of our perfection, and of our ruin and
mortality ; the figure of God's intention, of what man
has spoiled and God repaired. We may measure
the reality of the deliverance by the reality, which
we know, of the wreck ; we may measure the vastness
of what was wrecked by the greatness of the remedy.[1]
And so the world is changed, and what might but be
guessed at before is made certain now. We are of a
race that had lost its way ; and now we know it. We
are of a race whose prospects and destiny it is vain to
circumscribe by what we see ; it belongs to a world
to which this world cannot reach, and where we are
linked with God. So even the First man dared to
imagine before the Second came ; but he knew not,
and all the practical energy of his nature was directed

[1] Pascal, *Pensées*, ii. 85, 145 (ed. Faugère).

here.   He went forth and did great things.   As it is
said in those great Choruses which are the Psalms of
Heathenism,—he subdued the earth, he founded
states, he sought out arts,·he mastered powers living
and powers elemental, he found the secret of beauty,
and the spell of words, and the power of numbers,
and the fine threads that waken and order thought;
he made the world his workshop, his arsenal, his
palace ; generation after generation he learned to
know more of its inexhaustible magnificence, to use
more of its inexhaustible gifts ; his eye was more
opened, his sense more delicate, his hand more crafty ;
he created, he measured, he gathered together, he
enjoyed.   He is before us now, in his greatness, his
hopes, his pride, with even nobler aims and vaster
tasks, alleviating misery, curing injustice, bridling or
extinguishing disease.   But still he is the First Man :
of the riddle of his nature he has not the key, and
despairs of reaching it ; he passes in his˙greatness,
and never continueth in one stay ; sorrow and decay
baffle him, sin entangles him, and at the end is death.
" Of the earth, earthy " ; of the earth, bounded by its
barriers, invisible, impassable.   And now, side by
side with him, is the Second Man, from the Manger,
the Cross, the Grave,—dead, yet alive, and alive for
ever : attended by His train of sanctities, by unthought-of revelations of heart, by the " things of the
Spirit," by hopes and peace which for this ˌworld
were an idle dream, by the new Beatitudes.   He
comes in the greatness of His strength, He comes in
weakness : but strength and weakness to Him are
both alike ; for love, which is of God, in strong and
weak, is the life of the new creation, its " one thing

needful," the essential mark of its presence. So He comes, on the bed of sickness, in the lifelong burden, in the broken heart ; with the children in spirit, the poor, the feeble, the helpless, the unknown ; with the sorrows of penitence, the hunger after righteousness, the longings to be true, the longings to be pure, the joy of forgiveness, the hope that is for the other side of the grave. Strange attendants for the company of the Deliverer ; but they bring with them the victory which nothing else has gained. " The First Man is of the earth, earthy ; the Second Man is the Lord from heaven." O Soul of man,—called to this wonderful existence, so gifted, yet so rigidly bounded : made for such great things, yet turned aside by such poor ones : so promising, yet so transient : the breath of a day between the two eternities, yet rich with power, and thought, and beauty, rich in capacities of grace and goodness, ever unfolding, ever growing; conscious of such needs and such evils, longing for such firm reality and truth, responding to such calls, and then going hence, as if never having been :—where is to be thy part ? what wilt thou do with what is given thee, with that great and fearful thing which we call life ? Wilt thou rest in the portion of the First Adam :—great, lovely, as it often is, merely to live, to see, to be glad in the sky above and God's blessing on the earth, in our home, in our work ? It is enough, if we had no more ; it is enough to be thankful for, if our view closed here. But " the First Man is of the earth, earthy " : and there is "the Second Man, the Lord from heaven." And none but He dares claim the two great victories : the victory over sin, the victory over death. With Him only is it said, "Oh wretched man that I am, who shall deliver me from the body of this death? I thank God, through Jesus Christ our Lord." With Him only it is said, "that this corruptible must put on incorruption, and this mortal must put on immortality." Only He speaks to us here, of "mortality . . . swallowed up of life." With Him only it is said, "The sting of death is sin; and the strength of sin is the law. But thanks be to God, which giveth us the victory through our Lord Jesus Christ." He only

> Holds for us the Keys of either home,
> Earth and the world to come.[1]

O Soul of man, inheritor of the First Adam, new-born to the Second, which wilt thou choose?

[1] *Lyra Apostolica*, No. lxx.

VII

THE PROMISE TO ABRAHAM[1]

"And in thee shall all families of the earth be blessed."
GEN. xii. 3.

THIS promise is the foundation-stone of the history of the Church—at once of Hebrew and of Christian history. A man is chosen out of all his contemporaries: he is called from his home to be while he lives a sojourner in a strange land; and he has given him this stupendous blessing, this stupendous promise. "Now the Lord had said unto Abram, Get thee out of thy country, and from thy kindred, and from thy father's house, unto a land that I will show thee: and I will make of thee a great nation, and I will bless thee, and make thy name great; and thou shalt be a blessing: and I will bless them that bless thee, and curse him that curseth thee: and in thee shall all families of the earth be blessed." To be the minister and channel of God's blessing to mankind was he chosen and called: this was the inheritance of his children, the Patriarchs; for this was the nation into which they swelled chosen, and

---

[1] Preached in Norwich Cathedral at the Festival of the Society for the Propagation of the Gospel, 1876.

taught, and guided, and preserved, through the ages of their marvellous history—not for their own sakes, not because God has favourites, but because He puts upon nations as upon men, a charge, a mission, a work—which was in this case to be the witnesses and guardians of the promise—" In thee shall all families of the earth be blessed." And the Christian Church was hardly born on the day of Pentecost, when it claimed and appropriated the fulfilment of the promise. " Ye are the children of the prophets," says its first preacher, " and of the covenant which God made with our fathers, saying unto Abraham, And in thy seed shall all the kindreds of the earth be blessed." " The scripture," writes the great Apostle of the Gentiles, " foreseeing that God would justify the heathen through faith, preached before the Gospel unto Abraham, saying, In thee shall all nations be blessed." Thus from the first the eye of God's elect—man, or family, or people—was directed to look forward beyond their own fortunes to the hopes of the world ; beyond their own blessings to the universal blessing, which was travelling onward in their hands and drawing towards its full accomplishment. What had been given to them, was in due time to be the possession of man-kind ; what made the greatness and the crown of. their own blessing, was that in it all the families of the earth were to be blessed as well. God had made Himself known to them. God, the Lord of heaven and earth, the Maker and Ruler of all things, had vouchsafed to be their God, their King, their special Treasure and Reward. All around was darkness, with them there was this little speck of light.

C.S.,P   L

All round were "gods many and lords many"—
gods of the mountains and the valleys, of the
heavens and of the earth, of the living and of the
dead, worshipped and trusted in by each nation, or
tribe, or household.   Out of them all, they had been
selected to know the name of the One Almighty and
Eternal.   They, they alone, knew the truth about
the world, its origin, its government.   To them, He
who was before all things, and beyond the stars, was
the God of Abraham, Isaac, and Jacob.   But from
the first they were taught, that they knew this in
order that the world might know it : that He had
revealed Himself as their God, that He whom they
worshipped might be worshipped by all the families
of the earth.   This was God's secret : the mystery
hid for ages and generations till " the fulness of
time."   How it was to be—how the knowledge and
the blessing with which they were charged was to be
passed over from them to the multitudes of the
heathen—how the Gentiles were to be fellow-heirs
with them—this was not told them.   But, as the
end and purpose of their own calling, as the fulfilment
of their own wondrous blessing, they knew this—
that He whom they worshipped as their King and
God should become the King and Hope of all the
ends of the world : that in them should all the
families of the earth be blessed.   It seems to me that
this is one of the things which make the religious
history of the Bible unique in all that we know in
this world.   Israel looked forward from the first
to its religion becoming the religion of the world.
Confident of its own blessing, in knowing and
worshipping the one only God, it made no doubt

that at last He would be owned and honoured over all the earth.   This great and wonderful faith, rooted in the first promise to Abraham, ran through the history of Israel, persistent and indestructible in all their fortunes.   And consider what this was.   Here was a nation jealously separated from all its sister nations round, and deeply affected in character and temper by this necessary separation.   To the Israelite the heathen around him were the unclean, the godless, the profane, his own natural enemies, the blasphemers of Him who was the worship of Israel.   He must keep aloof from them ; he must not marry with them ; in time it came to be that he must not eat with them.   They had been the victims of his ex- terminating sword.   When spared they had been the fatal tempters to apostasy.   They had been used as the scourge in the hand of God, to chastise, to oppress, to overthrow.   Nowhere in all the world, not between Greek and barbarian, between conqueror and conquered, between slave and free, was the wall of partition so impassable, and the gulf so profound, as between the Jew and the heathen.   From the earliest to the latest times the objects of unceasing attack ; when best known and most active in the world, a byword of scorn and jealousy for fanatical arrogance ; they gave back with interest the hatred and contempt of the Gentile world.   Yet with all its narrow exclusiveness, with all its insignificance, with all its isolation, amid an uncongenial world, station- ary when others were advancing, lost in its little corner while others were dazzling mankind with their glory and their might, insensible to beauty, to the arts, to ambition, while the Western world was opening its

mind to the thought of Greece, and the statesman-
ship of Carthage and Rome — Israel obstinately
maintained the same conviction that its faith and
worship were to be the faith and worship of
mankind : that in due time these aliens and
strangers, hating and hated now, would join in
owning the God of Israel : that all the kindreds
of the nations should at last bow down before His
greatness and His truth. In the fierce bitterness
of oppression, in the fiercer pride of Pharisaic self-
righteousness, doubtless this belief was obscured or
distorted. But it was fixed where it could not be
lost : it was written deep and indelible in the
sacred Scriptures ; it broke out for ever, assured and
triumphant, in those Psalms and Prophecies which
enshrined the true hopes and faith of Israel. Is
there not something perfectly overwhelming to mere
human judgment in the *audacity* with which Psalmist
and Prophet—the Psalmists and Prophets of an obscure race, cut off by barriers physical and moral
from the great scenes of human history—dare to
claim for their faith, for their God, what no one else
dared to do—the inheritance of all the nations, the
spiritual future of all mankind ? " All nations whom
Thou hast made shall come and worship Thee, O
Lord, and shall glorify Thy name." " All the ends
of the world shall remember themselves, and be
turned unto the Lord ; and all the kindreds of the
nations shall worship before Him." " In that day
there shall be a root of Jesse, which shall stand for
an ensign of the people ; to it shall the Gentiles
seek : and His rest shall be glorious." " The earth
shall be full of the knowledge of the Lord, as the

waters cover the sea." Where, in the days when
these words were so boldly spoken, was there the
faintest indication of their accomplishment? Where
was the human likelihood of a universal religion?
where was the likelihood that it would be the
worship of the God of Abraham? If we want two
things in the Bible, absolutely without parallel and
unexampled elsewhere, we may find them, first and
foremost, of course, in the character of Jesus Christ,
and next, in the undoubting assurance with which
the Prophets and teachers of Israel claimed for their
religion, against every human likelihood, the future
allegiance of mankind.

They, dimly seeing all it meant, held fast to that
astonishing prospect, the conversion of the whole
world to God—the ultimate communication, to all the
families of the earth, of the blessing of Abraham.
They held fast to it in all the " sad vicissitudes of
things " that came on them ; in the darkest hours of
their history, beaten down and crushed by their own
sin and shame, they yet believed that somehow it
would be. They misunderstood it ; they abused it ;
in their pride and folly they allowed it to become to
them a snare and a daydream ; their ambition saw
in it the pledge of a reign like Solomon's, of a
Messiah more widely conquering than Alexander,
who should put under Jewish feet the empire of the
Cæsars ; they compassed sea and land to make one
proselyte—to make him—who would dare to use the
words if their Judge Himself had not spoken them ?—
" twofold more the child of hell than themselves."
But, anyhow, they would not surrender this wonderful, this most improbable hope. Their day has

passed away, with its failures, its delusions, its disappointments.   But   the   promise   still   remains,
handed on by the elder to the younger Church.
They built their hopes upon it, and now we build
ours.   But it comes to us with the illumination of
something yet more wonderful than even itself.   To us
it comes interpreted by events which have for ever
changed the whole aspect of the world, and history,
and human life.   To us it comes charged and
pregnant with God's nearest and most immediate
contact with humanity and its innermost realities—
the condescension of the everlasting Son to be made
Very Man.   What the promise meant is told us now
in the songs of Christmas, and the Lenten memories
of temptation, and the dumb awestruck contempla-
tions on Good Friday of the Agony and the
Passion, and the triumphs of Easter and Ascension
Day, and the new world and the new creation of
Pentecost.   There we came to know what the
blessing was, intended for all the families of the
earth.   There we learned how all, far and near, the
first and the last, were to be brought near in peace
and hope to Him who had chosen and called their
father Abraham, the "father of us all."   There we
learned how the religion of Moses, the worship of
the Tabernacle and Mount Zion, the local Church
of Judaism, was the first stage and the training
school of the universal and only religion, was to
break down all barriers and expand into the one
Catholic and eternal Church of all the nations, Jew
and Roman, Greek and barbarian, the nations of all
ages, those that have played their part and passed
away, and the unknown multitudes and yet unspoken

tongues, which are in due time to come upon the
stage of this world's history. Upon the Gentiles has
come the promise of Abraham in Christ Jesus :—
" If ye are Christ's, then are ye Abraham's seed,
and heirs according to the promise." To the eyes
of Apostles and Prophets has been revealed the
mystery, in other ages not made known to the sons
of men, that the Gentiles " should be fellow-heirs,
and of the same body, and partakers of God's
promise in Christ by the Gospel." " Aliens from
the commonwealth of Israel, and strangers from the
covenants of promise, having no hope, and without
God in the world," the nations once afar off are now
brought nigh by the blood of Christ, their peace,
their atonement, their reconciler ; and henceforth
they are " no more strangers and foreigners, but
fellow - citizens with the saints, and of the household of God." — " In thee shall all families of
the earth be blessed." Son of David, Seed of
Abraham, Saviour of the world, Very God and Very
Man, now we know : ' in Thee shall all families of
the earth be blessed.'

And now, we in our turn are entrusted with the
safe keeping and remembrance of that great promise.
We are chosen and called to remember and to look
forward ; to remember what God has promised to .
the world, to look forward to its accomplishment.
In this, at least, the ancient Church of Israel was
faithful to its calling. It believed, it insisted on
believing, that the world was to be its own at last,
that the world was to become the kingdom of its
Lord and God. It was set to keep this belief
alive ; and, with whatever mistakes and distortions,

it kept it alive.   Christians must indeed have
become dead to the truths to which their eyes have
been opened, whenever they have been indifferent
to the prospect which the Jew never forgot.   And
to remember it is to come under the obligation to
do our part in the purpose and design of our Lord.
Abraham was not called for his own sake alone,
and certainly those whom God's providence has
called by His sovereign predestination and choice
into the fellowship and family of His Church have
not only to take care of themselves, but to serve
as the ministers of His great dispensation to recover
and reclaim the whole human race.

We are met to-day to remind ourselves of this
great part of our religion.   We remind ourselves of
the declared purpose with which our Lord sent His
first Apostles to their work—of the mission which
He has laid on that Church which He called forth
to bear onward the light of His truth and promise ;
we set before us, in all its vastness and mystery,
that yet unaccomplished intention of God, which
first spoke in the Call of Abraham, which spoke
again in the Baptismal Commission, in the utterances
of St. Paul to the Romans and Ephesians.   And
yet, who can set this before him steadily, thinking
seriously what it really means, what has to be
done, how, as far as we see, it must be done,
and what are the chances of doing it, and not
feel that, as far as we see this great work going
on under the conditions of our own times, the disproportion between the object and the machinery,
between the end sought and all that is done to
attain it, is enormous and disheartening.   It is use-

less to dissemble or disguise this. If our efforts were tenfold what they are—and they are now doubtless tenfold or twenty-fold what they *were*— the disproportion would still be the same. Men of the world would still sneer at what they call our feeble spirit of proselytism. They would still accuse us of not understanding the very first elements of the problem, the mind and thoughts of those whom we wish to convert. And far beyond their sneers at our incapacity and our failures, rise up before us the huge impregnable bulwarks in a hundred lands, of custom, of tradition, of pride, of conviction, of interest, of habitual thought and motive, behind which the multitudes of the non-Christian world, separated from us in sympathies and ideas by gulfs which cannot be bridged and can hardly be measured, bid defiance to our attempts to make an impression on them.

Certainly when we think of ourselves and our own generation, as the heralds and instruments of this great promise to the world, the heart must be a strong one which does not fail sometimes. No wonder that all the words which denote what is extravagantly incredible and hopeless crowd into men's minds. What can we really expect to accomplish? We are attempting what is absurdly beyond our powers. Here are more than eighteen centuries past, and here is all that has been yet•done; and what is the rate of progress of to-day? How much nearer are we to the goal? Other human things advance, expand, and prosper : what, in comparison with trade, or colonisation, or science, or civil order, is the outlook of our missionary enterprises?

Are we spending our strength in vain? Are we desiring and aiming at the impossible? Is missionary enthusiasm a dream?

Faith and love and duty will have many answers to give to these doubts and misgivings. They will not shrink from ventures that seem desperate ones when the Master's voice clearly commands, when His love has awakened its new sympathies in the regenerate heart, when faith has risen above the phenomena of time into contact with the powers of the world to come. They will take refuge from the discouragement of the present in the remembrances of the past. " I call to remembrance my song . . . hath God forgotten to be gracious . . . and I said, It is mine own infirmity: but I will remember the years of the right hand of the most Highest. I will remember the works of the Lord, and call to mind Thy wonders of old time." They who have the Cross and Resurrection to remember may well bear to be called romantic, even in this busy and sceptical age, for still claiming the nations for the Crucified. They will recollect that they are workers together with God, and that He is the God of patience, who rests not but who hastes not ; who in all His works, as well of nature as of grace, reads the divine and wonderful lesson of enduring delay, of *biding the time*, of waiting, silently perhaps, through what we call ages, till the seed has sprung up, till the fruit is ripe, till the hour is come.

And when, in spite of all, our imagination is oppressed by the greatness of the contrast between the immensity of the task before us and the poverty of what we are doing, and of all that it seems possible for us to do ; when we see round us nothing but

machinery inadequate, ludicrously inadequate, to the
mighty revolution which we avow as our object ;
when the struggle and the labour seem in vain, and
" as things have been, they remain "—let us meet
the suggestions of despondency by widening the
horizon of our imagination and putting ourselves in
the place of other times and other men.   What is
the history, in detail and in its separate steps, by
which the promise has reached to us, by which the
knowledge of God has become our inheritance ?   How
many times, over and over again, in Jewish history,
did it not seem as if the hopes of the world were
wrecked ; as if it were impossible that the onward
march of God's great promise could continue ; as if
it must perish in the disasters of the Jewish nation,
in the perversions and narrowness of Jewish character?
Or again, put yourself in the position of a Christian
of the first or second century : with the words of the
Lord and His apostles ringing in his ears, what signs
did he see of their accomplishment ?   All round him
was the immensity, the unexampled strength, the
magnificence of the ever-present Empire, in its peace
so splendid and so calm, in its storms so terrible and
so remorseless ; and for him there was but an obscure
sect, apparently distracted by opposing voices, not
always exempt from folly and scandals, but anyhow
lost and helpless in the vast interests and powers
of Roman society.   Could there be a wilder dream than
that *that* sect, that those leaders should yet, within a
few generations, change the world ?   Or, once more,
suppose yourself in one of those troubled and confused
ages when truth and falsehood seemed entangled
together in the Church,—I do not say in some of

the dark days of blasphemy and rebuke, which
threatened the very existence of faith and religion :
the tenth century, when, amid profanations without a
name, the world seemed ending ; the fifteenth, when
the crimes of the old heathen Empire were outdone
in the high places of the Church,—I do not say these ;
but in some of those times when there was real zeal,
when Christianity was advancing, when the conversion
of the nations was really going on—the ages, say,
of St. Augustine the apostle of England, or St.
Boniface the apostle of Germany. You would have
seen unselfish devotion, single-minded purpose, large-
hearted charity, unstinted toil ; but you would have
seen, too, the other side of the picture. You would
have seen all the poor mean prosaic shortcomings of
common life, its littlenesses, its weaknesses. You would
have seen something worse. You would have seen the
skin-deep conversion, the unstable profession, the ready
apostasy, the revolting inconsistency. You would have
seen mixed motives, you would have seen force employed in the cause of Christ's Gospel. You might
have seen that cause supported by all kinds of un-
lawful means—superstition, exaggeration, credulity
—nay, imposture, false miracles. And you might
have despaired. But you would have despaired
unwisely. You would have missed the slow hidden
current of God's working under the accidents of
human folly and misdoing. God was preparing,
amid all that ignorance and error, the streams of
blessing which were to visit you and me. In that
imperfect, disappointing, sometimes repulsive process
the foundation was being laid of that great Christendom which has been the mother of saints, the nurse

of all the virtues, the utilities, the graces of modern ages, under whose shelter those whom we loved rejoiced in God's goodness and died in His peace, and in whose shadow we ourselves hope to lie down to rest.

It is owing to the enterprise, the courage, the faith, the toil of men who knew us not, and died ages before we were born, that the circle of God's kingdom has embraced ourselves. The conversion of the barbarians, of Goths and Franks, of the English and German and Northern races is, to us who look back on it, one of the most splendid and eventful achievements in the records of the Church. But we may be sure that, in the doing of it, it was, as our mission work is to us, very formidable, very doubtful, in its routine very dull and tiresome, in its results very uncertain and very chequered, and very long in coming. Grand and wonderful as the conquest was, the fighters saw only the dust and confusion of the fray. We shall indeed be without excuse, if with such experience behind us, with such daily and priceless blessings won for us by those who devoted themselves in faith for generations they would never see— if with all this, we fail and are disheartened in our appointed hour of work. And if there is much to daunt and chill us, yet, on the other hand, never since the old days has the ambition of extending the kingdom of God, of winning the fulfilment of the promise to Abraham, been awakened so strongly in the Church. And the tide has not yet mounted to its height : the men who have left all for this great war, the men who have died in it—the Henry Martyns, the Mackenzies, the Pattesons, the Livingstones, the Milmans—are, we may be sure, the pledges that more will follow. The race is not extinct of those high souls whom their Master's spell has called from their peaceful homes, whose hearts respond to His " desire," and who cannot rest till they go forth to win for Him " the heathen for His inheritance, and the utmost parts of the earth for His possession."

Let us, then, the heirs of His blessing, the witnesses of His noble acts of old, be patient, be enduring, be diligent, be hopeful. Let us not think of ourselves, or too much of what comes of our endeavours, of what we should like to see of the results. The present is a bad judge of everything but its own duty —a bad judge of determining forces, of the tendencies which are to prevail, of the changes which are impending. It is not for us, as was said to them of old, " to know the times or the seasons "—the times of success, the seasons of power. These the Father keeps in His own hand. It is for us to do what He has charged us with : to be faithful to our consciences, faithful to our opportunities. It is enough, if in the place appointed us we do not fail in our duty : if we do what we might do. It is enough for us to be links in the chain of that great process by which God for ages has been drawing mankind to Himself —links that can bear the strain put upon them, and may contribute to the strength and completeness of the whole. It will be enough if in our little hour of life, with our little measure of service, we may dare to look forward to sharing the triumph at last of Him who *must* conquer, who is the secret, unconscious, " Desire of all nations," in whom they will one day find their peace, in whom at last " shall all families of the earth be blessed."

VIII

THE KINGDOM OF GOD [1]

"Thy kingdom is an everlasting kingdom, and Thy dominion
endureth throughout all ages."—PSALM cxlv. 13.

THE Psalms are full of assertions—triumphant and
exulting assertions—of the Kingdom of God. " O
clap your hands together, all ye people ; O sing unto
God with the voice of melody. For the Lord is high,
and to be feared : He is the great King upon all the
earth." " The Lord is King, and hath put on glorious
apparel; the Lord hath put on His apparel and girded
Himself with strength." "The Lord is King, the earth
may be glad thereof; yea, the multitude of the isles
may be glad thereof." " The Lord is King, be the
people never so impatient ; He sitteth between the
cherubims, be the earth never so unquiet." " Tell it
out among the heathen that the Lord is King, and
that it is He who hath made the round world so fast
that it cannot be moved ; and how that He shall
judge the people righteously." " All Thy works
praise Thee, O Lord ; and Thy saints give thanks
unto Thee. They show the glory of Thy kingdom
and talk of Thy power ; that Thy power, Thy glory,

[1] Preached in Hereford Cathedral during Advent 1875.

and mightiness of Thy kingdom might be known
unto men."

I need not say how many lines of thought are
opened out by the mention of the Kingdom of
God, of which this solemn time of Advent reminds
us. If the idea of an earthly state, of an empire and
kingdom like our own, is infinitely manifold and
complex, presenting many sides, offering innumerable
subjects, all connected but all distinct, for contemplation, for inquiry and thought—if when you have
considered it in its relations to private life, to individual character, to social progress or decay, to public
interests and powers, to its neighbours, to its past
history, to its future fortunes, you still find that you
are as far as ever from having exhausted it—if this is
so with great ideas of things belonging to time and
our earthly state, it is natural that the name of the
Kingdom of God should waken the most diversified
trains of reflection. For it means that government
of which the history of our world and of our race, so
absorbing and so wonderful to our minds, is an in-
considerable epoch and fragment. It means the
calls and the issues of the Old Dispensation ; it
means the mystery of Redemption and Recovery in
the New. It means the dealings and sway of the
Ever-blessed and All-holy Father of Spirits in the
soul of each of His children. It means the continual
presence in His Church of the Incarnate Son. It
means the final unveiling of the Judge and Judgment-
seat of the world, and the bringing in of that new
creation to which all things here tend, and for which
all things yearn. We might be led into almost any
part of the field of religious meditation by the men-

tion of the Kingdom of God, of its Author, and Ruler, of its subjects, its citizens, its laws, its institutions, its hopes.

Among these various topics it may be profitable to consider—it can only be in the most general way —how we mortal men, with our limited faculties and limited experience, are in relation to that perfect and wondrous reign of power and righteousness ; how, as far as our knowledge goes, the Kingdom of God touches the confines of this present, visible state of things which we know and act in ; how it is made known to us, and what are the prospects which it opens to us :—what is at the bottom of our thoughts when we speak of the Kingdom of God ; what is our part in it ; what does it mean for our future.

What were the thoughts and feelings of Psalmists and Prophets about that Kingdom of God of which they said so much? They were men who felt strongly the reality of this present life, and of this visible scene which we call the world. They were alive to all the facts which it exhibited—its joys, its pains, its vicissitudes, its aims, its incessant restless activity ; in all that men do and suffer and desire and build up here, they had their part. And with this keen sense of its reality, asserting itself at every moment, they have an equally keen sense of its short-ness, its strange unintelligible vanity. " Yea, even as a dream when one awaketh." " We bring our years to an end, as it were a tale that is told." " A thousand years in Thy sight are but as yesterday . . . past as a watch in the night. As soon as Thou scatterest them they are even as a sleep." That was the feeling of the ancient Psalmist. " When the

breath of man goeth forth he shall turn again to his
earth, and then all his thoughts perish." This is the
state, the world, the life, they see and know; this is
the system of things of which they are part—so real,
yet so transitory ; which is familiar to them as
nothing else can be familiar ; which is with them
all day long, and every day ; which is fixed by unchanging laws ; which fills their eye and their ear ;
which they cannot alter, which they cannot resist,
which they cannot escape from ; of which, every
moment between birth and death, they test the
permanence.   And, as I said, to all its facts they are
keenly alive ; they are actors in it, sufferers, observers, directors.   But, in their minds, side by side
with this most important, most deeply eventful
system of things, there is another continually presenting itself to their thoughts, paramount, infinitely
paramount to the whole sum of all things here.
It is ever out of sight, it is ever near.   They believe
in another and a vaster order of things, as real, as
absolutely existing, as if we could see it and touch it
and feel it ; as real, as actually working and going
on, as what is within our present experience ; which
encompasses, like the invisible atmosphere, or the
invisible ether of space, all that we now see and do,
affecting, controlling, judging all things that happen.
It is the Kingdom of God.   Eye cannot see it, nor
ear hear it, neither hath it entered into the heart of
man to understand or imagine it.   It is as much
beyond the possibility of our comprehension as—
to compare great things to small—music, or the
height of mathematical science, are to savages, or to
men without the necessary faculty.   But there it is

—real, eternal, supreme ; and all that is, is within its
arms. It is the Kingdom and Sovereignty of One.
Powers there may be many and diverse in earth and
heaven, but there is one only King of this world. It
is the Kingdom of perfect righteousness, of perfect
goodness, of perfect holiness. Besides and beyond
this mixed scene of good and evil which we behold,
this perpetual conflict, with its great efforts and
great defeats, its ceaseless jar, its ceaseless alternations of advance and recoil, there is really a Kingdom, existing even now, where sin and evil cannot
enter, where the law is justice, and love, and wisdom,
and peace ; and the law is fulfilled. The earth, this
little earth that we men tenant for our little lives,
is full of the glory and beauty of the Lord ; we know
much of it, but even here there is more to know ;
the thought and eye of man have not yet mastered
it, the tongue and art of man never will. exhaust it.
But who has beheld or who can imagine the magnificence of *His* glory, who spake the word, and all
things were made, who commanded, and they were
created : the beauty which surrounds the throne of
Him from whom all that we know of greatness and
of beauty flows, in form, in sound, in expression ?
" O Lord, how manifold are Thy works : in wisdom
hast Thou made them all ; the earth is full of Thy
riches." The earth alone calls forth such a burst ;
but the Psalmist's thought rises to where the earth is
lost. " Praise the Lord, O my soul : O Lord my
God, Thou art become exceeding glorious ; Thou art
clothed with majesty and honour." The voices of
the prophets and messengers of the Kingdom of God
answer one another in distant ages : the New Testa-

ment echoes back the Old—" Holy, Holy, Holy, is the Lord of Hosts : the whole earth is full of His glory . . . the King, the Lord of Hosts." " Holy, Holy, Holy, Lord God Almighty, which was, and is, and is to come." And the Church on earth still answers what they heard in heaven, " Holy, Holy, Holy, Lord God of Hosts : heaven and earth are full of Thy glory ; glory be to Thee, O Lord most high."

This is that ever-present belief which possesses the minds of the sacred writers, and is distinctive of them ; which expresses itself in every imaginable variety of form, and is equally evident in every change and shade of feeling, in despair and misery as well as in triumph and hope. They believe in two worlds, and that they are standing on the confines of both. They belong to both ; they are subjects of both ; what they do has its consequences in both. As surely as nature is real and substantial and true, so there is something as real beyond nature. As surely as what we see concerns us, so surely there is something that we cannot see which concerns us more. As surely as we cannot withdraw ourselves from the dominion of tangible facts, from the inevitable conditions of our life, from the ideas and judgments of those with whom we have to live, so surely there are laws out of sight from which we cannot release ourselves ; there are judgments passed on what we think, and wish, and do, which, though we hear nothing of them now, sub-sist among the realities of a government from which nothing is hidden, and in which everything is mea-sured according to what it really is. Man and nature strive, as it were, for mastery here ; and within limits, yet very truly, man is master now ; but both have

a Master beyond. And this earthly system, this kingdom of men, has not only a counterpart out of sight,
the two kingdoms are contrasts. There is a Kingdom
where what we never experience here is realised ;
where what is weak here is strong ; where what fails
here is victorious; where what is imperfect here is complete ; where what is the exception here is the rule.
Our justice is partial and maimed, and consciously
blind ; in God's Kingdom His justice has no flaw.
The world, the present constitution of society, bears
hard on the friendless, who cannot take care of themselves, rides rough-shod over the poor, the obscure,
the feeble ; but there is a great King, outside this
world—it is the recurring burden of the Psalms—
whose " eyes consider the poor," who forgets not
their complaint, who hearkens to their desire, whose
awful voice may be heard amid the silence of nature
and the boasting of the proud. " Now for the comfortless troubles' sake of the needy, and because of
the deep sighing of the poor, I will up, saith the
Lord, and will help every one from him that swelleth
against him, and will set him at rest."

We, in our poor and feeble measure, try to provide against the evils which embitter life, to remedy
what we cannot prevent, to soothe what must be
endured, to set mercy, loving-kindness, sympathy,
patience, in array against the sternness of law, whether
of nature or of society ; but among the .deepest
anxieties of good men is the little, the very little,
that human mercy and human forethought can do to
abate the ever-swelling sum of human wretchedness.
But there is a Kingdom, though we cannot scan its
ways, of which the faith of the Psalmist sings—" Praise

the Lord, O my soul, and forget not all His benefits ; who forgiveth all thy sin, and healeth all thine infirmities. Who saveth thy life from destruction, and crowneth thee with mercy and loving-kindness. . . . The Lord is full of compassion and mercy: long-suffer ing, and of great goodness." "The Lord is loving unto every man, and His mercy is over all His works."

Our common rules of judgment are suited to present appearances, and are framed on the feeling that this short time is our only life. It is pleasant to be rich, to be honoured, to be powerful, to have the desire of our hearts ; it is dreadful to be poor, to be spoken against, to be sick and weak and in pain. But there is a different estimate of these things, which values them by the measure of interests far larger, far more permanent than those which affect our opinions now.

If there is one certainty in the present order under which we live, it is the certainty of death, of a final break in work and hope, of the utter incompleteness of human life. None ever felt it more strongly than the Psalmists. But over against it was the permanent everlasting Kingdom of the God who was the Maker and Friend and Lover of mankind. " Hast Thou made all men for naught ? " " Yes," was the answer of the visible course of nature. " It cannot be," was the certain conviction of those who, though they could not solve the riddle, remembered "the years of the right hand of the most Highest " ; who felt, brooding over the fate and the hopes of man, the loving wisdom of God, reaching from end to end of the ages, which would not despise the work of His own hands ; who felt that around our incompleteness and vanity was

God's unknown and immeasurable greatness ; that
around and above the fall and extinction of the hopes
of man were the everlasting mercies of the Father
who gave him life.   In their conviction of the reality
of the Kingdom of God lay their sure hope, not
knowing the *when* or the *how*, of deliverance from
the darkness and ruin of death.

The belief, absorbing and pervading, of the
Kingdom of God, was the heart and strength of the
Psalmists' religion.   With this belief they interpreted
their own marvellous history ; with this belief they
looked abroad on nature, they trained and quickened
their own souls.   Translated into our modern ways
of speaking, it was a profound, ever-present conviction
of the reality of the supernatural and unseen.   I say
" supernatural " for want of a better word.   I mean
that, beyond and around this great familiar order of
things under which we live, and our fathers have
lived before us, whose general conditions and laws we
have faculties to discern, there is another and greater
order implied in the very mention of the name of
God ; an order whose laws and ways, except that
they must be moral ones, we know not and cannot
know.   To the Psalmists the Kingdom of God is not
merely an ideal, but, though they cannot explain or
grasp it, an actual present reality.   The things unseen
are ever accompanying, bordering on, influencing, the
things that are seen.   That real existence, which we,
with our habits of thought and imagination, confine
to things which we can handle and test here, belongs
as certainly to the works and doings of the unseen
Lord of the world in that vaster universe which even
our thoughts cannot reach to.   And it was not only

the reality of this unseen system and order which
had such hold on the Psalmists' minds: it was its
supremacy over that order to which we are here
accustomed, its continual presence, its uninterrupted
permanence. The things which are seen — it was
their faith as well as St. Paul's—are for the time ;
the things which are not seen are eternal.

And we, with St. Paul, know so much more than
they did. They had been taught by the long chain of
wonders which made their history unique in the world.
It had awakened, and it had justified the growth in
their minds and consciences of those clear and strong
and bold ideas about the Kingdom and Government
of God, of its certainty, of its action, of its righteousness, which were theirs alone, among all the aspirations and all the wisdom of the ancient world. But
that long history has ended in events which have
brought the Kingdom of God in a manner from the
region of the invisible into the very companionship
with flesh and blood. That history, which in flashes
or dim shadows revealed the eternal Kingdom of
God, led up to and closed in the sign of signs, the
wonder of wonders, which attested its presence.
" The Word was made flesh, and dwelt among us, and
we beheld His glory, the glory as of the only-
begotten of the Father, full of grace and truth." In
darkness and afar off the Prophets *felt*, rather than
discerned, the Kingdom in which they believed. It
descended and disclosed itself in the very realm of
nature, when human eyes beheld and human hands
touched Him, who was " declared to be the Son of
God with power, Jesus Christ our Lord . . . according
to the Spirit of Holiness, by the resurrection from the

dead." God hath shown us the very King Himself,
one in essence and eternity with Himself, the Head
and Lord of all things, the Man by whom " He will
judge the world in righteousness . . . whereof He hath
given assurance unto all men, in that He hath raised
Him from the dead." There is one veil the less
on the unfathomable mystery of that still unseen
Kingdom. He, in ways we cannot conceive of, is
ever with us. " Lo, I am with you alway—all the
days—even unto the end of the world." One veil the
less—for there are many veils, many veils still,
between us and the knowledge of God's Kingdom.
We know, indeed, much : who that steadily thinks
about it but must be amazed at all we know, so infinitely beyond all we could have once been expected
to know ; so overpowering to our intellect, so subduing, so absorbing to our affections, so transporting
to our hope ? But no one who thinks steadily and
soberly about this knowledge can ever allow himself
to think of it except as fragmentary, imperfect knowledge—as the knowledge, as it has been called, of a
" scheme imperfectly understood." We know much ;
but what we know is out of all proportion to the immensity of what we do not know, of what we cannot
know. Our knowledge of God's Kingdom, of its
works and ways, is like all our knowledge of the
highest kind, a combination of light and certainty
on some great points, with ignorance and darkness
on others equally great. There are those who,
because we cannot know all, or all that we should
like to know, think that we can know nothing.
There are those who think that no question can be
asked about the ways of God which cannot be

answered.   Neither remember the most familiar
conditions of our knowledge.   The most awful, the
most certain, the most inexplicable thing *within* us,
is our own soul, our own consciousness, our own
existence ;   the most awful, the most certain, the
most inexplicable thing *without* us, is that unsearch-
able, but not therefore "unknowable," or, as it is
said, "unthinkable" Being, whose name is so familiar
to us, whom we name God.   We know, if we have
ever tried, how difficult it is to escape contradiction
and inconsistency in describing the common experiences of our mental and bodily constitution.   But
boldly and without doubt, as if all lay clear before
us, we take on us to pronounce on what *must be* in
God's unseen Kingdom and working ; what *must be*
if we are to believe in God, if we are to accept the
hypothesis of His Being ; what *must be* because we
believe in God and are sure of Him.   We assume
our experience here as the measure of what is beyond,
far beyond, the bounds we know of space and time.
We draw consequences from our narrow range of
knowledge, and call them necessary.   From God's
certain promise, we advance, absolutely to affirm or
absolutely to deny, this or that way of fulfilling it ;
from God's certain attributes, we proceed without
a suspicion that we may not understand all His
counsels, or all His possibilities, to lay down the
course that He must follow.   And yet, we both know
and know not.   We know in part, in part only ;
we see but through a glass darkly.   If there were
no depths in man's nature which have never been
sounded and fathomed, it would still be unreasonable to assume that our knowledge of God must be,

if worth anything, complete. But if man is himself
a compound of the clearest certainties and the most
hopeless of mysteries—if he, too, with so much
experience and so much search into himself, is yet
so profoundly in the dark about what is yet most
inward, most familiar to him, we need not wonder
that we should know at once so much and so little
about the Kingdom of God : so much about its
greatness, its purposes, its laws, its blessings, its
hopes ; so little about the vastness of its range ; so
little about the conditions of its contact with this
visible scene of life ; so little about the limitations
He has imposed on His own working, about possibilities in it beyond our power even to guess ; so
little about the links that bind in harmony the
opposite, and apparently inconsistent truths that
we have equal reason to believe. Our fuller knowledge, our larger experience, our vaster science, have
not made void those solemn ancient words, " Canst
thou by searching find out God ? canst thou find
out the Almighty unto perfection ? It is as high as
heaven; what canst thou do ? deeper than hell ; what
canst thou know ? " " No heart can think upon these
things worthily, and who is able to conceive His
ways ? It is a tempest which no man can see : for
the most part of His works are hid." " Hardly do
we guess aright at things that are upon earth, and
with labour do we find the things that are before us
—in our very hands ;—but the things that are in
heaven who hath searched out ? " " God is in
heaven, and thou upon earth : therefore let thy words
be few."

There is a better way for serious men to think of

the Kingdom of God, than either affecting an incapacity to recognise it, or than seeking to know in
it what they cannot know, and dogmatising on what
God keeps secret from us on this side the grave.
There it is, ever about us, ever perfect ; and in it,
unknown as is its greatness, we men have even here
our wonderful communion and fellowship with Him
its King, "Who loved us, and gave Himself for us."
So, in far inferior measure, it was to the Psalmists.
But to them it was the subject of unceasing rejoicing.
Just as men feel themselves on a bright day in spring,
when the earth smiles, and the sky surrounds them
with light, and their whole nature opens out and
answers to the glory and gladness of the hour, so did
those ancient saints rejoice in the light of God's
countenance, in the consciousness that His Kingdom
encompassed them, and shone upon them, and blessed
them.   And their hearts burst forth in those ever
marvellous songs in which, in all its aspects, its
magnificence was sung, and the children of Sion
were joyful in their King.   It was to them no dead
phrase, no subject for criticism, no theory of the
mind ; it was the reality in which they lived and
trusted.

And can it be less to us than it was to them?
Do we ever think of what it means ?   And if we do,
is it not true that the prospect opened to reason and
imagination and hope is simply and soberly overwhelming.   Think of what, in outlines which we are
utterly unable to fill up, it promises to men ; and
measure this by what we know too well here.   It
promises a life without sin, without suffering ; a life
where there shall be no death.   It promises a life of

happiness.   It promises a life of which love shall be
the unfailing spring.   It promises to bring us near,
to make us like, to God.   That, in its soberest, most
certain expression, is the hope of the Kingdom of
God.   That is the inconceivable change reserved for
man.   And on that we have leave, we are invited,
to meditate, to hope.

One of the lessons of Advent is that of increased
attention to the Holy Scriptures, in order that
through patience, and the comfort of the Scriptures,
" we may embrace and ever hold fast the blessed hope
of everlasting life," given us in Jesus Christ our Lord.
We cannot open a book of the New Testament without coming upon this " hope " expressed in words,
which, if they were not so familiar to us, would startle
and thrill and haunt us with their astonishing import.
Those who wrote them, felt them ; felt themselves,
in all seriousness and earnest, the heirs of a prospect
passing infinitely anything known or possible here,
but as real, as sure to be, as anything that we can
prize and count on in our life.   What we need, dulled
and bewildered as we are with our present experience
—what we need is to feel this too.   What we need
is to fix our eyes and our thoughts on these records
of a higher experience than our own, till the words
which have become dim and dull and pale by use,
recover their true and original force, and kindle before
our minds into the fire and light of their writers'
meaning.   Then, as we read such parts of the Bible
as the Epistles to the Romans and the Ephesians,
and the first Epistle of St. Peter, it would come home
to us what is really awaiting, at the end, those who
believe, and try to live as St. Paul and St. Peter

lived.[1]   Then we should understand better the solemn
adjuration, " Having therefore these promises, dearly
beloved, let us cleanse ourselves from all filthiness of
the flesh and spirit, perfecting holiness in the fear of
God." Then, feeling the reality and the greatness
of the Kingdom of God, in which we are, we should
find it less hard than we often do, to sympathise with
St. Paul's hold on the future : " I reckon that the
sufferings of this present time are not worthy to be
compared with the glory which shall be revealed in us."
Then we should understand better, and by God's
grace be led to share, that sober and certain, yet
piercing and rapturous exultation, which filled prophets and apostles when their souls rose to things
unseen, and they thought of what was one day to be
—the revelation of the Kingdom of the Most High
—the " manifestation of the sons of God "—the
Advent again of the invisible, yet ever-present, Lord,
" Whom," says St. Peter, " having not seen, ye love ;
in whom, though now ye see Him not, yet believing,
ye rejoice with joy unspeakable and full of glory."

[1] O princely lot ! O blissful art !
E'en while by sense of change opprest,
    Thus to forecast in heart
    Heaven's Age of fearless rest.

Vanity of Vanities : *Lyra Apostolica*, xliii. (First Ed.)

IX

THE INCARNATION OF GOD[1]

"Paul, a servant of Jesus Christ, called to be an apostle, separated
unto the gospel of God, (which He had promised afore by His prophets in the holy scriptures,) concerning His Son Jesus Christ our
Lord ; which was made of the seed of David according to the
flesh ; and declared to be the Son of God with power, according
to the spirit of holiness, by the resurrection from the dead."—
ROM. i. 1-4.

WE are invited to-day to turn our thoughts with
special devotion to that great truth upon which the
Gospel, as St. Paul here says, is founded, the awful
and overwhelming mystery of the Incarnation of the
Son of God—the truth expressed in the beginning
of St. John's Gospel—"the Word was made Flesh." It
must be, indeed, to Christians, their continual thought.
But, year by year, Christmas brings it back, as if it
were something fresh and new, and calls upon our
minds to make a fresh effort to master its significance,
and pay it the homage which is its due. It is no
new thing. It is that which has supported the life
and the growth of Christendom for more than
eighteen centuries, and yet, in a sense, it is new once
more every Christmas Day. There is a sight which
happens every day we live, which if it happened only

[1] Preached in St. Paul's Cathedral, Christmas Day, 1874.

once in a long period of time, would excite a wonder and admiration beyond anything that the strangest phenomena, or the most glorious scenes we are acquainted with could call forth. Darkness changes into light, the sun arises on the earth every day ; but because the sunrise happens every day, we are unconscious of the wonder and magnificence of the event, till something or other makes us *think*, and opens our eyes to what custom had blinded us to. Christmas Day is given to awaken us afresh to the Rising of our Eternal Sun over the darkness and despair of the world. Once at least in the year, we are made to remember what ought to call forth our adoring wonder every day and all the day long. To-day let us awake to it. To-day let us prepare our hearts to receive the impressions which Psalm and Hymn and Lessons of Scripture are meant to make. To-day " let us go even unto Bethlehem, and see this thing which is come to pass, which the Lord hath made known unto us."

What is it that we shall find ? What did the shepherds see there ? They saw, we know, " a babe wrapped in swaddling clothes, lying in a manger." And it is the Babe lying in the manger, the scene of the Nativity, so like, yet so unlike what has happened to each man born into the world, which is before our minds and memories now. Even in its outward aspect, it has its lessons, its deep and overpowering appeals, to our thoughts and affections. But we shall ill answer to the call of our great festival if we stop here. We have been taught what was behind that veil of helplessness and poverty. We know that it was no mere entrance on a career in this world of time, amid circumstances of commonplace obscurity, made striking to us by their contrast with a mighty future, of one who was to be great and do great things in the sphere of our mortal life. It was no birth of one who was to be a great Lawgiver, or Conqueror, or Prophet, or King. There is one and one only thought which can adequately fill our minds at a time like this—a thought beside which all other marvels, all other instances and displays of God's interest in the concerns of His creatures are thrown into the background. It was the coming into this world—as the child of a Virgin mother, but otherwise under the conditions, the common conditions, of our humanity—of the Everlasting and Almighty Son of God.

1. Such an event as that can have nothing like it, or parallel to it, while this world lasts. It is the turning-point in the history of the world. The Gospel of Christ, which, as announced by His Church from the first, has made the Incarnation of the Eternal Son what St. Paul made it, the centre and heart of all teaching, worship, and obedience, the fulfilment and end of all that was old, the starting-point of all that was new—the Gospel of Christ refuses, and must ever refuse, to compromise with any view of religion which puts this tremendous truth in any less than its paramount and sovereign place. It has been forgotten at times ; it has been displaced, for a season, by ideas and doctrines which the exigencies, or the accidental disputes, or the fashions of the age brought to the surface ; it has been fiercely assailed, or subtly explained away, or shrunk from as something too overwhelming to human imagination. But it

C.S.,P. ·   N

reasserts itself in the latest century as in the first.
Let the Christian Church become serious after being
careless and frivolous ; let Christians become thoughtful after having been superficial and shallow ; let them
become alive after having been dead, and the first thing
which meets them, the first thing that occupies and
stirs their minds from their depths, is this amazing
and transporting mystery, of the Eternal Son, born
man indeed, to live and die. You may as well
divide the soul from the body, and hope to leave the
living man, as attempt to separate from the Gospel
of the New Testament, from the religion which calls
itself Christianity, the belief in the Word made
Flesh.

This is the great thought, the great fact, that
faces us this morning. God has been made man.
God has indeed taken human form and flesh, this
form and flesh that we bear. God, our maker, our
upholder, the maker and upholder of all the worlds—
God has been with us ; has trodden our earth, has
spoken with human words, has worked with human
hands, has suffered human pains, has wept with
human tears. God has been with us, the Eternal,
the Ineffable, whom the heavens, and the heaven of
heavens cannot contain—here, in certain of the years
of time, on the hills of Galilee, in the streets of
Jerusalem. God has been with us, the most mighty,
the most merciful, in the form of a servant, as the
carpenter's son of Nazareth, as a little child. Men
have looked upon the face of God, and it was the
face of One who called them His friends, His brethren.
God has been with us, and seen our life, what we are,
and what we do, all our sin and all our need, our

madness, our anguish, our helplessness—seen it with the eyes of a man, with a heart as human in its sympathy and brotherhood as it was divinely perfect in its love and righteousness. God has unveiled Himself to us here, to be as man the Healer and Restorer of mankind, to regenerate them by His word and truth, to shed the blood which was to redeem the world. Is it possible that such a thing should be, and that all things else should not be changed by it? Can such an event have had its real place in what has passed in the ages during which mankind has lived and acted here, and must it not have made a change which nothing else could conceivably make, in the world, and life, and all things belonging to them? Can we steadily fix our thoughts on what it means—on the words which enshrine it in the Creed and the *Te Deum*—and not see that after such a Day of God, such a Visitation and Presence as nothing can be compared with except the First Day of Creation, and the Last Day of the World—that after the Incarnation in this our world of the Eternal Son, nothing could be henceforth, in fact or in our thoughts, as it was before : " neither death, nor life . . . nor things present, nor things to come, nor height, nor depth, nor any other creature." All things are made different, are absolutely, irreversibly altered ; and from that moment a new world begins, as truly as the old one began, with new knowledge, new hopes, new powers, new laws. How could it be otherwise, when it pleased the Eternal Father to work so wonderfully and so strangely for us men and for our salvation? How could it be otherwise, when " God so loved the world that He gave His only begotten Son," to take our nature upon Him, to be as at this time born of a pure Virgin? What a profound and complete revolution in the conditions of our state, what renovations, what unimagined prospects, must surely follow on such an act of God? Think of what was promised, think of what was expected, even by those who waited for the consolation of Israel, before *He* came—the Seed of Abraham, in whom all the families of the earth should be blessed ; the Son of David, who should reign from sea to sea, whose kingdom should be as long as the sun and moon endure ; the Anointed One, with wondrous and mystic names, the Child born to us, the Son given to us, the mighty God, the everlasting Father, the Prince of Peace, " Immanuel, God with us,"— think of it all, and at its highest, as it was thought of in the darkness, or in the twilight before the dawn, before He the Sun arose, before the Dayspring from on high visited us in the manner in which He *really* was to visit us ; think of the promise and expectation, and then, of what was in fact the fulfil- ment, and surely we are not able to measure the gap between them—the infinite distance between the loftiest mysteries and enigmas of prophecy, and the clear certainty of the truth, most incomprehen- sible, most sure, of the advent of the Word who was God, the Word made Flesh, and dwelling among us.

2. The Incarnation was the turning-point in the history of this world ; and as a matter of fact, we have before our eyes the consequences which have followed from it. In the good and in the evil, in what the world seems and what it is, in its tendencies, its motives, its efforts, in what is visibly on its surface

and in its secret forces, in the depths of men's hearts
and their strongest purposes, that awful Presence
which was once visibly in the world has made things
different in it from what they ever were before. They
are incommensurable in the nature of the case, the
ancient and the Christian ages : there is no common
measure between them, and vainly do we try to
invent one. But I turn to another aspect of the
subject. We have each of us, one by one, our
concern with this great truth. For each man, as
for the world, the Son of God was made man, to
help and enable man to reach the perfection for
which he was made ; for each of us, did He humble
Himself to this awful condescension of His love; for
each one, He was born and died ; for each one's
restoration and strength and blessing, He has in
store all that has been done by His becoming man.
His Incarnation has been made known· to us not
only for the public creed and confession of the
Church, but for the private needs and private use, for
the personal hope and stay, of each of our souls.
And to know and master what it means, to *realise*,
as we say, what it is, and what it is *to us*, is the
turning-point of each man's belief. Like the realis-
ation and bringing home to our own selves of the
idea of death ; like the becoming alive to the great
questions—Whence am I ? What am I ? Why am I
here? Whither am I going?—like as it is when, in
the stillness of meditation, there opens on the mind
the overwhelming and absorbing thought of what God
is, of what God must be,—so is it with us, when first
we are able to catch hold of the meaning of those
amazing words, the Word was made Flesh—God was

made Man. Once let a man grasp the idea, not only
that some Great One came to save, and teach, and
forgive, and justify him ; not only that some one came
to die for him, and rose from the dead that his whole
moral nature might be raised and restored ; but that
He who came was in simple truth no other than the
Very and Eternal God ; that He who came, came by
being born of woman, came in the substantial truth of
human nature ; and not only is the whole Gospel
lighted up with new glory, but its reference to himself receives a new force, breaks upon him with inexpressible and tremendous meaning. " Who loved
me, and gave Himself for me "—to think that He
who did this for each one of us, that He who loved
with such self-sacrifice, is He, of whom all may be
said that the mind of man can conceive and the
tongue of man can utter of the Almighty and Ever-
living God,—*this* is a revelation to a man's spirit, which,
whether it come gradually, or come, as it may do,
suddenly in a moment, is one of those things which
lift him up out of the commonplaces of routine
religion, one of those things which bring him face to
face with the real questions of his being, with those
fateful alternatives, the choice of which decides the
course of his life and its issues. We may not know
it or take it in : the Creed, the Gospel of St. John,
the Epistles of St. Paul may be a matter of words,
into which we may not be able to put a living meaning ; we may overlook and cloud the fact of the Incarnation with subordinate doctrines, with the theories
and traditions of men, with a disproportionate mass of
guesses on what it is not given us to know, of subtleties and reasonings in the sphere of human philo-

sophy ; we may recoil from it and put it from us, as something which oppresses our imagination and confounds our reason ; but we may be sure that on the place which we really give it in our mind and heart depends the whole character of our Christianity, depends what the Gospel of Christ means *to us.*

We see in the Incarnation and the Nativity how God fulfils the promises He makes and the hopes which He raises, in ways utterly unforeseen and unexpected, utterly inconceivable beforehand, utterly beyond the power of man to anticipate. And further, we see exemplified in it that widely prevailing law of His government, that in this stage of His dispensations with which we are acquainted, which we call this world and this life, that which is to be greatest must stoop to begin from what is humblest—the greatest glories must pass through their hour of obscurity, the greatest strength must rise out of the poorest weakness, the greatest triumphs must have faced their outset of defeat and rebuke, the greatest goodness start unrecognised and misunderstood.   Is it not something almost too great for the mind to endure—the contrast between what the eye of man saw and what really *was,* between what *was to be* and its present visible beginnings—when we go back to that first Christmas morning, and think of that poor manger in that poor Jewish town, and of Him who lay there?   Must we not feel as if there'was a spell in the world to blind our eyes to what is real, and that we are passing through it in a dream, when that was the first sight that human eyes ever had of Him who had made all things, of Him men's only Hope and Joy, of Him who was to be their Judge?

Is even the Cross itself so overwhelmingly marvellous
as the Humiliation of the Little Child? But so it is.
So He willed. So it should be, in the perfect harmony of the eternal purpose. So, then, in those
depths of lowliness and self-abasement, of feebleness
and neglect, began that path which was to lead the
Son of Man, through shame and death, to the right
hand of the Father. So began here, *in time*, that
reign of all the ages, which was to win back to Him
who had made them the world of souls, and fill
heaven with the multitudes of the redeemed. From
such a level did He start on His course of warfare
and sacrifice for man, the second Adam, at whose
name, at the end, every knee shall bow, of things
in heaven and things in earth, and things under
the earth, King of Kings, and Lord of Lords. St.
Paul himself, St. John himself, cannot find words to
tell the mystery of accomplished purpose, by which
God gathers together in one "all things in Christ,
both which are in heaven, and which are in earth;
even in Him"; "and hath put all things under His
feet, and given Him to be the Head over all things to
the Church, which is His body, the fulness of Him
that filleth all in all"; and here, in Bethlehem, wrapped
in the swaddling clothes, He was one in whom the
shepherds could see no difference from any other
new-born babe.

Christian brethren—you who are as much interested
as they in this disclosure of God—you who know
more than they did of its awful meaning, don't let
this time pass without an effort to bring home to
your hearts the things you have to do with—the
Person who is the centre of it all, the lesson which,

as far as men can follow it, He teaches you. When
wonder and adoration—and thanksgiving, if it were
possible, without bounds—have had their due, there
remains the practical impressions to be laid up for
the actual, serious, definite work of life. You are the
heirs—you cannot doubt it in presence of that
manger cradle—of a hope which passes measuring
here ; you are the object of a Divine solicitude and
love, of which human language is absolutely incapable
of revealing the fulness. But in the meanwhile, you
are men and women, with your appointed parts to play
on this earthly scene, with lives to waste and spoil,
or to improve and elevate ; with the risks of unfaithfulness and carelessness, with the sure rewards of self-
discipline and sincerity; with a heart and character to
fashion after the mind of Christ, with an allotted and
fast-shortening term to finish your work. What can
you learn for your own guidance from the mystery
of His Incarnation, His nativity and childhood—from
these stages of His work, from which He would not
excuse Himself? Is it not surely, that *we* must
begin *our* eternal work, as He was pleased to begin
His, according to that law which He has laid down
for the kingdom of God, by which those who are to
reach the highest must have known and welcomed
the humblest and the lowest ? " Except ye become as
little children," is His characteristic word, " ye shall
not enter into the kingdom of heaven." We must
learn the lesson of patient waiting, of lowliness of heart
and self-estimation, patiently and faithfully fulfilling
the tasks of the present, patiently waiting as time
moves insensibly on and keeps us still from much that
we stretch our hands to ; of patient resolution, in try-

ing again and again, for love of Christ, what we have
often failed in; of patient endurance of the facts which
make us conscious of the scantiness of our powers and
knowledge, of the poverty of our character, of the ill-
success of our endeavours; of patient determination to
learn and bear the truth about, and against, ourselves ;
of patient courage to feel that we are but beginners,
and that we are without the gifts, the strength, the
excellence that others have ; of patient waiting, and
patient hope, till, of the seed which we sow in faith,
the years shall bring the fruit.   Lowliness, in such as
we are, and in our condition, means simply truth—
truthfulness in our judgment of things and of ourselves;
truthfulness about ourselves before God.   To become
as little children is to recognise the reality of our condition in this life of time—its disproportion to the endless life before us—its weakness, its failures, its sin, its
vanity ; the humiliation of our knowledge, the poorness of all we are doing now.   And yet, through such
poorness of doing and dimness of knowing has all
that has been ever worthy here to be called great
worked its way.   It is sown in weakness, it is unknown in growing, it is despised in its first appearings;
and it is, after all this, that it bears its blossoms and is
crowned with its fruit.   So is it in the work of the
kingdom of God.   What is there, according to this
world's standard of greatness or interest, in the dull,
dreary, disappointing struggle against our own faults
and selfishness, the long labour of self-conquest, the
detail and the trouble of watchfulness and self-correction, the often wasted, and yet still repeated prayers ?
But through such a discipline—who can say through
any other?—have human characters, hardly conscious

of what was going on, waxed strong and holy and fit for their Master's triumphs, and sprung up to the heights of nobleness and saintliness.

We look on, some of us almost with a shudder, at the drudgery of Christian labourers—plain, simple people, dull in themselves, dull to the dignity of their calling—in the squalid courts of our cities, in the loathsome dens of vice, by the cold, dismal sick-beds of the poor, in crowded school-rooms, amid misery and darkness, and lives without joy and hope. We are glad, perhaps, that there are some to do it; and glad, perhaps, that it is not ourselves. And yet, will not one day declare, that in these uninteresting, repulsive "poor and sick and ignorant and naked," it was Christ Himself who was visited and ministered to—that what was done for the neglected children was done for Him who blessed the children, was done for the Child of Bethlehem? And can we doubt that when that great multitude which stand in white robes and golden crowns, with palms in their hands, before the Lamb, and from whose eyes God has wiped away every tear, look back to the conflicts through which they came to their great beatitude, they will wonder at the littleness, the meanness, the paltriness of the trials which were then their daily experience, their daily cross, the commonplace diffi- culties of their lives—poor things, of "the earth, earthy"—which yet were in their appointed hour the trial-ground of martyrs, the steps by which here the saints made their approach to the likeness of their Lord?

We cannot but be children, do or think what we will, in the face of the powers and mysteries of

this immense and awful universe of nature which surrounds us. We cannot but feel ourselves children,
in the presence of the chances and uncertainties of a
dark and menacing future, impenetrable, beyond man's
control. But He who made us, He who guides all
things, descended, even to the lowliness and helplessness of childhood, that He might comfort us,—
descended, as the first step of His everlasting triumph.
Let us entreat Him to help us to descend from our
ignorant pride, from our vain and self-wise confidence,
to the level of what we are in His eyes. Let us
think of ourselves as children, in the presence of
that supreme mystery with which all our destiny is
bound up ; children, before the incalculable Humiliation of the Son of God, before the infinity of His
greatness and His love ; children, on the brink and
threshold of that vast, unchanging life, to which this
one is but a playtime and a trial-ground, knowing
nothing except in part, yet with the fortunes of an
eternal existence in our hands. May He who loved
us, and in all things gave Himself for us, convert us
to become in heart and spirit like the little children
whom He blessed—convert us from our blindness,
our folly, and our sin, to the lowly trust, the purity,
the simpleness, the cheerful readiness, the joy, of
childhood ; so that we may grow up to Him in all
things, to the measure of the stature of the fulness
of Christ ; *here*, even here, as we are able, amid the
errors and miseries of our mortality ; *there*, in the
completeness of that perfect and stainless world.

X

THE LIVING HOPE [1]

" Who hath begotten us again unto a lively hope by the resurrection of Jesus Christ from the dead."—1 PETER i. 3.

THESE words speak of a change which can only be described in language to which nothing in human experience can possibly answer. There is no such thing in nature as being begotten again, as a new and second birth. That word " regeneration," which from Scripture and the Church has passed into the common phraseology of historical and political speculation, involves in its proper meaning an impossible conception—the conception of life once begun, beginning again ; and it is no wonder that Nicodemus, with his thoughts moulded and limited by experience and custom, stumbled at it. But no less than this strange and violent word would suffice to express the change which the Incarnation of the Eternal Son was to work in the souls of men. And no less a word will suffice for the Apostle, to express the change made in the condition and prospects of God's chosen by the Resurrection of Jesus Christ.

Here, as in so many other cases, we are not startled, we are not struck, from the long effect of

[1] Preached in St. Paul's Cathedral, Easter Day, 1875.

use and habit. These amazing words of Scripture, we have heard them all our life long ;—every Sunday in church, and to many of us on week days or out of church, the language in which Prophets and Apostles set forth the wonderful works of God, has been before our minds—minds often inattentive, often wandering, and anyhow seldom adequately alive to its full import. In God's great goodness, these words have been made to us "current coin" ; but, as in current coin, the sharpness and freshness of their first impress has been worn away by long familiarity, by the sin and the misuse of centuries, by the irreverence and unfaithfulness of human custom. If we could be carried back to the days when they were written—if we could hear or read an Epistle of St. Paul or St. Peter, as its words fell for the first time or the second on the ears of those to whom it was originally written, and who were living in the midst of the things and events to which it referred— language which we now listen to with so languid an interest would take our minds captive with astonish- ment ; what seems so trite, so tame, so vague, would start in every syllable into life and definite meaning and overpowering surprise ; we should feel that we were hearing or reading of things never yet spoken of by the tongues of men, or of thoughts too mighty even for inspired minds. The language is indeed astonishing, but not more astonishing than that which it represents. That which had come to pass in this world of ours when Jesus Christ died on the Cross and rose from the dead on the third day— that change of all beliefs, all suppositions, all hopes, all motives—that great change required a new outfit

of words for its expression. To those who could not
break with what they had been accustomed to, who
could not imagine it possible that the Son of God
could die for men, that any breathing mortal breath
could come back from the grave, the new language
was simply unintelligible. " To the Jews a stumbling-
block—to the Greeks foolishness." But to those who
did believe it, even the loftiest and most startling
language must have seemed too weak : nothing but
that sustained tone of expression, raised to its
highest power and boldest strain, which prevails
without exception throughout the Epistles of the
New Testament, could in any degree correspond to
what had now become the supreme realities of
men's existence. To speak of a " new creation," to
speak of " death being swallowed up in victory," of
" life and immortality " being " brought to light," of
men being " born again " into the sonship, and household, and inheritance of God—all this to them was no
extravagance of Eastern rhetoric, but the plain " words
of truth and soberness." Such a change as had been
in the order of things here when Christ died and
rose again, more than authorised it. How could
such things happen, and all things not be made new ?
The anomaly would have been that men should have
seen and should believe such wonders, and yet should
only speak in the language to which the world had
been accustomed before such things had happened.

The first Easter Day divides two worlds, the old
and the new : this is not speculation or opinion,
but fact. From the faith in Jesus Christ raised
from the dead, has followed all that is characteristic
of modern ages, of the highest forms of human

society,—their ideas of good, their essays after improvement, their hopes of the future which sustain and encourage mankind. This deep and permanent change, so extensive, so antecedently incalculable, has passed over the condition and prospects of man even here, and it is evident and undeniable as a matter of history. But this is the least of the great change to us, to whom Jesus Christ, Crucified, Risen, Ascended, is the Redeemer and Hope ; to us, to whom life is what it is, because He was indeed raised from the dead. The change to us means something more than can be measured by any bettering or elevation of our circumstances or our ways of thinking in time. We are still bound to time, but the significance of this change is that it opens to us something beyond time. We are still subjects of nature, and citizens of this visible world which Christ's Redemption has done so much to interpret and exalt. But that Redemption to us means something which imparts to us what is above nature, and makes us sharers in the realities and powers of the invisible world. This it is which makes to Christians the difference between what they would have been *without* Christ dying and rising, what they would have been *before* that Passion and Victory, and what they now are, *after* it—*because* of it. This it is which explains and accounts for such strong words as the Apostle's—" Who hath begotten us again unto a living hope,"—" being born again, not of corruptible seed, but of incorruptible, by the word of God, which liveth and abideth for ever."

Let us dwell for a few moments on two points in this " living hope," to which we have been "born again

by the resurrection of Jesus Christ from the dead."
(1) One is, the abiding presence of Jesus Christ with
us, in this mortal and passing state. (2) The other
is, the certainty and assurance it gives that what
man was made for shall be accomplished ; that his
nature is to be made perfect ; that his destiny as
God's creation is to be fulfilled.

1. Who among the most favoured of Prophets
could have raised their souls to the hope, that the
day would come when God should be made known
to men, as God *was* made known in the Person
of Jesus Christ — that what their prophetic words
signified was such a manifestation of God to man
as the Gospels record? Who among them could
have imagined, that He who came and disclosed to
men that mystery and nature of the Godhead which
had been veiled to Moses and Isaiah, was to abide
with those whom He had redeemed, till He returned
to judge the world? And yet this is the "living
hope," to which the successive generations of Christian people are heirs, by virtue of that great change
in their condition made by the Resurrection of Jesus
Christ. He who made man and knew what was in
man, knew what was at the bottom of man's heart,
of his purest love, of his blind longings. What man
was made for,, what man consciously or unconsciously yearned after, was, not merely God's gifts,
but God Himself; what he wanted in the world,
what he needed to stay upon in its darkness and disorder, what he imagined to himself, as the highest
of conceivable blessings, was a Divine Presence.
"Verily Thou art a God that hidest Thyself," was
the awestruck reflection of the Prophet, even while

recounting the power and providence of the "God of Israel, the Saviour"; and nature and conscience, His witnesses throughout all the earth, yet echoed the confession—"A God that hideth Himself." This hidden God made known, made certain, this was what man sought after—this was the "Desire of all nations." And this was given. God came forth from the depths and uncertainties of nature, from the clouds and terrors and enigmas of Providence, from the veil and mystery behind which Israel worshipped Him, from the silence in which yet He was the dim hope of all the ends of the earth—He came forth and showed Himself, He came forth and gave Himself to the love and hearts of men. He taught with human words; He healed, He forgave, He blessed; He drew souls to Himself with new and Divine affections; *with* men and *for* men, He passed from this life through that dark gate of fear and humiliation which we call Death. And if this had been all—if He had passed at once from the grave which could not hold Him to His glory above—who among us knows enough to dare to ask why He should have stopped at this, why He should have vouchsafed no more, whether with only so much His promise could have been fulfilled and His work accomplished? But this, as we know, was not all. On earth itself He was again, alive from the dead. On earth again, as He had been before, and yet *not* as He had been before: passing across the scene of life, yet no longer mortal—conversing, walking, eating with men, but vanishing the next moment from their sight; in form, in love, in power the same, but no longer bound by the body of

humiliation which He had worn with His brethren ;
lifting their thoughts above all that is natural, carnal,
earthly in the body, fixing them on all in it that
is real and personal. And this was the beginning
of a Presence of God which was nevermore to be
withdrawn from the sons of men. It was a Presence
not limited to the thirty-three years during which men
saw and touched Jesus Christ. The Presence which
then began, such a Presence as never had been in
the world before, was to continue in His Church to
the end of all things. " Lo, I am with you alway,
even unto the end of the world." The promise of
that ancient name of prophecy was to be fulfilled,
not merely for a short time, and to a small band
of disciples, but to His Church for ever—" Immanuel,
God with us." The thirst of the soul and mind
and heart of man for the Presence of God—a God
known, and adored, and loved—was to .be satisfied
by a universal blessing : it was to be no privilege
even of Apostles. His Ascension out of our sight
was a change in the manner of His presence, not
in the reality of His presence itself. It ceased to
be verified by sense or sight, it was not less real to
that which is the real inward self of man, that in
him which feels, and thinks, and loves ; that in him
which alone lasts on for ever ; that deep, unsearch-
able, yet most certain personality of his existence, conscious only in part of the facts of its life, which is only
less mysterious to us than the Personality of God Himself. *There*, the Word who had become man was to
be present. There, in all His truth, in all the grace
and blessing of such a Presence, the Risen Saviour,
who was dead and is alive for evermore, was hence-

forth to meet men, henceforth to give Himself to them,
henceforth to be one with them, and they one with
Him.   " I will not leave you comfortless: I will come
to you.   Yet a little while, and the world seeth Me
no more; but ye see Me : because I live, ye shall live
also.   At that day ye shall know that I am in My
Father, and ye in Me, and I in you."   Again, "he that
eateth My flesh and drinketh My blood, dwelleth in
Me, and I in him."   What explanations can reach
or exhaust these amazing words : the utterance of
the Son of God Himself, passing all created thought,
beyond all imaginable created power.   And as such
in their plain meaning, as the most certain of realities,
the most unutterable of blessings, the Apostles received them.   " I am crucified with Christ: nevertheless I live; yet not I, but Christ liveth in me."   "Who
shall separate us from the love of Christ ? "   Such
words sum up the feeling under which all the Epistles
are written : the feeling of that immediate nearness
of the unseen Christ, of that immediate dealing,
through the veils and mystery of our present state,
with the Risen Lord of Life, which implies the con-
tinuance and the perpetuity of His Presence with those
for whom He died : " Whom having not seen, ye love;
in whom, though now ye see Him not, yet believing,
ye rejoice with joy unspeakable and full of glory."

2. The Resurrection was the answer to the cry of
human nature after the Presence of God—the cry, as
we hear it in the Psalms, to have God near, to know
Him, to possess Him.   The Incarnate Word, Risen
from the Dead, is ever with those whom He has made
members of His body—at the Father's right hand,
yet walking in the midst of the golden candlesticks—

with us in our secret chamber and solemn worship,
with us in the breaking of bread at Holy Communion,
with us in those depths of conscience and feeling on
which no eye but His can look ; *how* near, *how* awfully
close and present no tongue can tell, but He has
said, "ye in Me, and I in you"—the very words
which He had just used of His oneness with the
Father.   But further, the Resurrection is the Divine
answer to the old, sad lament of human nature, over
the mystery of its contradictions, its vanity, its abor-
tive purpose.   "Wherefore hast Thou made all men
for nought ? "   Why was the creature made subject
to vanity ?   Why is life so wonderful, so enjoyable,
and yet more idle than a dream ?   Why does man
live only to go hence and perish ?   Why is he so great,
so largely endowed, capable of such powers of reason,
capable of such high goodness and nobleness of soul,
capable of such affections, of such love, only to be
lost and thrown away in the waste and vastness of
the universe ?   Why, just as he comes to the ripeness
of his wisdom and power, is he cut off, as if at random,
like the meanest insect, like the summer leaf ?   Why
are those taken who could serve and bless their
fellows, and the useless, the worthless, left ?   What is
the meaning of that destiny which starts with such
wonderful promise and such high hope, and in the
midst of its achievements suddenly and abruptly
drops into nothing ?   What is the meaning of that
force and energy of will, that penetrating and
victorious intelligence, that infinite play and charm
of character, that loveliness and sweetness, which are
just shown to the world, and then pass, "like as a
dream when one awaketh ? "   Where is it gone, what

has become of it, what was it made for, that great
heart, that richly-furnished mind, which was with us
yesterday and is with us no more for ever? What
does it all mean, this irony of human glory and human
fate? "Wherefore hast Thou made all men for nought?"
What a world is that in which "those who most enjoy
life, and those who best employ it, must close it amid
the same impenetrable shadows."[1]   And that is not
the worst. What a destiny is that which, as long as we
can trace it, sin and evil cross and thwart and spoil?
Why does man know and desire what is good, when
against his will, and yet by his own fault, he drifts off
so persistently into evil? Why those continual aims
at what is excellent, realised in miserable and heart-
broken failure? What is the meaning of that cruel
obstinacy of custom, which puts such difficulties in
the way of those who wish to do better? Why is
evil so easy and good so hard? What I would I do
not, but what I hate that I do. " I find then a law,
that, when I would do good, evil is present with me.
. . . Oh wretched man that I am! who shall deliver
me from the body of this death?" What is man
meant for, that such should be his universal cry?
There is no subject in the whole compass of experience on which the greatest writers, poets, moralists,
preachers have spoken their greatest words with such
pathetic sincerity as on this strange argument of the
appalling disproportion between the endowments of
man's nature and what comes of them; between promise
and fulfilment ; between achievement, and its worth
when done ; between what man seems to have been
made to live for, and what his career is seen to end in.

[1] Greg, *Enigmas of Life*, p. 189. (Ed. 1891.)

"But now is Christ risen from the dead, and become the firstfruits of them that slept." " For in that He died, He died unto sin once : but in that He liveth, He liveth unto God." There is the answer. Failure and disappointment are in the world; and to men He too failed : the hope He had raised ended in despair. Love and goodness spend themselves here, and seem to leave little mark on the misery and selfishness of the world : He loved as no one loved ; human hearts were in the presence of His goodness—yet He was the "rejected of men." Pain, mysterious, terrible, irremediable pain, is in the world: He suffered it in its fiercest pangs. Sin is in the world : He was counted as a sinner, and endured its shame, its curse, its doom. Death is in the world: He underwent it. But failure, and pain, and a sinner's death, were but the short transitory passage to the fulfilment of what He came for : ."made perfect through sufferings," He entered into His glory. And in Him, the First-begotten of the Dead—of those dead who seem to human eyes to have perished— the riddle of human existence received its solution : man was not made to come to nought, but to be made perfect. That wonderful being, made in the Image of God, fitted for his course with the choicest gifts from God's treasury, capable of so much, aspiring to so much, with such capacities for delight and happiness, was not born for Death but Immortality ; he was not sent here for defeat, and incompleteness, and disappointment, but to grow "from grace to grace," into the likeness of the Son of God. We talk of life cut short, of great hopes extinguished, of vast usefulness arrested, of high powers given only to be taken away ; but indeed there is nothing lost, nothing has been in vain—the incompleteness and the failure are only relative to us, and while we are here in the darkness. Sin is no longer man's fatal master, from whom no conscience can get free, over whom no will can assert its supremacy. The Resurrection has brought assurance of forgiveness unknown before : the spirit of Him who raised Jesus Christ from the dead has brought into the moral world a strength which can break the tyranny of sin. Language, feeling, thought, may exhaust their strength in dwelling on the darkness and doubts of man's existence and fortunes ; there is but one answer, but *one* there is. He was not made in vain, for whom Christ died ; he was not made to perish, with all his thoughts and perfections, in the dust of death, for whom Christ rose again. " As we have borne the image of the earthy, we shall also bear the image of the heavenly." "He that spared not His own Son, but delivered Him up for us all, how shall He not with Him also freely give us all things ? . . . Who is he that condemneth ? It is Christ that died, yea rather, that is risen again, who is even at the right hand of God, who also maketh intercession for us."

My brethren, if these things are true, let us not merely talk about them, but *think* them and *live* them—think of their reality and greatness, live according to their unspeakable importance to us. If there is one thing certain in the teaching of St. John and St. Paul, it is that the Risen and Ascended Christ is still in very truth present with His Church for ever. They assert it in every varied form of thought and expression ; and we accept their teaching. Well, then, what is it to us, that we have Him so present, that we know Him to be so near? You know how, in the days of His visible presence on earth, the multitudes who stood before it were composed. Then He was before them, and they sought Him; but all sorts were there. There were the earnest and the idle, the heartless and the generous, the tempted, the heart-broken, the prosperous, the critical, the thoughtless. Those who believed, and those who half-believed; those who loved Him, and those whom His sweetness could not move or touch; those who were ready to give up all for Him, and those who would give up all but the one secret, darling idol; those who saw what He was, and those who seeing saw not and hearing heard nothing; those whom misery and sin, the pangs of disease, or the hunger of the soul, or the longing to be true and good, drew to Him, perhaps drove to Him; those who came because others came, because it was fashionable, who looked on, curious, or amused, or indifferent, or scorning, or hating. Is not every congregation which assembles to worship Him—nay, every gathering of those who seek His Presence in Holy Communion—very like those multitudes, composed in the same way, of elements equally various, equally opposite? What a thought that any should be in that Presence, apathetic, thankless, stony-hearted! Have we not reason to ask ourselves, What is it to us, that He still continues to us His Presence? Let us ask ourselves once more on this great Day of the Lord, what we are doing to break through the dreams and doubts of earth, and to fulfil that destiny and calling which the Lord's Resurrection

points out and assures to human nature, to each
living soul which hears that He is Risen. That
destiny which now we know, that promise of a running which may reach the goal, shall it be *to us*,
indeed, in vain ? Knowing that we are not made for
nought, shall we be content with a life that must
come to nought, with wishes that must at last be
baffled, with strength and energy that must at last
have been spent in vain ? What awaits all that is of
the earth, earthy, that is no matter of question.
The alternative only is, between the "living hope,"
the destiny of man, revealed, assured in Christ, or
else that death of hope, that philosophy of plain-
spoken and obstinate despair, that open-eyed, frank,
resigned abandonment of all thought of the future,
that passionate reaction to heathenism, which seems
to be taking possession of some of the finest minds
and greatest intellects of our time. There is no
choice but these ; and yet we go on, saying to ourselves—" The tone of the Bible, the ideal of the Bible,
is too high for us : we do not pretend to much, we
can do with something less ; leave us to get through
life as we may ; leave us our small sins and faults,
they are but little ones ; leave us our trifling interests,
we are not made for greater ; leave us our petty
selfishness and our commonplace, harmless worldliness, our frivolous whims and tempers, our quiet lazi-
ness, our trivial shabbinesses, our mild dishonesties :
we were not made for troublesome improvement, for
high aims, for bold ventures. Leave us with our
life as we lead it, not trying to rise higher, keeping
out of serious wrong, keeping out of the sense of
responsibility. Leave us our easy conscience, our

content with what we are." Yes, it might be, perhaps, if the emptiest worldling, nay, the most
abandoned of sinners, did not bear within him the
germ, the possibility, the intention on God's part
who made him, of a redeemed and saintly life. It
might be, if man held only of the earth and time, and
had no fellowship with what is divine and eternal. It
might be, if only, by forgetting, by not choosing to see,
we could make that *not* to be which *is*, and which
must be—all that there is in the world of misery, all
that must make us know one day something of that
misery ourselves. No, if this is so, the philosophy
of despair is right. If this is the way to live, there
is nothing to contradict the old dreary complaint,
that life is but a cheat, luring forward by hopes
that never can be realised, cutting off the best,
separating the dearest, mocking the greatest. There
is nothing to contradict the cynic's melancholy sneer
at the utmost stretch of life even if it is reached :—

> Then old Age and Experience, hand in hand,
> Lead him to Death, and make him understand,
> After a search so painful and so long,
> That all his Life, he has been in the wrong.[1]

But there is another supposition on which men
may frame their lives. There is another conviction as
deep, as founded on realities, as well tested by experience, as to what man's life, even the humblest,
was made for and meant to end in. It is no supposition of dreamers. It has been the conviction of
the most serious men in their most serious hours.
It is the one belief which attempts to give a mean-

---

[1] Rochester, quoted in Goethe, *Aus Meinem Leben*, Book XIII

ing to human life ; which accounts at once for what
is great in it and what is poor, for its hopes and
their visible defeat.   Christians, hear once more on
Easter morning, how St. Paul has taught us what
man was meant for, why Christ rose from the
dead :—

"The eyes of your understanding being enlightened ; that ye may know what is the hope of His
calling, and what the riches of the glory of His inheritance in the saints, and what is the exceeding
greatness of His power to us-ward who believe,
according to the working of His mighty power, which
He wrought in Christ, when He raised Him from the
dead, and set Him at His own right hand in the
heavenly places, far above all principality, and power,
and might, and dominion, and every name that is
named, not only in this world, but also in that which
is to come : and hath put all things under His feet,
and gave Him to be the head over all things to the
church, which is His body, the fulness of Him that
filleth all in all."

XI

ASCENSION-TIDE[1]

"Go to My brethren, and say unto them, I ascend unto My Father, and your Father; and to My God, and your God."—St. JOHN xx. 17.

As we enter on this week, the week of the Ascension, two great subjects take precedence of all others in our religious thoughts, and strike the keynote in the treatment of every topic of Christian teaching or exhortation. One is the triumphal close of that ministry on earth which the Eternal Son of God undertook for the redemption of mankind; the other is the fellowship, so close, so certain, so incapable of change, which has been established by the Ascension of our Lord between Him who sits at the Father's right hand and the race to which we belong. Our first thought is of our Master's glory, of that final attestation of His mission and work of which the voices from heaven at His Baptism and His Transfiguration were the prelude; of the opening and beginning of that new kingdom in which the Son of Man has all power given to Him in heaven and on earth; in which He has the Name given Him which is above every name; in which He reigns

[1] Preached in St. Andrew's Church, Wells Street, on Ascension Day, 1874, for the Bishop of London's Fund.

" far above all principality, and power, and might, and dominion, and every name that is named, not only in this world, but also in that which is to come," King of Kings, and Lord of Lords. And our next thought is, how deeply, how mysteriously we men are affected by this mystery of Christ ; by what awful bonds we are bound to that nature which once was mortal like our own, and which is now in Divine Majesty on the Eternal Throne ; by what near, and intimate, and undecaying relations He has united and incorporated with Himself our whole race, even its outcasts ; how, amid the darkness and the overthrows of time, we are able to believe in One who is beyond them and unchanged through them all, who once shared, as we share them, the conditions of life and time, and who now has all things, all life and death, all time, all being, beneath His feet ; how we are able to think of Him as One who has not ceased to be man, and how we can stretch forth our hands to Him, through the veil, sure of His regard, sure that He knows us, sure of His sympathy. The Eternal Conqueror and King was not ashamed of His brotherhood with us, which was to be His for ever. In the very hour of His triumph, He salutes us as His brethren. He calls on our souls to go along with His, and bids them con-verge with His on the one centre of all existence and of all love. " I ascend unto My Father, and your Father ; and to My God, and your God."

There is yet a third thought, which the purpose for which I am here to-day seems naturally to elicit from the impressions which the memory of the Lord's Ascension awakens in us, and which, at no time out of place, is now emphatically in place. This amazing relation of our race to its Eternal Lord must, if we believe in it, influence deeply our feelings of our relations to one another. Men who are our companions and fellows in life, are recognised as *His* brethren, joined to Him by the ties and claims of a common nature—to Him whom we worship as our Lord and our God. To all of them He has the same relation that He has to us, who are called by His name, and trust in Him as our Deliverer from sin and from the ruin of the grave. The life and the death that they know, He knew; to make them what their Father meant them to be, to redeem their souls from death, He became man, He laid down His life. He associates them too, like us, in His own supreme and transcendent relation to the Father; to them, as to us, belong the words which gather and bind us all to Him— " I ascend unto My Father, and your Father ; and to My God, and your God." This is what they are to Him, the multitudes of our race, baffling the imagination in their swarming and thronging crowds, infinitely various in all that makes men different here ; this is what they are to Him, the numbers of those living souls, which along with us are now passing through their allotted time on earth. This is what they are to Him, near to Him and far off; those who know Him best and are most like Him, and those who know not even His name; those who in their various degrees, each in his own 'order, realise the greatness of His benefit, and those too who are cut off and estranged from Him by deep moral opposition, alienated and enemies by wicked works. Yet they all bear the humanity which He has taken, which He has redeemed, which He has

glorified.   As men, they are all His brethren, for
whom He refused not shame and death, for whom
He is at the Father's right hand.   This they are to
Him.   What are they to us ?

This subject of thought naturally at this time
forces itself on all who seriously believe in that
wonderful article of the Creed—" He ascended into
heaven, He sitteth on the right hand of God."   Our
human nature, our human race, is linked with Him
by bonds which will never be broken.   How does
this bind us, one to another, among ourselves ?   We
are bound together by many and powerful ties of
fellowship, by our common origin, our common
necessities, our common experience of life, our
common exposure to the blows of fortune, our
common longing for good, our common capacity for
pain.   We are bound together by that great law of
right and wrong, which more or less clearly is
written on all our hearts, and before which our
conscience bows even when we disobey.   We are
bound together by having one and all to share the
changes and chances of this short-lived, mortal
state, by the quick sense which we have of its felicity
and its anguish, by having, one and all of us, to die.
With all our endless and sharply-contrasted differences
of condition, of education, of character, of opinion,
of our views and uses of life—in all these things
we know that we are as all men are, and that all
men, high and low, far and near, are as we are.
But beyond all these natural and universal bonds of
human fellowship, there are others, founded on even
more solemn and more wonderful realities, having
relation to things that are even more serious than

life, more final and more unchangeable than death. We are all one in that common disaster which we call the fall and corruption of our nature. We are all one in our need of redemption, healing, restoration. And for us all the Eternal Son humbled Himself and was made man, and lived. For all of us, He has created a new bond of union, of the deepest and most awful significance, in that Cross and Passion which He endured for all men. For all of us He rose from the dead, and removed the darkness and doubts which hung on man's immortality. And now, as if these bonds of union were not enough, He shows us a new wonder in heaven. For all of us, the Son of Man is gone up above the heaven of heavens to the right hand of the Father. For all our classes, for all our conditions, for all our inequalities of state, for all our varieties of opposing and clashing purposes, and mutually repellent tempers; for those to whom life is easy, and those to whom it is so hard; for those who are masters of their course and position, and those who are helplessly overwhelmed and swept along by the merciless currents of the world,—for all of us, make what distinctions we will among ourselves, He, who has taken to the Throne of God that nature which is common to us all, holds up before us that new and profound bond of sympathy and of common hope, which He has added to all those bonds by which we were united before. That old and natural brotherhood of flesh and blood which made us one, He has strengthened and made closer, by revealing to us that we are one in a brotherhood, not only of earth but now also of heaven, in which He is not ashamed to be our

brother.   Our distinctions disappear, our inequalities
are lost, all that keeps us apart or uninterested in
one another sinks, and all that attracts and unites
us revives in fresh power, before the amazing
message, " Go to My brethren, and say unto them, I
ascend unto My Father, and your Father ; and to My
God, and your God."

At this season of overpowering prospects and
hopes, with this its message to you, I come to lay
before you what I am charged with.   I have to ask
you to consider, as Christians ought, not now the
natural and bodily needs, but the spiritual wants of
the multitudes of this great city in which you live.
They want many things ; but their wants of which
I have to speak are their wants of teaching, their
wants of light, and truth, and comfort ; the wants, in
what touches their highest and permanent interests,
of those for whom we believe Christ died, whom He
in heaven knows of and sympathises with in their
temptations and distresses, who, with us, are running
the race we all of us are running, for life or death,
for the eternal gain or the eternal loss.   On what
a scale these wants require to be faced and met
no one here needs to be told.   No one can pass
through those wastes and wildernesses of population,
which spread thicker and thicker every year round
our homes, no one can pass in or out of London,
without feeling the oppression of those crowded but
dreary regions.   What would He, our Master, have
said, He who was so moved with compassion for the
few thousands whom He saw before Him, because
"·they were as sheep not having a shepherd," if He beheld the unshepherded, wandering, untaught crowds,

who toil, and endure sickness and pain, and die,
without consolation, without hope, in the alleys and
courts, and under the dreary lengths of melancholy,
monotonous, squalid roofs which fill our overgrown
suburbs.   And He *does* behold them, from that Throne
of Judgment, where He still bears the nature of those
who are so miserable, and of those to whose care and
charity He commends them.   To *your* care and
charity—yours, who, pardon me for saying so, have
no more original or special claim on His favour than
they have, yet whose condition He has, in His good
pleasure, made so vast and strange a contrast to theirs.
All that they want of light and opportunity, of religious atmosphere, of high Christian teaching, of
elevating and consoling worship, of the things which
protect the soul against the pressure and fascination
of the sensible and the temporary, He has bestowed
in full measure on you.   While your hearts rejoice
and go up in the devotion which is to you as your
familiar breath of life, to them the thing itself, the
very possibility of it, is as absolutely an unknown
experience as any unimaginable condition of their
existence.   They wander about, hearing that there
is such a thing as religion, about which men quarrel
and call names, knowing it mainly by the meannesses,
or extravagances, or follies by which men caricature
the highest of human ideas and human affections,
thinking that they see nothing but a maze and hubbub
of bewildered sects.   Of that which you believe that
you have, of teaching, steady, and certain, and re-
assuring in its great outlines and foundations; of gifts
which have come down unimpaired through the vicissitudes of history, from the very hand of the Incarnate

Redeemer; of all those ties which bind Christ's Body together, clergy and people, the Church of one age with the Church of another, the Church on its human side with the Church in its Divine relations and eternal perfection,—of all this they know nothing.   It was in the face of these stupendous wants that this great Fund was created ; great, but not great in proportion to these necessities ; great, but not great in proportion to what might be done in this, the richest city in all the earth.

It is with the appalling contrasts in the condition and opportunities of men, forced on the notice of all of us by the appeal made on this Sunday, through the diocese, for the Bishop of London's Fund, that you are asked to make your offerings to-day.   And you are asked especially to contribute to that part of the Fund which is appropriated to increasing the number of the clergy employed.   For what is wanted is to plant the Church in its fulness and solidity, in its complete and long-proved ministries of teaching, and grace, and discipline—of guiding, and building up, and recovering, and comforting, the souls which are wandering aimless and uncared for through their pathless wild of life.   *You* know, in this place, all that the Church in its Divine order, in its truths commensurate with all human thought and human life, in its manifold and continuous ministrations, has done for you.   You know how, in its system, the personal is combined with the impersonal, the visible with the invisible, the ministry of men with the unfathomable influences of God's grace, and how each presupposes and acts with the others.   You know all this and the value of it. Nothing less than this would satisfy and sustain you, in your passage through this difficult and unsettled world. Let us face the thought that the crowds which fill the streets of extending London, need all this as much as we do. These are the necessities of this day, and to-day comes the call to you to consider what is due from you, when you recognise and realise them.

These dreadful waste places of London—London where, side by side with those who are the most prosperous and the happiest of living men, are those who seem doomed to the most hopeless wretchedness and degradation—are filled with the forlorn and out-cast brethren of the Redeemer. They, with you, have His Father for their Father, and His God for their God. For them, as for you, comes down through the centuries His message of encouragement and hope : " Say unto My brethren, I ascend unto My Father, and your Father ; and to My God, and your God." All that is dear to us in life and death is wrapped up in that assurance, and all it implies of promise. What can we do that they may know it too ? Surely it is uncomfortable to enjoy so much, to have so much, as many of us have, of the blessings of either world—the blessings and gifts of this, and the powers of the world to come—and to do what is below our fair measure for those who have so little ?

XII

EDUCATION[1]

" When I was a child, I spake as a child, I understood as a child, I thought as a child : but when I became a man, I put away childish things."—I COR. xiii. 11.

THESE famous words express one of the many forms of that unceasing change which is the law of human nature and human life. But this law of change, which is an irresistible necessity, is accompanied with another condition, which is not a necessity, not a thing of course, not inevitable, but depends on the will and choice and foresight of man. It is, that this change, which *must* be somehow, may be for the better ; may be not only a change, but a progress. And the law of change, transformed into the nobler and higher law of progress, is what gives all its excellence and all its hope to our existence here. Be we at what stage of it we may, we see in ourselves something which, as time rolls on, *must* be different, but which, thanks to Him who has made us what we are, and compassed us with His blessings and His grace, may be, ought to be, something much better. . And that great law of change which is going on

---

[1] Preached in the Church of St. Botolph, Aldersgate, for the Ward Schools of the Parish, 1873.

in us all, silently but certainly—going on in the
stoutest frames, the most unshaken health, the most
settled habits, the firmest and most resolute characters
—is shown to us in its most touching shape in that
contrast between childhood and age of which the
Apostle speaks in the text.

" I have been young, and now am old "—what a
world of history, of chances, of thoughts, of memories,
of regrets, do these words of the Psalm realised call
up in those of whom they are true.   The change by
which a human being passes from infancy and childhood to the ripeness of his age and powers, is the
greatest and most eventful of our state here : greater,
really, than all subsequent changes of circumstance,
of employment, of fortune, of success or failure in
life.   For it is the change from what he, as yet, only
may be, to what, in the deepest and most momentous
sense, he *really is* in his very self.   There is no
greater in the natural course of our lives, except that
change by which we pass at last from this visible
scene, by the mysterious incident in our existence
which we call death, into the further stage of being
which is now beyond the veil.

And this great change—this growth and ripening
of each single human being, from the very extremity
of insignificance and helplessness, to the complete
and developed man—is committed to the care and
direction, and left to the responsibility, of the generation which is already grown up, which has reached its
stage of maturity.   This change *we*, as children, have
all made under the guidance and influence of those
whom, at our coming into the world, we found in
possession of the world ; of those who, as a great writer

says,[1] "children find here settled in a world where they
themselves are strangers." This change, those who
are to succeed us are now making under the guidance
and influence of *us*, who at the present have the
work of the world to carry on. It is part of the
duty of each generation, in all its infinitely varied
departments, to watch over and control this great
change in those who are now so tender, so feeble, so
unknown, but who a few years hence will have
inherited our strength and our possessions, and whose
names will have put out our names. It is our duty,
I say, to watch over this change ; it is the certain
and inevitable necessity of things that, whether we
are mindful of our duty or not, what we do or leave
undone must profoundly affect those who, under our
shadow, are going through this great change. Yes,
my brethren, it is part, and perhaps the most solemn
and affecting part, of that wonderful dispensation in
which we find ourselves, by which the happiness of
one set of people is placed in the power, and made
to depend on the conduct of another set of people—
that whether our children grow up as they ought to
grow up, whether the change from infancy to age in
them is not merely a change but a progress—a change
of the right sort, a change to knowledge, to power,
to goodness—that this, in a degree which we cannot
possibly measure, but can hardly over-estimate, is
dependent on what *we* do to help and guide them.
Unable to provide for themselves, unable to guard or
guide themselves, knowing little of the terms on
which they will have to pass through life, unable yet

---

[1] Bishop Butler, sermon for Charity schools, preached in Christ
Church, Newgate Street.

to distinguish between those tremendous and in-
exorable laws of life which nothing can bend, and
those forces which yield to human effort and will, our
children are hurried on by the tide of the years, and
are being changed into men and women ; but what
sort of men and women they shall be changed into,
this rests, to an extent which is incalculable, with
us : what their happiness shall be, what their usefulness, what their goodness, hangs on the thread of our
present decision to take up and fulfil our task—rests
on our sensitiveness of conscience, our faithfulness to
what we know, our readiness to perform the part which
God has given us to do in this world, not merely in
what concerns ourselves, but in what concerns others.

The conduct of this great change by which
children pass into men, and by which they ought
to pass into good and useful men, fulfilling their
part here, and preparing for a still greater life hereafter, is what we call Education.   And education is,
as I have said, one of the greatest and hardest tasks
which it lies on each generation of human society to
fulfil.   So great, so difficult, so full of unexplored
and unknown conditions, and opposite and apparently
contradictory requirements, that human thought and
wisdom are not wide enough to take in the whole
field it presents to them : they still stand perplexed
and baffled before many of its most important
problems.   But still the experience of ages, and the
sincerity of honest efforts, have not gone for nothing ;
and we see enough, amply enough, to encourage us
to fulfil our duty.   Our thoughts have risen, not of
its necessity—that was always obvious and always
felt—but of the *possibilities* of its extension.   The

feeling of our responsibilities about it has been quickened and deepened, our knowledge of its methods and processes has been raised and increased. We come more and more to see how in all its parts it must be a combination of authority and liberty ; how essential it is that, with discipline and control, there should also be frank confidence and trust ; how teacher and scholar act and react on one another, how much the scholar has to give and to teach, how greatly he must be induced to contribute to his own education, if it is to be a successful one. And our ideas have widened, consciously and distinctly, of its true aim and scope. In the eventful and hazardous interval which all must cross between childhood and manhood, two terrible powers of evil are to be met with in each man's path—ignorance and sin. If education is to have its perfect work, both must be encountered, both must be defeated. It only fulfils half its office, it works with a maimed and distorted idea, unless it deals with character as well as with intellect ; unless, again, it opens and enlightens the mind, as well as directs, and purifies, and fortifies the will.

We may, we do, vary greatly as to the degree in which instruction, which has to do with intellect, and moral and religious discipline, which has to do with character, help one another ; how far one may, by its indirect influences, be a substitute for the other ; how far excellence in one may make up for imperfections in the other ; how far, when they seem to clash, one must give way to the other. On such points, as we know, opinions vary widely ; and it may be that, in this or that condition of things, we may have to put up with something that falls short of our standard of education. But there is but one true and adequate conception of education, worthy of its place in the history of men, worthy of what it can do and ought to do for human good. Education deals not with any one part of man, but with the whole man ; it really does so whether it will or no ; for a one-sided education damages by its neglect what it refuses to care for. It must embrace the child as a creature with wonderful capacities for knowledge and thought, with great risks from ignorance and mistakes ; it must embrace him as a creature endowed with conscience, capable of goodness, sure to be tempted, meant for immortality. It must prepare him for opening his eyes to the truths and necessities of his condition here ; it must acquaint him with the laws of his moral nature, with the dangers of his moral weakness, with the hopes of his redemption. Education is true and noble, and has the promise of success, in proportion as it fulfils these two conditions ; in proportion as we are able to make it not only a ministry of light, but a discipline of duty ; in proportion as it not only ex-pands the mind, and trains its powers, and furnishes it with the skill and knowledge which are the imple-ments by which we do our work on earth, but also finds its way to the heart, and moulds and strengthens character, and fits the soul for the fierce conflicts of passion which await it in its course,—for that " fatal " and terrible " war " which " our desires wage with our destiny." Education is worthy of its name only when it deliberately sets before itself as its purpose, however it may be hampered in realising it, that its office is to make the change between childhood and manhood, as God meant it to be made ; not merely to sharpen wits,

or impart information, or cultivate faculties, but to
ensure, as far as possible, that when children pass
into men they shall recognise their Eternal Father ;
they shall know who died to save them ; they shall
feel from whose hands they came, and what they
were made for ; their eyes shall be opened to their
high calling of duty now, to that unspeakable future
of holiness, and love, and rest, which is the goal of
all our running.

On the present occasion I have to ask you,
keeping these great principles both of social and
religious progress in mind, to give your aid to the
local institutions where these principles are carried
out and realised : the schools of this Ward and
parish.   They rest on old foundations.   The Ward
school   was   founded   in   1702.   We   sometimes
assume rather hastily that interest in education is a
thing   of   modern   times.   Doubtless,   it   has   been
largely developed of late, and its responsibilities more
widely felt.   But   no   one   can   be   but   slightly acquainted with the history of this great municipality,
without learning how early, how earnestly, and with
what liberality our predecessors here recognised the
great claims of true education.   They did for their own
time what they could ; if their forethought sometimes
came short, and their provisions have not reached to
all the changing and enlarging necessities of the
times which were to follow them, they but exemplified
the universal condition of limitation, imposed on all
human wisdom and human efforts.   As time went
on, it became advisable to alter the form in order to
improve the substance.   Separate schools have been
merged together, and what was done piecemeal has

been more successfully done on a larger scale. The material requisites so absolutely necessary for efficiency — space, air, convenient arrangement — have been carefully looked after. The schools, I am assured, are in high working order, judged by the impartial test of Government inspection. They are still, what our fathers, with a true and deep conception of the function of education, meant them to be, religious schools ; and they still give that help which our fathers were so ready to give, to the wants of the poor : they clothe as well as teach. And their usefulness to the neighbourhood might, I am told, by improved arrangements, and by the amalgamation of smaller schools, be largely increased. These improvements have not been done, cannot be done, except at a large cost. As I said, our fathers did not spare cost, when they were persuaded that a work of this kind was worth doing. They did what we now often have to alter ; but they did what was in proportion to the needs of their time : they did what they could ; they did things nobly and generously.

My brethren, shall we be behind them ? Shall we be degenerate children of such a stock ? Shall we hang back in doing what is wanted in our day to meet the day's call, the day's obligations ? Here in this centre of English wealth and enterprise, here in this great focus of English thought and purpose, surrounded by the memorials of what English minds and English characters have wrought in the most splendid of histories, no good work, surely, can possibly languish for want of means : much less, I am convinced, a work of this kind ; a work which connects itself with the special interest, the neighbourly sympathies, the local feeling and most praiseworthy local pride of one of the great and ancient divisions of our historic city ; a work of which the object is, that, where so much wealth is created and stored up, that which is far above wealth,—English hearts, English intelligence, English souls,—shall grow up to use and to honour.

Let us then, with thoughts not unworthy of the object, try to do our part for those who are to come after us.   It is one of the great prerogatives of Christianity that it has stimulated our care for posterity.   Amid the dark uncertainties of heathenism, men knew not enough of their position in the world to make it worth while to take much trouble to provide for the benefit of a future race.   They lived their time and knew no more ; why should they think about the generations after them ?   Deterioration seemed the unvarying lesson of history, the fatal rule of life and character ; and it was lost pains to strive against it.   But Christianity opened a new view of the destiny of the human race.   Christianity, among its many glories, is the parent of popular education.   It gave a new incentive to every care and every effort to direct the great law of change towards ultimate and permanent and widely-reaching improvement.   By disclosing what man was made for and might become, and what God had done for him, it furnished to each generation a new and overwhelming motive for caring for their children, for caring for posterity.   They are indeed worth caring for, they are worth all our forethought and our efforts for their improvement, who have such an endless life before them, for whom Christ died.   We are now in our measure entrusted with their fate. How they shall grow up, with what furniture of thought, and habit, and knowledge, and principle, they shall meet their time of trial when it comes, depends very much upon us their elders, us their fathers, us, by position, and opportunity, and power, the natural guardians of those who, in the great change they are going through, cannot take care of themselves, but must rely on the sympathy, the large intelligence, the public spirit, the Christian charity of their grown-up brethren.

Think then of this great matter of education whenever it comes before you, not as it is involved in the disputes and misconceptions and difficulties of the moment, but in its true and deep significance. It will help you to meet these difficulties to have cherished in your minds true and fit ideas of it. Look at it, therefore, with warm sympathy and with wide thoughts. Lift up your views to what is the true interest of those who will soon be in our places ; —and, beyond them, of the great generations yet unborn. You cannot doubt, in the " increasing pur- pose " which manifestly runs through the ages, how great your posterity will be. Show yourselves then worthy to be their progenitors. Show yourselves worthy to be associated with. their destiny, by your wise, and generous, and timely providence for their wants. Take care, as far as you are able, that; when they shall come upon the scene, they shall find it fit to act their part in. Our fathers, knowing less than we do, seeing less- clearly, yet seeing with a high spirit of duty the great necessities of education, have provided nobly for us. Let not our children after us have reason to say that we, with our greater light, our deeper insight, our wider experiences, were less large-hearted, less far-sighted, less unselfish than those before us—less worthy to fill our place in the chain and succession of the generations of Christian England.

I will end in the words and with the prayer of one of the greatest of Christian and English thinkers, in the sermon which he preached on a kindred occasion in a neighbouring church in this city—in the concluding words of Bishop Butler. "And may the blessing of Almighty God accompany this work of charity, which He has put into the hearts of His servants in behalf of these poor children ; that being now 'trained up in the way they should go, when they are old they may not depart from it.' May He of His mercy keep them safe amid the innumerable dangers of this bad world through which they are to pass, and preserve them unto His heavenly kingdom."

XIII

PAIN AND REMEDY [1]

" And Jesus went about all Galilee, teaching in their synagogues, and preaching the Gospel of the Kingdom, and healing all manner of sickness and all manner of disease among the people."—St. Matt. iv. 23.

PAIN is the first, the most familiar, the most enduring experience of man. I suppose it is almost the earliest of our childish recollections ; but with the remembrance of pain we have also the remembrance of the remedies of pain, of what soothed and removed it. And what we remember, as far back as we can carry our memory, we have found, throughout, to be one of the fixed and prominent conditions of our state here. Many great and striking and wonderful things belong to this state. But that which is the thing of course with us all, that which must be assumed and taken into account as unavoidable in all our views of life, that which is the groundwork on which half of all our arrangements are made and half of all our forethought expended, that which especially accentuates human life as we know it, is the universal

---

[1] Preached in the Church of St. Anne and St. Agnes, with St. John Zachary, Gresham Street, for the London Dispensary, 1873.

C.S.,P.　　　　　　　Q

presence of these two great facts—pain, on the one
hand, and the possible remedies for pain, on the other.
" The whole creation groaneth and travaileth in pain
together," is the expression of one side of the truth.
The Lord " healeth those that are broken in heart, and
giveth medicine to heal their sickness "—is the other.

This is the constitution of things under which we
find ourselves at this stage of our existence. Pain
is with us all our lives long, from the hour of our first
breathing this air of ours, to the moment when we
breathe it for the last time. In pain we begin life,
in pain we leave it ; and in the interval between these
points we each of us have our various experience of
its strange and manifold companionship. Its actual
presence is infinitely varied : some of us it never
leaves, some of us, as we grow into life, it seems
almost to spare ; but as the strongest and healthiest
man knows certainly that he has to die, so one of the
certainties of our lot, be it what it may, is our liability
to pain : we have the frame, we have the feeling, we
have the mind, which are ever open to it, ever capable
of admitting the dread visitor in ways and in intensity
beyond present conception : it lurks within us and
about us when we think least about it, ready to spring
forth from its ambush, unsuspected, undreamt of ;
ready, perhaps, to take up its abode with us and to
make us learn a new lesson and widen our thoughts
of things, in a way we can little realise till it comes.
Among the many riddles of our existence it is, at
least as far as nature can inform us, one of the
strangest. Some of the common conditions and
trials of our existence here, we have only to be
humble to understand. A limited term of life ; a

certain time, and no more, allotted to each creature
to play its part in ; decay of strength when the functions and work are done for which strength was
wanted ; the unequal distribution of gifts, of success,
of enjoyment; final dissolution and passing away, as
the leaves fall when summer is over,—this, though
we lose ourselves in seeking to comprehend the
reasons of it, is not so very perplexing to the mind
which compares our state here to the vastness of the
universe.   But pain is something beyond this.   Pain
is not merely a negative thing, the absence of something we should like to have, a maiming of powers, a
failure of enjoyment.   Pain is something over and
above, superadded to our mere weakness, and littleness, and fewness of days.   Pain means that wonderful power of feeling, which seems as much meant to
give us pleasure and happiness as the eye is meant
for seeing, turned back against its natural purpose
and use, turned back upon us, turned back *against* us ;
made the means of driving the iron into our very
soul ; fitting us for a new life which is filled with
new and amazing energy, but one that qualifies
us for tasting deeper and deeper the cup of suffering.   Pain means that consciousness of life which
can give our soul delight, not merely defeated of
its hope, not merely baffled and balked of its natural
end, but raised to a new power, the power of agony.
When we think, too, of those whom pain strikes
with indiscriminate severity—the poor, the helpless,
the children—when we think of what seems the
needlessness of pain, its mystery becomes great
and oppressive.   And the strangeness is the
greater, because the higher we rise in the scale of

being, the keener, the deeper, the more intense the
pain which may visit us.   As life is developed
and made perfect, so is the capacity, I might almost
say the faculty, of pain.   In its more terrible forms,
in its variety, in its prevalence and extent, it is the
awful prerogative of the highest nature, man.   On
the lower forms of life, its burden is not imposed ;
but as brain is developed and nerves become finer
and more multiplied, and more complex and delicate,
its presence announces itself, its sting becomes keener.
But no creature, I take it, can be supposed to suffer
on the same scale, much less in the same way, as
man : disease does not make the same diversified
ravages ; suffering, when it comes, is fitful, is com-
monly short, and is not complicated with all the
aggravations of imagination and forethought which
add so heavily to its pangs.   And in the same
way in men themselves, with the finer organisation
and higher training, goes also a superior quickness
to pain, a more piercing and exquisite anguish.
And yet our experience tells us, also, that pain,
though so terrible, is one of the most salutary—in
the end the most beneficent—of the conditions of our
nature and state here.   It does not account for its
mysterious presence, but it reconciles the wise and
the thoughtful to what is in itself so hard to understand, to consider, how pain has been the occasion
and groundwork of some of the greatest of human
virtues and the most glorious of human actions ;
how it has called forth in the human soul energies,
affections, sweetness, strength, goodness, which only
its awful but mighty touch could have quickened
into life ; how, under it discipline, character—even

commonplace character — has been elevated and made beautiful, heroes have been created, martyrs have triumphed, saints have been made perfect. The world and life require *pain*, to make them as noble as they may be, as noble as they have been. We look in vain for anything to take the place which in the dispensations of Providence it has held, in schooling men to higher things. If fortitude, courage, patience, endurance, resignation are among the parts of human perfection, it is pain under whose benignant severity they have grown—it is pain which has been the schoolmaster who has taught them.

And, on the other hand, side by side with the familiar but mysterious fact of pain, is the familiar but also mysterious fact of the existence of remedies. God has appointed pain to be a portion of our experience, but not pain unmixed and alone, not pain unconquerable and overmastering, not pain without alleviation and relief. The natural world is in this the counterpart to the moral and spiritual world. God has indeed freely and bountifully given us the pure and unmixed blessings of His goodness. But much of His gracious dealings with us has taken the shape, not merely of goodness, but of *mercy*— mercy, in undoing mischief, in repairing ruin, in retrieving life—of compassion, repair, restoration. We have gone astray, and He has called us back. We have fallen, and He has raised us. We have been lost, and He has come to seek and to save. We have sinned, and He has forgiven us. We have been in misery, and He has pitifully comforted us. We have been in sorrow, and He has dried our tears. We have been sick, and He has healed us. We have

thrown away what He gave us, and He has made it
up. We have to die, and He has given us the pledge
of our resurrection. This is the general character of
His dealings with us. He has not seen fit to take
out of life its evils, its pains : they remain, as all
whom we know of have found them ; but He does
give us their remedies and their antidotes ; and, further,
He puts these to a great extent in our own power.
Pain cannot be banished ; but it can be greatly kept
within bounds, it can be greatly soothed. Disease
cannot be extirpated ; but it can be cured, it can
be greatly prevented. There are mischiefs which
nothing can make up for ; but there are countless
more which can be entirely repaired, still more
which can be alleviated. And it is a point to be
observed, how more and more it appears that pain,
disease, all but the last end of life, is within the
control of remedies. Think of the interval between
the simple surgery and medicine of the savage, and
the enlarging discoveries and daily increasing skill
of our great hospitals ; and we see how we are
called upon to work *ourselves* for our own relief ;
how we were to win for ourselves, but to win by
care, and effort, and honest pains, the remedies which
were to be within our reach. Century after century,
new knowledge, new contrivances have added to our
store ; and, for the most part, God has made these
the reward of sincere and diligent searching. We
know now, we might perhaps have known much
earlier, how much may be saved of misery and
suffering, how much of disease may be staved off,
by the commonest attention, by the commonest
forethought : it is our own fault, if we know this in

vain. If pain is one part of our mortal condition,
we know also that there are great and merciful forces
which can keep it within bounds ; and we know, too,
that their efficacy has been made to depend on
our own faithful and manly discharge of the duties
which increased knowledge has brought with it : on
our conquering the selfishness, the indolence, the
prejudices, the indifference which have done so much
to prolong and aggravate the dominion of pain and
disease.

The matter comes before us in a practical shape
in the appeal which I have to recommend to you.
You have an opportunity given you to help in the
great struggle to restrict the range of suffering, and
to soften those cruel visitations of disease which
cannot be wholly cured.   Here in your midst is one
of those centres, where the remedial energies of our
condition are brought to bear skilfully and method-
ically on the pain which is inseparable from it ; you
may be fellow-workers with the great Healer, who has
appointed the remedies which are the counterpoise of
pain, and who has put them into our hands, to use
them if we will.   The pain, the suffering, which
come for relief to a hospital, a dispensary like this,
are sufferings which it is now too late, for you or for
any one, to turn aside or prevent by knowledge and
prudence.   We know not how they came : we know
not whose fault they may be traced to ; only we
know that there they are : terrible facts, which it is
no use speculating about or complaining of, which
cannot be undone, but which perhaps may be
ministered to and relieved.   They are the very class
of sufferings which appealed to the mercy of our

Blessed Lord in the days of His earthly life, and which met at His hands with so much tender compassion and help. In His great strife with evil, it was bodily pain and disease which He made the special object of His personal work on earth. It was in them that He recognised the sharpest, if not the deepest and most fatal, wounds of human nature ; and He won men's hearts for His higher message by showing how He felt the wretchedness and bitterness of bodily infirmity and anguish. When we consider what the ultimate end and purpose of His coming was, His deep, varied, inexhaustible sympathy for bodily suffering and disease is very remarkable. He came, as we read in the text, "preaching the Gospel of the Kingdom," and He came also "healing all manner of sickness." He did not care to make men rich, to make men great ; He showed no interest in their philosophy, in their public affairs, in the business of the kingdoms of this world ; He *did* care, He was never tired of caring, to relieve their pain, to cure their diseases. You follow closely in His divine footsteps, when you take to heart seriously, and with the sympathy which it deserves, that sad eminence which our nature has, in the intensity and the variety of the pain which it may have to go through.

We have two duties, with respect to pain and disease and physical suffering. As regards ourselves, we have to learn to bear them as they come, with patience, with courage, with self-command. We have to extract from them the discipline they are meant to minister to us. We have to accept their often hard lesson and turn it to account. There is

no saying to what extent this chastisement may
profit men, if they will meet it nobly and bravely,
in refining, softening, fortifying character.   That is
its office to ourselves.   But it has another call on us,
as regards others.   Pain is for men to *bear*, in
themselves ; it is for them to *relieve*, in others.   It
is in this latter view that it appeals to us to-day.
There stands before us this strange, appalling fact of
our nature and condition—almost more appalling to
men in health than to men themselves in suffering—that multitudes of our fellow-creatures round
about us are, intermittently or continuously, lan-
guishing or agonizing in disease or pain.   We see
them not.   We do not hear their groans and cries.
Their pale faces, their hopeless eyes, their writh-
ing forms, are hidden from us—hidden in dark
alleys, and squalid courts, and mean and wretched
lodgings.   Yet there they are.   Behind this screen
of opulence and busy life, *there* they are.   It does not
require an effort of faith or imagination to realise
all the misery which is going on not so far off
while we are here : it only requires us to open our
minds to what we know to be certain ; it only needs
to make leisure in our souls, to attend and to think
of what there is no doubt about.   This great mass
of suffering and pain cries to us for help : all the
more solemnly that the appeal is a silent one, and
we are not allowed to see the suffering which yet
we know exists.   It makes its mute entreaty for
relief.   And it is not as if the entreaty were an idle
one.   It is as certain that there are remedies to be
had, as it is certain that pain exists.   And the power
of opening these remedies to this suffering, God has

placed, my brethren, *just as* we are willing to use it, in our hands.

I ask you, then, on behalf of all the pain and suffering which must be in a great city, to use this power.   I ask you to do what you can to co-operate with an institution which exists to minister relief and healing to the numbers who could not otherwise obtain it.   There is in this matter, between different classes of men, a tremendous equality and a tremendous inequality.   The equality is that in the pangs and horrors of disease all of us are on a level.   In the dreadful scale of human suffering—from its most homely to its severest forms, from a cold or a toothache or a headache to those extreme forms of torment which it makes us shudder even to think of; in those strange visitations of it which have a kind of tragic interest about them and are thought worthy of special record and special pity, and in its commonplace vulgar shapes, which, when we are not suffering ourselves, we are apt to smile at—in this liability to every kind of pain, in feeling its bitterness when it comes, all of us, the highest and the lowest, the richest and the meanest of us, are all equal.   The man on whom an empire depends, the man whose name written on a bit of paper can dispose of millions, can decide on the peace of the world and the happiness of nations and the course of history, is as much open to pain in its direst form, is its subject and perhaps its victim, is as absolutely at its mercy, as the weakest and most miserable of his fellow-men.   Here all are equal. But when we think of what may be done to ease pain, to arrest disease, to help the sufferers to bear

it, oh, brethren and fellow-men, is it not almost
terrible to think of the inequalities and contrasts in
men's lot? Two men are racked with pain: the one
with everything round him which can give the chance
of even a moment's relief; with everything that money
can buy, or skill devise, or tender affection minister;
with everything to amuse him, to soothe him, to console him: the other, starved, and cold, and destitute,
with all his power of earning stopped, with all his
small possessions, all his small comforts gradually
slipping away and disappearing; a prisoner—perhaps
a solitary prisoner—through dreary days and sleep-
less nights, in a close and unwholesome garret. Two
young girls are touched by the hand of consumption:
for one of them there is a respite, perhaps a cure:
she has the chance of a change of scene and climate,
of softer air, of the reviving influences of Southern
warmth and brightness: the other—she cannot be
moved—no one can afford to move her, though that
alone can save her—not even to an English hospital;
she must stay where she is, and in the cold and
damp, the raw mornings and chilly nights she cannot
escape from, gasp out her life. These are the inequalities under which men have to meet pain.

Shall we not, we whom God has prospered and
perhaps enriched, do what we can to make these
inequalities at least a *little* less? Shall we not, in the
name of our great Master, who has made us all
fellows in suffering, but put into the hands of some
of us the remedies which make suffering tolerable,
do what we can to co-operate with His purpose?
One was once on earth who came from God, and
whom we now recognise as the Example and Hope

of humankind. To Him no form of human suffering appealed in vain. Miracle after miracle in His wondrous history tells of His compassion and pity for sickness and pain. To express that never-failing sympathy it is said of Him, " Himself took our infirmities, and bare our sicknesses." The Lord and Master of pain, quelling it in a moment with His touch, yet for our sakes He made Himself subject to it. His fellowship with us would not be complete unless He shared the sufferings He came to cure. He calmed the fever, and cleansed the leprosy, and gave power to the palsied, and sight to the blind, and speech and hearing to the dumb ; and then, for us men and for our salvation, He was in agony in the garden, He suffered, and was crucified, and died.

He who has voluntarily tasted what you suffer for the sake of your endless good, may He not commend to your tender and generous sympathy those sufferings of the poor which He was always so ready to relieve ? Has He not earned the right to bid you console and soothe those pains and hours of anguish which neither poverty nor riches exempt us from, but to which poverty adds an additional and frightful aggravation, of which those who have not known poverty can hardly take the measure ?

XIV

THE LIFE OF INTELLECTUAL SELF-SUFFICIENCY [1]

"Thy hands have made me and fashioned me : O give me understanding, that I may learn Thy commandments."—PSALM cxix. 73.

WHEN I was asked to take this subject, against which Psalm cxix. is by anticipation so remarkable a lesson and so comprehensive a counter theory, I hesitated. I hesitated for this reason. "Rationalism," the "Life of Rationalism," expresses undoubtedly a very real and grave thing ; and if there was nothing to do but to speak of it with a clear and definite meaning, there would be no special difficulty about it. But Rationalism, it is to be remembered, which expresses a habit of mind or method of thinking rather than any definite set of opinions, is also one of those vague words, which mean very different things in different mouths. It is one of those words to which men often do not take the trouble to attach clear ideas, but which they charge with evil associations and strong condemnations. It is often used as a mere nickname ; and nicknames, though very convenient and often very powerful, are not safe weapons. The Puritans would

[1] Preached in the Church of St. John the Baptist, Frome, 1876.

have called Hooker a rationalist, if the word, as a
term of reproach, had yet been invented. And there
are those who would apply the term to such writers
as St. Augustine and St. Anselm, the great Schoolmen,
Pascal, Leibnitz, Bishop Butler. It is dangerous to
be loose in using such terms in reference to difficult
questions ; and I need not say that the use and place
of reason in religious matters is one of the most difficult of questions, and one which has exercised the
most powerful and most devout minds ever since men
began to think at all, down to our own day. The
difficulty is no reason why we should be blind to the
obvious and certain dangers attending the relation of
reason to religion. But there is clearly good ground,
when we are handling a hard and difficult matter,
that we should speak carefully, modestly, and with
self-distrust.

I wish, then, at starting, to guard myself. I am
not going into the great question of the relation of
reason to faith, or to authority. I am not going to
discuss systems. But, considering what the subject
of this course of Sermons is—the object, the employment, the direction and use of life—I shall venture to
speak of the dangers, of the sins, accompanying the
exercise of one of the great powers of man's condition
here, his intelligence, his reason. I mean, by the life
of Rationalism, the life of intellectual self-sufficiency ;
a life which fails in the essentials of self-discipline
over the intellect and its temptations, which fails in
humility, self-distrust, reverence, modesty, in the use
of our faculties, in the pursuit of knowledge. And it
must be remembered that such habits of mind, though
naturally tending to produce error and unbelief, and

the formidable phenomena characteristic of our time, are yet compatible with a right belief, which they are capable of so deeply injuring.

Each man has his life to live and to order, not only with reference to the necessities and the business of this present system and framework of existence— to the natural constitution of his mind and body, the number of his years, his decay, his mortality—but also with reference to feelings, thoughts, affections, duties, which pass beyond this world of time and sense into a world unseen. He comes into life and consciousness, and he meets the facts and phenomena of his state. Some of them are outward and open to the testing and verifying of his senses. Others are moral, inward, spiritual, yet they are phenomena and facts just as real and inevitable as those of the external system of which he finds himself a part. As he finds himself in an atmosphere of air and light, and meets the phenomena of nature and the powers and inventions of man, so he finds himself in an atmosphere of conscience, of duty, of home, of society, of rules of right and wrong, of happiness and sorrow ; and, do what he will, he can no more get rid of these primary and fundamental conditions of his life, even by rebelling against them, than he can get rid of the natural conditions to which his life is subject. They are parts of a moral order ; but he is, and cannot help being, a creature of the moral order as well as the physical. He may wish, but it is an idle wish, that his life was longer, his faculties more perfect, his knowledge more certain and greater, that he had not to grow old and to die. So he may wish, but that it is an idle wish, that there were no moral law over man, that men

about him, his brethren and his fellows, were not moral
beings. He may imagine a different state of things
morally, as he may physically, but what he imagines
does not exist. He is what he is, by a different law to
what he imagines ; and even if things were different
in other times and in other places, yet to *him* here, to
him at the stage of human history at which he lives,
life comes with these great living laws of duty and the
affections, with this encompassing moral atmosphere,
in which he cannot draw a breath without being
dependent on it. And further, he finds round him
another atmosphere—the atmosphere of religion, connecting the right and wrong of daily life, its affections,
its efforts, its hopes, with something above nature and
above time, invisible and eternal. He finds round
him the fact of diffused, inherited, long-existing belief ;
not a dead set of opinions, but an array of living and
fruitful convictions, which, as a matter of fact and
history, have for ages affected, and are still affecting
in the profoundest way, what men are, what men do,
what men feel, and without which they would be
absolutely different from anything we know them to
be. He finds round him a great Institution and
Society, with a life of more than eighteen centuries,
and having its roots in the earliest beginnings of
human history. He sees the earliest and most venerable records of all this in every one's hands about
him, the guide of conduct, the comforter of sorrow, the
source of the noblest thought, the expression of the
deepest feelings. And above all, he sees One like
unto the sons of men and yet absolutely different ;
a character, a life, a Person, such as experience never
shows him now, yet responding with the widest and

fullest sympathy to all that experience makes him long for ; One who presents Himself as answering to the " Desire of all nations " and all ages, the link between man and God, in whom alone human nature comes into contact with God, in all His holiness, in all His power—that " Light of the world " who, if He were supposed absent for one moment from the firmament of our thought and belief, the whole moral world, the very ground under our feet, would sink beneath us into darkness and the abyss.

How shall a man, when these things open upon him, use his life ?   How shall he do what is right in regard to them ?   Shall he ask no questions about them ?   Shall he be blind to their awfulness, their wonder, to the interval that separates them from what we are most familiar with now ?   Shall he go about his work here, taking them for granted, not caring to understand, not caring to deny ?   All round him, he hears, he cannot but hear, high and self-confident, the questioning voices ; how, amid the tumult and contention of jarring opinions, with the dangers of mistake, and the certainty that men *do* mistake, how shall he order his life ?   Blessed and happy indeed is he, if his training has been such, and he has so answered to his training, that his religion has been harmoniously and deeply interwoven with his outward and inward experience so as to be raised, like the certainties of his very being, above the strife of tongues ; if, on the same sort of evidence on which he trusts and honours his parents and gives his home the first place in his affections, on the same evidence on which he accepts his duty to his country even unto death, even to the length of

laying down his life in its service, so he accepts his
Gospel heritage, so he feels that he has tasted that
" the Lord is gracious." Christianity has been long
enough in the world and shown itself for what it
is, to protect him from the charge of mere blind
following of custom. Say what men will to confound it with other religions, the mature and
unperverted judgment of mankind pronounces that
it stands by itself, unique and unapproachable. The
very evils, the abundant evils, which men have done
in its name, are only a greater proof of its inherent
divinity ; for it would have perished long ago under
their weight and enormity, if it had not been
altogether different from everything else in the
world. " The Christian thought," as a great statesman [1] has recently said, " the Christian tradition, the
Christian society, are the imperial thought and
tradition and society of this earth " ; and its inward
power over the heart and will of men, the lowest
and the highest, corresponds to its august majesty
without. The authority of the Christian Church,
the witness of Christendom, however disturbed and
impaired by divisions and sins, is yet the master fact
of our history and our society, the master fact of all
our own lives. There is enough to warrant any
reasonable man, brought up to know what Christianity is, on the strength of his Christian education,
to make his venture on it for this world and the next.

But Christianity addresses inquirers as well as
believers. It challenges the world to inquire. " He
that seeketh findeth." " Prove all things ; hold fast
that which is good." God calls many souls through

---

[1] The Right Hon. W. E. Gladstone.

the trial, the distress, perhaps the agony, of intellectual difficulty ; and the circumstances and results
of intellectual trial are often as mysterious as moral
trials. I don't know anything more pathetic, more
awe-inspiring than what moved Pascal's deep sympathy—the case of a man, to human eyes honestly
seeking the light and not finding it. But without
trying to fathom what we know but imperfectly,
our business is with ourselves. Our business is to
recognise the dangers of intellectual trial—of the
trial of our moral nature, of our will, our motives,
our characters, through our intellect, as others are
tried through their passions. Christianity does
address itself to inquirers. But it assumes in all
religious inquiry three great axioms. 1. It assumes
the existence and the supremacy of goodness, of
justice, of love, and with this, the converse, the
terrible reality and mystery of *sin*. 2. It assumes
that the object of life here is to *do*, and not merely to
know : to meet a trial, to form a character, to fulfil
a charge, of which knowledge, such knowledge as is
possible in this short life, is but a part. And lastly,
3. It assumes that all good gifts, of light and truth,
as well as of power and holiness, come from God,
to be sought by faithfulness and prayer, to be given
to those who seek rightly. It recognises no other
safe conditions of inquiry. If a man chooses to
inquire on any other principles, he must take his
chance—he must go his way : that any other should
be possible, as a way of reaching truth, is not its
presupposition. " If any man will (θέλη) do His will
—is willing and desires to do His will, *wills* to do
His will—he shall know of the doctrine."

And surely these conditions have the full sanction of the natural conscience of man.   Perhaps the experience of mankind presents no more alarming spectacle than the plausibility with which they can be set aside.   The plain, gross, open sins of the world and the flesh bear on them their own mark : they are " open beforehand, going before to judgment." We know also that there are the veiled and disguised sins of the self-deceiver and the double-minded ; but besides, deeper and more impenetrable still, passing, it may be, through the world under the semblance and with the confidence of virtues, there are the subtle, refined sins of the intellect—sins of the hard, unbending, ungodly will, under the mask of passionless reason.

And no one can cast ever so superficial a glance on the wild turmoil of opinions all round without seeing the fatal marks which point to sins of the intellect as surely as others point to sins of the passions.   First and foremost, perhaps, there is the sin of not caring: the sin of indifference and negligence amid the most awful issues that can be raised to man.   It is the sin which raised the indignation of Bishop Butler ; it is the sin which it taxed the powers of Pascal to express his scorn of.   And of all the amazing things in the world it is indeed the most wonderful, not that men should reject the Gospel, not that they should hate religion, not that they should disbelieve in God, but that they should write and speak continually, in the character of serious men and public teachers, as if they were insensible to the infinite and inexpressible import and gravity of these things ; as if it really did not matter whether or not a man made up his mind and took his side about God, about immortality, about the Cross and Resurrection of Jesus Christ. They hold religion in their hands and look at it, as if it were a curious product of nature, to be examined, and turned round, and coldly taken to pieces ; and they are holding, they *must* be holding, in their hands their own life *or* death. They play with doubts. They amuse themselves with views. They who know so well what agitation and anxiety and alarm mean in their households, in their business, look on, as they call it, dispassionately, at questions on the decision of which must depend all that interests man —whether life is a shadow and delusion or the most inconceivable of treasures : whether a key can be found to its enigmas, so fatal if they cannot be answered, or whether all explanation of them is hopeless. Men sin against their reason itself, who trifle with interests which reason itself shows them must be so tremendous.

This off-hand, lazy-going fashion of disposing of the most solemn of claims by smart and shallow audacities is the sin of the negligent and the unthinking. But then there are the sins of those who do think. There is the sin of self-confidence and pride, of trusting to ourselves to find our way. No man who knows anything of himself can be ignorant of these two things : 1. How the look of theories and the force of arguments alter, with persons, with times, with varying knowledge, with force and ability of handling, with situations, with frames of mind, with moral habits ; and 2. How a man's own reasonings and conclusions need the check of something

out of himself, to test, to qualify, to correct them.
He who has not learnt this, knows nothing of the
real conditions on which sound reason acts and by
which truth is gained. But in religion men make
the specious novelty, which has caught their imagination as much as their reason *to-day*—though in
contradiction to the gravest, the holiest, the most
ancient voices round them—the last word, the final
verdict of modern wisdom. The experience of a
long history, which has made them what they are,
is against them ; but they are not the less confident
that they see clearly where all others have bewildered
themselves. There is, as we all know, the sin of
resisting the light, of refusing to see the truth before
us. But there is also the sin of lightly or impatiently
yielding to a plausible objection to our whole belief,
without waiting to see what it is worth ; of hastily
letting ourselves be shaken by a clever imposing
argument, feeling our own cleverness and superiority
in acknowledging its force. Men must bow, they say,
to facts : they must follow where logic leads them.
Yes, but the facts which they bow to are those, out
of all the multitude, to the right hand and the left,
which they choose to see ; and the facts which they
exclude bar and traverse that logic which seems so
straightforward and so plain. A man may see what
he pleases, and not see what he pleases, if he will but
choose his point of view and take no account of what
is on either side of him : if the disciple of criticism
will argue as if there were no broad vast lines of
general history and of human nature, to which he
must subordinate and proportion his results ; if the
student of material nature chooses to ignore that he

is a moral agent amid the facts and certainties of a
moral world ; and allows himself to forget, amid the
immensities, great or infinitely small, of the physical
world, the incommensurable superiority of moral and
spiritual interests.

We all know how one engrossing pursuit is apt
to dwarf and starve all other ideas. We know the
narrowing and blinding effect of an unresisted fascination by one special line of thought, one order of ideas.
It is the besetting sin of all absorbing studies, (such is
the admission of one of the most distinguished students
of physical science,) that they lift a man so entirely
above the ordinary sphere of daily duty, that they
betray him into selfishness and neglect of duty—and
not only of duty, but of thoughts and interests as great
as his own. Dr. Johnson's solemn irony expresses one
of the deepest truths of our one-sided nature. " He
who is growing great in electrifying a bottle wonders
to see the world engaged in the prattle about peace
and war,"—he whose soul is in the stars or the depths
feels small interest in such commonplaces as sin
and repentance, pain and despair, death and God.
Theologians have at times forgotten that the God
of the Gospel is the God of the universe, the Lawgiver whose are those wonderful laws of nature
which science has discovered ; and the depth and
fulness of their teaching have suffered accordingly.
But no pedantry or narrowness of theologians' ever
equalled theirs who, being what they are, feeling,
willing, choosing, thinking, contriving—the champions
of all freedom, the advocates of all progress, the
discoverers of the most refined analysis—teach us as
the latest certainty of philosophy, that the mind

which feels and thinks and wills is not mind at all ;
that mind is a phrase or an assumption, that man's
freedom of choice and action, his goodness, his
sin, is the freedom of an automaton ; that our consciousness, as we think, of a responsible self and
immaterial soul, is, in theory at least, a delusion.
Slaves of an imagination moulded and coloured by a
single uniform set of familiar phenomena, slaves of
customs and modes of thought which they have lost
the power to review and control, by rising above them
and beyond them, they are, with the latest and
richest eloquence of the English language, as
formal and rigid, as childishly unreal, as much in
antagonism with plain things which are certain if
anything is certain, as the most fantastic of the
Schoolmen.   It seems as if in such a fatal labyrinth,
without ending or escape, life would be unendurable.
No ; the pleasure of reckless and arrogant theorising,
of thoughts for which they owe no account to
any one, of pushing things to startling extremes,
of contradicting and flouting what is received as
most venerable and sacred, have their charm ; and ·
not even the absurdity of the results is enough to
check them.

And yet there is something worse.   It is when
intellect and reasoning persuade us that this world
after all is our best and satisfying portion ; that
we are wisest when we most follow our pleasure ;
that the lusts of the flesh and the pomps of the
world have a good deal to say for themselves ; that
we were made for this world—made for things *seen ;*
and that of another, as we can *know* nothing, we were
best *believe* nothing.   Intellect will do this for us if

we will let it ; it will do it in hard-headed and powerful systems of abstract thought ; it will do it in rich
and passionate poetry, pathetic or tender or rapturous ; it will do it in the beauty and magnificence
of art. And descending to a yet lower deep, the
questioning spirit which has called evil good finds
it no hard task to prove that good is evil. Then
intellect has indeed sinned its deadliest sin, when
it has not only beguiled the will to break down
the eternal barriers between goodness and sin, but
has argued the soul out of its instinctive recognition and admiration of goodness ; when by specious
reasonings, the most easy of all things, it has taught
the soul to revolt from its natural estimate of purity
and unselfishness, and undermined its veneration of
holiness—taught it to be disloyal to its own ideas
of the highest and the best. This terrible insensi-
bility, this terrible sophistry, reaches its climax when
it assails, as we have seen it do, the moral character
of our Lord, and deliberately vindicates the Pharisees'
judgment about Him and the policy of the Pharisees.
It is a saying of an unbeliever of this day, a serious
and able man, that it will be impossible to get rid
of Christianity among civilised nations, till their
reverence shall have been destroyed for the moral
character and life of Christ. In this spake he truly :
but when that reverence is destroyed, there will have
been first destroyed the conscience, the affections,
and the love of good in human nature.

These, of course, considering what Christianity is,
and has done, are outrages, unnatural and monstrous,
shocking to all serious men, and condemned by
public feeling. They belong to the same order as

the morality which would disturb the relations of
parents and children, or merge citizenship in some
league of humanity. But there is yet another sin,
not so hateful as the sin of despising and explain-
ing away goodness, yet very subtle and very fatal,
which hangs about the excitement of religious inquiry. It is the sin of requiring undue and impossible conditions of proof. I call it a sin, because
it is a rebellion against the natural conditions of
the world and of our own constitution—a rebellion
against those limitations and imperfections of our
knowledge amid which we find ourselves—a demand
that God should give us what it has not pleased
Him to give us. He has given us conscience, and
the knowledge of right and wrong : He has *not*
given us demonstrative proof—the proof which we
get by sight, and touch, and number, or by mathematical reasoning, of the truths of our moral
condition. The most elementary of these are open
to the "all-corroding, all-dissolving scepticism" of
the intellect which chooses to make difficulties and
start objections, perhaps insoluble. But there can
be no question about the madness and the wickedness of refusing to be true and just, because there are
half-a-dozen contradictory theories of morality, and
we are not satisfied which is the right one, which
meets all the objections against it. The fault is the
same, when, on evidence on which we are daily
acting without scruple or misgiving—evidence not
without difficulties, and open not merely to cavils
but to serious objections, yet on the whole full and
decisive—evidence surrounding us and perpetual
and converging—evidence on which we stake the fate

of a nation and take in courts of justice a fellow-creature's life—on evidence of this kind we refuse to admit the claims of the Gospel. Such evidence as that of the Gospel, and the Church which is its preacher, is that common to the whole world of action—of responsible, eventful action—bringing about its results, its achievements, its judgments. And in religion, the most practical of all things, that in which a man can least afford to indulge his fastidiousness and his hesitations, men demand more : they demand the evidence which belongs to the world of speculation, which implies either a problem which can never be exhausted, or else one which can be brought definitely to the verification of experiment. " Except I shall see in His hands the print of the nails, and put my finger into the print of the nails, and thrust my hand into His side, I will not believe." No ; to you that test will not be given. It is not part of the law of your condition. You know it is no part of it. Yet here you *must* make your venture. If you resolve not to believe, you must equally make your venture— as much, as practically, as eventfully, as if you do. If you refuse to believe, still you cannot have the certainty you want. Anyhow, you cannot have everything that you would like to have. Will you throw away so much, as if it were worthless, because you cannot have all ?

What is the object of life ? Why is it possessed ? What is its worth ? There is the heathen, the non-Christian estimate of it : in its noblest form, to *know*, to search, to inquire with the widest imagination and the most delicate methods,

to balance and hesitate, to make and unmake hypotheses, to detect mistakes, to accumulate the splen-
dours of discovery and the riches of intellectual
satisfaction,—a life to which our partial knowledge
gives its highest value, the aspirations of our poetry
and art its highest charms, but which knows nothing, and thinks little, of anything beyond. And
there is the Christian estimate : life, great for the
present, but immeasurably greater for the future, for
what it is to be ; and it is great now, if, by knowledge and power indeed, yet *doubly* by faith, and
love, and hope, the will is strengthened and directed
to all that is most like Him whom we worship and
trust in, and expect one day to see. Here are the
two rival estimates of life, which divide the allegiance
of all who aim high in their use of life. But man
has but a poor heritage, if knowledge is his all,
and his best :—knowledge, with all the meannesses,
jealousies, hatreds, with which its votaries reproach
theologians ; knowledge which lights up so tragic-
ally the abysses of man's condition and can show no
escape; knowledge, which with all its glories is consistent with what is poorest in character, and most
selfish in aim, and gloomy and unloving in temper.
Intellect is no moral safeguard. We may see the
clearest, strongest, soundest intellect joined with a
hard, ungenerous, malignant heart, with petty vanity,
with gross self-conceit, with hateful pride. God forbid that we should disparage knowledge—that we
should, as Bishop Butler says,[1] "vilify the faculty of
reason, which is ' the candle of the Lord within us.' "
But, as he adds, "it can afford no light, where it does

[1] *Analogy*, p. 351.

not shine ; nor judge, where it has no principles to judge upon." Knowledge is God's precious and wondrous gift. It is the glorious crown on the head of goodness and love and purity. But knowledge, like beauty, is of time ; and goodness only is eternal. Knowledge is the queen of our merely earthly life ; but her realm is bounded by the grave : in the next life, she whom we know here is nothing. Shall we then be content to take her for our all ; to resign all that is given us, all hope, beyond her. With whom shall we in life—life which is so short and so practical—cast in our lot ? With Christ and His servants, those who have served their brethren even to death, who have hoped most, and loved most, and attempted most, for man ? or with those whose one thought—a noble one, if it had not stood alone—has been *to know :* who have had the season and the bloom of a brilliant career— brilliant researches, brilliant discoveries, brilliant lectures, brilliant criticism—and who, when energy decays, and they are succeeded by others as brilliant, have nothing more to tell us, except that men are astray, wrapt in delusions, powerless to dispel them ? This may seem the more attractive, the more reasonable view of life, in the summer days of brightness, and health, and excitement. Will it seem so, when death and the end are near ? " Alas for those," says the Divine Speaker, in the *Invitation of Christ,*—" alas for those, who busy themselves with men about many curious inquiries, but care little about the way of serving Me.

"The time will come when the Master of masters

¹ Book III. chap. xliii.

will appear, Christ, the Lord of angels, to hear the lessons of all ; that is, to examine each man's conscience. And then shall He 'search Jerusalem with candles,' and 'the hidden things of darkness shall be made manifest,' and the strife of tongues shall be still.

" There will come one hour," He proceeds, " when all tumult and all toil will cease.

" Do, therefore, that thou doest. Labour faithfully in My vineyard. I will be thy reward.

" Write, read, sing, mourn, keep silence, pray : bear like a man all that is against thee.

" There is that which is worth all these and greater conflicts—everlasting life."

XV

STRONG WORDS [1]

" By thy words thou shalt be justified, and by thy words thou shalt
be condemned."—ST. MATT. xii. 37.

ONE of the subjects which must come, I suppose,
before a serious man at a time of self-trial and self-
discipline like this, if he makes any use of it at all
for his own correction and improvement, is his
employment of the great gift of language, his habits
of speech. The Bible, I need not remind you, lays
great stress on men's duties in regard to it, on the
mischief and the sin of a careless and uncontrolled
exercise of a faculty which is such a mighty instrument for good or harm. Given for the highest
purposes of man's nature and end, it may be
degraded to the meanest and vilest uses, it may
be wasted in the most miserable and emptiest folly.
We are tempted in days like ours, of freedom, and
boldness, and activity, to forget our responsibilities.
"We are they that ought to speak, who is lord
over us?" is the expression of no unusual or over-
weening arrogance. Yet for this, we know a real
account is finally to be given. "For every idle
word that men shall speak" (whatever be the

[1] Preached in King's College Chapel during Lent, 1874.

meaning of the expression, none can doubt that it
is most emphatic and most solemn), "they shall give
account thereof in the day of judgment." Men's
words, and their use of them, are to furnish at last a
test of character, and of the true state and general
bent of will and life. " By thy words thou shalt be
justified, and by thy words thou shalt be condemned."
I will venture then, to-day, to ask your attention
for a few minutes to one, and only one, portion of
this great matter, which ought, as much as anything,
to give us something to think about if we will make
proper use of Lent.

I am going, then, to say a few words on a very
old-fashioned and homely subject, a branch of that
great department of self-ruling and self-watching
which we speak of as the government of the tongue.
I am going to say something on the duty of self-
restraint in the strength of our words and general
tone of speech, on the obligation of conscientious
and real care when we are induced, or tempted, to
use strong words. The solemn language of our
Lord in the text shows that it is a matter which
we cannot afford to put on one side.

We most of us know how easy it is to get into
the way of using strong words in our statements,
in our opinions, in our expressions of feeling, in
our praise or our condemnation. It is convenient.
It is pleasant. It is, with many people, what we
call natural. It saves much trouble. A strong and
summary phrase dispenses with the effort of finding
and stating reasons. A loose but tempting exaggeration seems to bear witness to our earnestness,
and to make us sure that we have manfully taken

our side.   A bold sweeping sentence of approval or
censure seems to put us in a position of superiority
as judges, and to show the breadth and largeness
of our view.   It is easier, often, to see and feel
what is right and true than it is to prove it : and
to put our conviction into the most energetic words
which occur to us, while it favours our indolence,
seems at the same time to give us the gratification
of an intellectual victory.   And, at any rate, there
is a kind of natural satisfaction in using our strength
of language, just as there is in using our strength
of body, or limbs, or mental gifts.   We can be at
our ease while we talk strongly, and yet seem to be
doing something strong.

Strong words are one of two things, supposing,
as I am supposing, that they are not the words of
conscious hollowness and intended hypocrisy, and
leaving out of account, of course, the question of
professed fiction, and all that comes fairly under
playfulness in our intercourse.   They are the natural
and fit expression of deep and strong feeling, or
passion, or judgment, right or wrong ; or they are
the cheap expedients and favourite resources and
instruments of weakness ; and, so far as they are
resorted to, they betray it.   There are occasions in
all our lives which call for them, oftener, perhaps,
than we always recollect.   But this very thing makes
it all the more necessary that we should not get into
the way of using strong words at random, and wasting
force which ought to be husbanded to do the work, and
to produce the effect which deep and genuine feeling
often has to do and to produce in our intercourse.

When I ask you to be on your guard against

a careless and loose strength of language, I do so
first in the interests of truth.   There is no more
insidious enemy to that value and respect for truth,
which must be the foundation of all that is good,
and noble, and manly in character, than this un-
intentional but habitual slighting of its claim.   A
man has to make a statement, or he tells a story.
In nine cases out of ten it does not seem to him
to matter whether he gives it a turn which his
imagination suggests, or adds a touch natural, prob-
able, it may be, but for which he has no warrant.
The statement is made more intelligible ; the story
gains in point.   And in nine cases out of ten,
perhaps, it does not matter, except in the unseen,
impalpable interests of the great law that word and
fact ought to correspond.   But the tenth case may
be one in which all the difference is made by
the simple truth, or by additions to it ; and the
nine, apparently harmless and innocent exaggerations or colourings, have helped to strengthen a
custom of exaggerating and colouring.   A man gets
to confuse, and to not mind confusing, what he is
sure of with what he guesses.   He *imagines* where
he thought he saw or heard.   He thinks that he
believes what he does not really believe.

And it is so easy to lose the limits and distinctions
between what is true and what might have been true.
" Conversation," says a shrewd novelist,[1] " consists a
good deal in the denial of what is true."   At any
rate, conversation is often impatient of the limits of
what is true, and I don't know a man more to be
.honoured than he who prefers being awkward,

---

[1] George Eliot in *Felix Holt*.

and seeming to be clumsy and blundering, to saying more than he knows or means. The temptation to a clear mind to round off and order its facts, to an imaginative one to give them the significance which it creates, is often enormous. The interests of accuracy seem petty beside the call for a vigorous, forcible, telling account of a thing, beside the charm of quaint or suggestive anecdote. These claims seem petty ; they would seem overwhelming if we could only see what comes of the difference between exaggeration and truthful self-restraint in the long run. This habit of accuracy will doubtless often impair the effect of a sentence, or spoil a good story ; but even at that risk, we shall be well paid at last, if we keep before our minds the saying of a distinguished writer about some case of, perhaps, prosaic exactness : " It *is* rather a minute accuracy. But I have a respect for all accuracy ; for all accuracy is of the noble family of truth, and is to be respected accordingly, even to her most menial servant." [1]

And next I plead in the interests of soundness and reality of feeling and character. Words, as we are told, which we think our slaves and instruments, may become our masters and tyrants. In times when thought is keen, when great principles are in conflict, and great interests are at stake, when aims and prospects are unexpectedly opening and enlarging, and all minds feel quickened and strung by the atmosphere they breathe, our common language reflects the highly wrought condition ; reflects it, exaggerates it, and contributes to make it more intense.

[1] John Davison, Newman's *Essays, Critical and Historical*, vol. ii. p. 385.

Then is the time when it seems to become men to take,
in thought and word, advanced positions, the more
advanced, the more creditable to their thorough-going
manliness.   Then is the time when it seems the brave
and honest thing to commit ourselves to strong and
uncompromising professions.   I need not tell you
that excitement, though it may be most sincere at
the moment, does not always cover real purpose.   It
does not always know the ventures which it under-
takes, and the responsibilities to which it binds itself.
But time, all-trying, all-revealing time, goes on.
We have spoken strongly, our strong words have
been deep pledges of what we believed and meant ;
and, by and by, the course of things, the development
of events, bring out their significance and bearing.
We make to ourselves, perhaps, the excuse, the sorry
excuse, of the great advocate for our old over-state-
ments, our old rashnesses : they belonged to the
occasion, they were " temporis, potius quam veritatis."
But it will not prevent their recoil.   The future
takes us at our word and mercilessly exacts its
redemption.   And then, if we did not really know
all that our words meant, if we did not really mean
all that their strength and decisiveness implied, one
of two things happens : we have to back out of
them, or else they drive and sting us on into more
than we really meant at first.   I cannot tell which
is a sorer trial of the soul, which is more dangerous
to our integrity and wholeness of mind.   To have
to retreat where we were so confident of our position,
to have to unsay what we said perhaps so loudly,
is indeed a humiliation to which a brave honesty,
which feels in discomfiture and shame its sharp but

wholesome medicine, may submit with profit. But
all cannot bear it. To find themselves caught and
entrapped in their own strong words brings with it
the painful sense of hollowness which leads men to
disbelieve that any one can be in earnest ; or else,
to escape this, they let a one-sided consistency which
they call logical drag them into extremes, they lash
themselves into violence and excess. In any case
they are not what they meant to be, when they
could judge more freely ; often, not what in the
depths of their conscience they know they ought to
be, and *would* be. Character has received a shock
and a wound. They have talked too fast for what
was really in their mind ; and either in scepticism or
feebleness, or in forced exaggeration and intemper-
ateness, they suffer the penalties of their unreality.

You will not suspect me of recommending the
safe reserve of the cowardly and selfish. · But our
words must be, as our Lord says, the standard of
our deeds, and of the judgment on them ; and it is
of the deepest moment that our words and deeds
should make " according music." And no man can
have lived long without having seen, over and over
again, and, I suppose, without having himself deeply
suffered from, their fatal discord. Our words have
outstripped our · convictions and our knowledge,
whereas they ought, if we are wise, I do not say to
lag, but to be curbed and kept back behind them.
And indeed, if we could but believe it, there is
nothing lost in force and power by understatement,
by words deliberately subdued. Contrast the weight
of a statement of the same set of facts, in the hands
of undisciplined and exaggerating ability, and as

represented in the calm clearness and light of a
passionless judicial summing up, and we shall feel
that measured and temperate words need not want
strength.   But I urge on you the care of this self-
discipline on higher grounds than that of the power
it bestows.   I urge it for the sake of the depth, the
truthfulness, the Christian manliness and reality of
your characters ; for the sake of the seriousness of
your purposes, the genuineness of your plan and
course of life, in the sight of Him who will make
our profession the standard to judge our deeds.

> Prune thou thy words, the thoughts control
> That o'er thee swell and throng ;
> They will condense within thy soul,
> And change to purpose strong.[1]

"So speak ye, and so do, as they that shall be
judged by the law of liberty."   Remember that you
have always a listener, One who abhors all ostentation
and pretence, all insolent carelessness—One who
takes men at their word in ways they think not of.
We instinctively lower our voice, and limit our
words, when we are in the presence of one whose
wisdom or whose greatness awes us ; and we are
never out of the presence of Him who judges us
with equity, and with all the loving-kindness and
largeness of His perfect knowledge, but so also with
wisdom measuring our folly, with truth measuring
our insincerity and show.   Learn to speak as owing
an account to Him, and to your conscience, not only
of what you do but of what you say.   Don't be
afraid of being dull because you measure your words
and check them.   Better be dull than learn to be

---

[1] *Lyra Apostolica*, lxvii.

extravagant and exaggerated ; than to get into habits of saying what you don't mean, and of not caring whether you mean what you say or not. Better anything than, in any shape, habitual, unregarded, unconscious untruthfulness of language. But, indeed, believe that in fact no interest matches the interest of truth. There is no limit to the unexplored treasures of living and varied interest assured to those who have faith in truth and truthfulness. Don't confound honesty of speech with strength of words, with extreme unbalanced phrases: strength is indeed one attribute of truth and honesty, but measure, controlled and ordered, is another. Your care, your self-restraint, may deprive you of a momentary sparkle, of a momentary triumph ; but you will be glad of it by and by, when you see the issues of things, when you come to die. Don't waste the force of your soul. Depend upon it, the day will come, if we have anything to do with the real affairs of life, when we shall want, with the best reason, to feel strongly, to speak strongly. Don't let us come to those occasions with our power impaired and dulled, because we have accustomed ourselves to use it at random, in idle, disproportioned vehemence, in excess of what we really meant, in excess of what the subject called for, and of what we had a right to say. Trouble of this kind and self-control are not always pleasant, but they are well worth the effort. Alas ! how many strong words shall we, all of us, wish unspoken, when that day comes, in which, in the presence of the Lord of Truth, "by our words we shall be justified, and by our words we shall be condemned."

XVI

THE MINISTRY OF WOMEN[1]

" Having then gifts differing according to the grace that is given to us,
whether prophecy, let us prophesy according to the proportion of
faith ; or ministry, let us wait on our ministering : or he that
teacheth, on teaching."—ROM. xii. 6, 7.

IN the Church, as in the world, every man has two
great departments of duty to think of, one relating
to himself, the other relating to that body of which
he is a member. In one point of view, every one is
as if there were no one else in existence but himself
—none but himself face to face with God, none but
himself face to face with nature. He lives within a
circle which no one outside can penetrate ; he owns
allegiance to a law of conscience which speaks to
him alone ; he knows what none can possibly know
but himself ; he feels what none can feel for him
or instead of him ; he has interests which are his
absolutely alone ; there is a solitude in which, in the
midst of the most crowded and active companionship,
he is isolated : as he lives alone, so he dies alone.
But in another point of view, it is not as the individual
but as the member of a complex organisation that

[1] Preached at the Festival of the Community of St. Mary the Virgin,
Wantage, 1875.

we view him—an organisation in which he and his place, even if the highest, are subordinate to the claims and interests of the whole. The soldier may be brave, generous, accomplished as a man and a soldier, and we may think of him as such and admire him as such ; but there is also another standard of judgment, by which we decide what sort of soldier he is in the army of which he is a member, or in the particular work on which he along with others is employed. No lesson was earlier or more emphatically impressed on Christians than this : that none of them lives merely for himself or stands alone in what he has to do to fulfil God's will. Christians are the children or the servants of a great family or household. Christians are the subjects and citizens of a great kingdom ; and a great kingdom means ranks and classes in ordered gradation, and offices and duties dependent one on another. The Church as portrayed in the New Testament is a body as "fearfully and wonderfully made" as the natural body, in which each living portion has its life on the condition, the absolute condition, of contributing according to its due function and ministry to the combined working of the whole. The organ or the limb which will take no part in the general movement loses its own proper powers ; the muscle which will not play becomes wasted and obliterated ; the sense or the faculty which is not exercised becomes dulled, paralysed, extinguished. All are wanted : none can be spared. For the service demanded of them is most complicated and most varied, and each single fibre of our nerves, each single cell in our tissues, has its part to do or has its part to spoil and thwart in the tasks which the greater and worthier members of the body are called on to discharge. And to these calls it is impossible to fix the limit. The circumstances change in which the body is required to act or to endure : no one can tell what novel conditions it or each several member may have to encounter and suit itself to ; no one can enumerate the infinite employments to which its primitive and original faculties and endowments may be applied. Its forces may be strained in rude battle with nature or with men ; or the subtle harmonies of eye, and ear, and touch may be summoned into co-operating exercise in the execution of some delicate and elaborate work of art or music. And the circumstances to which the body may have to accommodate itself, the services for which each of its parts may be needed, cannot be more different, more changing, more uncertain, than the altering conditions of human society and human necessities under which the Church has to carry on the work imposed on it by its Master, or the varying character of the services which, as things change around it, are wanted from the members who are united in its Divine organisation.

In that great " City of God," to which we belong even here, though all that is greatest in it is still unknown to us, God its Master has, in the words of our prayer, " ordained and constituted the services of Angels and men in a wonderful order." And in the same kind of " wonderful order " has He constituted here on earth the services of His mortal creatures in their several places and degrees. Thus has He constituted the several ministries and services of men and women. No one

has ever doubted the law, the obligation, the variety
of service in the case of men.   Nothing has been
more often overlooked, in those tacit assumptions by
which life is so much governed, than the force of this
claim of service—distinct, definite, personal service
—in the case of women.   It is not that the Bible over-
looks it.   There, the idea from first to last is that
God's call to His creatures and servants for co-operation
with Him in His work comes to women as much as
to men.   To women, in their homes primarily, as
primarily to men in the open field and battle-ground
of life ; to women, primarily, as charged with the
care and training of the family, the original and
fundamental unit of God's kingdom, out of which it
grows, and which must be kept pure and sound in
affections and order, unless everything else in human
society is to be ruined.   But though primarily to
women in their homes and families, not exclusively
so.   They, too, have borne their full share in the
movements and events recorded in the Bible, by
which the course of God's dispensation has moved
on.   They, too, have been charged with its responsibilities.   They too, like men, have been called
to a great trust, and have betrayed it.   They have
lost the world, wounded its dearest and most sacred
interest.   And they have been partners in its
redemption and deliverance.   Their Master has
claimed their service, their self-sacrifice, and they
have given it.   The voices of ready obedience to the
great demands of God respond, in the history of the
Bible, like the voices of two sides of a choir.   "Speak,
Lord ; for Thy servant heareth," and " Here am I ;
send me," are answered by the self-dedication,

" Behold the handmaid of the Lord ; be it unto me according to Thy word."

But that nothing is strange in a world in which, after truths have been keenly and strongly grasped, they are so soon and so easily forgotten, it would seem strange that so obvious a principle of God's kingdom as this, the use which our Master has for the ministry of women, should ever have passed out of sight. The Early Church seized it and turned it to full account. The Early Church found a place for women in all the Gospel offices spoken of in the text —in prophesying, in ministering, in teaching. Women were among her missionaries : women were among her most willing martyrs. The Church of the Middle Ages, amid all the confusion and ignorance following the extinction of a corrupted civilisation, and the slow regeneration by a barbarian triumph, never forgot what women might be as the special servants of Christ. New and fruitful ideas of usefulness were struck out. Women aspired boldly, and not only aspired but reached, to brave and noble deeds of self-sacrifice and love. The Church was enriched by fresh applications of its eternal rules ; by new types of charity, of sanctity, of sympathy with things unseen ; by methods which presented a new front to the undying evils of society. Women took their part in the Divine work : they taught the ignorant, they reclaimed the lost, they rescued the perishing, they comforted the miserable, they helped the poor to bear the load of poverty. In time these systematic attempts felt the fate of weakness and degeneracy which attends all human things, and all human plans even to reform, to improve, to elevate. They

languished, they were turned out of their course,
they went astray. The form remained, the functions
slackened, the spirit failed. Institutions, organisa-
tions, which once had been sacred to the highest
purposes, let in the subtle corrupting air of worldliness, and fell as they deserved. In their fall they
take their place among the accumulating lessons of
the world. But the truths which they embodied
remain the same ; the great things which they
sought to do, still remain to be done. And I am
afraid that the lesson which was for a long time
drawn from their failures, was that what they had
failed in needed not be tried again ; at any rate, that
it was safer and better not to try at all, than to try
with the risk of mistake and ill-success. For a long
time, among ourselves at least, it seemed as if there
were no room for any special application to the
service of the Gospel of the gifts and faculties of
women. Partly the dulness of custom, partly fear of
the prejudices and sneers of the world, partly distrust
of enthusiasm, discouragement at the breakdown of
ancient attempts, and recoil from the corruption in
which they often ended, kept us from fairly considering
what the sufferings and sins of mankind wanted, and
what women could do to make them less. I do not
like to hear the modest religion, the unobtrusive piety
and benevolence of the last century depreciated. It
undoubtedly did exist. I believe that there was a great
deal of unheeded, unremembered religion in it which
may put us to deep shame. But the idea of an
English Sister of Charity was one which, I suppose,
never rose in even good people's minds. No, in
this, as in many other things, that which properly

belonged to the Church, that which long ago the Church had used and ordered to great purposes, was now revived by those without the Church, and was left to them by the Church, afraid of her own powers, distrustful of her own strength, shrinking from the fulness of her own calling. The person who in our later times first grasped the conviction of a special mission for women—beyond those offices of kindness and mercy which lie in every one's power, and which doubtless are so amply and so modestly fulfilled by numbers whose only profession is to make home happy—the first person who recognised a call for special self-devotion to a definite work, was not a Churchwoman, but a Quaker, Elizabeth Fry. And when in our own days the Church woke up to a more true and more generous conception of her duties, it broke upon us almost like a discovery—so fast had custom sealed our eyes—that among human occupations and employments, among the special activities which the Church enlists in its service, there was a large space for the employment of women : there was work which they could do, and none could do but they.

I cannot help remembering that I am speaking here, in one of the places where that great but obvious thought first took practical shape. We are, I suppose, in some sense commemorating the birth of that ancient, but to our times in England new idea—the idea of a life devoted by women to the service of religion, in the same sense as a soldier devotes his life to whatever the country calls him to undertake—a life of definite, orderly, regulated duty. This is one of the places where an experiment which

once seemed a bold one was earliest made. It is a
place which has helped to reconcile our jealous
English nature—jealous of all mere imitations and
revivals, jealous of what has once been insidiously
harmful, jealous of extravagance and pretence,
supremely jealous of all that might disparage family
affections and household duties—to a view of life,
and a use of it, which are so manifestly Christian.
Here the plan of a life of labour for women—intelligent, beneficent, fervent labour for Christ—labour
serious, habitual, sustained, like the labour of men,
broke through the spell which condemned it as unnatural and unprecedented, and became a reality.
The idea has by this time had a history. It has
learned from experience. It has made mistakes and
disclosed its weak places. It has gained, too, in
firmness, in sobriety, in knowledge of the conditions
under which it is to be carried on. And on this
anniversary, we have a right, we have cause, to bless
God that the ministry of women has again become
one of the recognised institutions of the English
Church ; one of the proofs of its power to stir up
the gift that is in it, and to meet the calls of the
day as well as the permanent needs of the wonderfully manifold society round us.

1. What should be our thoughts on a day like this ?
Who can refuse to us,—even to us who are outside of
your work here, and are bound to it only by the tie of
sympathy,—that the first feeling of us all should be
one of exultation—exultation that what was once de-
cried as visionary and impossible should be before us
as a living and vigorous work ; exultation that a great
venture for the love of Christ has not put to shame

the faith and boldness of those who made it ; exultation that, in this ancient Church of England, after all
the conflicts and exhaustion of centuries, the spring
of youth is yet so strong ; exultation that, in spite
of great hopes cast down, in spite of the misgivings
of those who most believed in her, and the prophecies
of helplessness and decay from those who despaired of
her and those who hated her, she has met the strain
of one of the most critical trials of her history, and
disclosed unknown and unsuspected sources of force
and power, to answer to new emergencies.   Many of
us can remember the days when the question was
anxiously asked, Can the Church of England bear
the test of a loftier standard, a higher aim than those
of the traditions of her later history ?   Can she bear
to look with unflinching eye on the words, on the
deeds, of her Master, on the necessities of those for
whom He died ? Can she bear originality of thought ?
Can she bear the spirit of enterprise, in carrying on
the redeeming and consoling work of the Crucified ?
Without disguising from ourselves that there was
reason to ask the question, we have lived to see, I
think, the unwisdom of despondency.   We have lived
to see the undeserved grace of God wakening in many
hearts and in distant points at once a life which seemed
extinct.   We have learned from facts, assuming every
day larger proportions and more distinct significance,
a reassurance which some only can find in the most
self-consistent theories.   After languor and sickness,
the old lineaments are reviving, the well-known
lineaments of the Bride of Christ.   We recognise the
·tokens of an unearthly presence, in the sympathy
which cannot rest before the infinite wants of men,

in the lowly boldness to attempt and to endure hard things to accomplish the Master's purposes. God does not desert those whom He calls from sleep and death to life and work.

2. " Thanks be unto God for His unspeakable gift." But the gift is to us men, and men may fail. He has given it to others, this precious gift of the ministry of women, which He has restored to us ; and others have failed. There are not wanting those who say that we shall fail. What is certain is that it depends on those against whom the evil prophecy is spoken, whether they shall shame it or shall fulfil it. But it is a warning to us all to fear, to watch, to pray, to be sober. This great service is not a light one. It is one which, in spite of all prejudices, is essentially so reasonable, so noble, so full of blessing, so adapted to uses to which nothing else is equally adapted, that it cannot in the end be gainsaid : it recommends itself, even if it be often against the grain, to the daring and serious mind of England. But it must fulfil its promise. It cannot afford to be weak ; it cannot afford to play with its arduous and exacting tasks ; it cannot afford to disguise, under the forms of its austere unselfishness, the temper of self-pleasing, of vanity, of petty and fanciful and fantastic waywardness. It must be kept pure by deep and sincere devotion, and by the strong spirit of self-government and honest self-mastery. So ruled, so balanced, so fortified, the religious ministry of women opens a prospect of good things to England, which we may look for in vain in any other direction, and to which it seems hard to put a limit.

3. For the wants of English society are great and

C.S.,P.   T

are increasing—increasing in their pressure and in
their variety. Take but one great and tremendous
department of them. What war is to men, merciless,
devouring, hopeless in its natural destructiveness, vice
is to women. It is idle to make ourselves giddy
with thinking of this mystery. But there it is : the
fatal mischief, without natural remedy, after which
hope seems to go. It overthrows, it wrecks, it consumes. And none but women can dare to deal with
it hand to hand. In former days, society almost
accepted its horrible tyranny and ruin as something
as inevitable as death. Its scale was so immense,
its range so wide, its power so uncontrollable, that
it seemed idle to grapple with it. As generation
followed generation, the tribute of victims which it
levied seemed fated, and beyond human power to
arrest or diminish ; and it claimed them in all ranks
of society. At least, *we* have learned to think, that
huge and monstrous as it is, we *must* try to encounter
it. We must not sit still, as if we could do nothing,
and were excused for being passive. We *must* try
to open paths of escape to its miserable captives.
We, who have coped with slavery and bridled disease,
must try *not* to look upon it as something which it
is useless to resist or to remedy. The Penitentiary,
the Reformatory are not, indeed, the invention of
our times ; but the imperious sense of their overwhelming necessity is a thing the growth of which
many of us can remember. We see that there are no
limits to their need as long as there are souls to be
rescued. Such places of refuge require to be multiplied indefinitely. They must be local and dispersed
through the country. They must be as varied in

their management and system as there are classes of
society whom the mischief invades, as there are ages
and characters blasted by its poison.   And who is
to supply all this amount and all this versatility of
service?   If there were nothing else to call for and
occupy the ministry—the deliberate, systematic ministry—of women,—if there were no schools to teach,
nor poor to be visited, nor hospitals to be tended,—
think of the field on which none but they can dare to
venture, in which none but they can hope on a large
scale for influence and fruit, in reclaiming, restoring,
comforting those whom sin has ruined—among rich
and poor, the ignorant and the refined.   If any one
wanted to see a proof of the varied adaptation of the
same ministry and the same self-devotion in the
various times of history, he might find it here.   That
ministry which once was thought to have found its
chief place in the sanctuary, and its function in wit-
nessing to penitence and self-devotion by seclusion
from the world, has, without altering its spirit or its
ends, reversed its methods.   Without leaving the
sanctuary, it has found a wider field outside : it no
longer shrinks from the world and abandons it to its
fate ; it associates itself in loving sympathy and help
with the penitence of others.

May the God of power and love guide and rule
His own good gifts.   May He point out and direct
their manifold applications, and correct our ignorance
in using them.   We trust that He has been mindful
of us, and hopes much from us, by the flame which
He has lit up in so many hearts—the desire to serve
Him, the will which seeks to reflect His Perfect Will.
May He who has kindled zeal give with it sobriety

and strength. May He who has taught us new ways
of glorifying Him and of serving His creatures save
us from wasting His blessings by self-will and folly.
There are great and untold things before those who
have been led to make His definite service the work
and object of life. There are great hopes and great
dangers; there is sure to be difficulty, opposition,
distrust, annoyance. May He help all who have
entered on this road, to put to shame the accuser's
sneers by the simplicity and perseverance of a noble
life—noble with the noblest of all noble things,
the nobleness of unconscious humility. May He
strengthen, refine, steady us all in our several paths
—many of them dizzy and hard ones; in our
several tasks—many of them as perilous as they are
great. May He help us, by using the openings His
good Providence has made for faith and for true life,
to attract more and more of those unexhausted and
unimagined gifts, to enrich and adorn His Church,
which are in *His* keeping, who led our captivity captive, and ascended up on high. We are still within
the memory of the day of that great Apostle who
derived his name from the power bestowed on him,
of strengthening, animating, comforting others, by
the spell of his words, by the force and charm of his
character—Barnabas, "the Son of Consolation," the
earthly reflection of the Paraclete. The closing
words of the Gospel of that day may well serve as
the mingled warning and encouragement of this :—
"Ye have not chosen Me, but I have chosen you,
and ordained you, that ye should go and bring forth
fruit, and that your fruit should remain : that whatsoever ye shall ask of the Father in My name, He

may give it you." The prayer of that day may well be the prayer of this—" O Lord God Almighty, who didst endue Thy holy Apostle Barnabas with singular gifts of the Holy Ghost: Leave us not, we beseech Thee, destitute of Thy manifold gifts, nor yet of grace to use them alway to Thy honour and glory ; through Jesus Christ our Lord."

XVII

FOREIGN TRAVEL[1]

" The earth is the Lord's, and all that therein is : the compass of the world, and they that dwell therein."—PSALM xxiv. 1.

THE object of the present course of sermons has been, I suppose, to bring home to the thoughts and consciences of the hearers the special conditions surrounding that particular form of high civilisation under which they are passing their lives, and going through that trial of character and behaviour which under the most varied and contrasted shapes all men have to meet. The great and familiar facts of our actual life have been disengaged from the generalities under which they are usually spoken of in the pulpit : they have been named as we name them in our ordinary conversation and in less sacred places, and have been boldly subjected to the severe testing ot being confronted with the moral and religious principles which we acknowledge as Christians. The time in which we live is rife, for many of us, with new gifts, abounds with new fields of enterprise and enjoyment, opens the most varied directions for intellectual and imaginative activity; no graver

[1] Preached in St. James's Church, Piccadilly, 1873, being one in a course of Sermons entitled " The Use and Abuse of the World."

question can be asked than how all this shall be harmonised with the Divine ideal of life left us in the New Testament : not only how all these things can be made safe for a Christian, but how they can be made to strengthen, adorn, elevate his spiritual nature. They are condemned at once if they cannot do this : they are condemned at once if, in that discipline of which they are part, they cannot do much to fit the children of time for the tasks and the ministries of eternity. But to show the office which they discharge in this continual and manifold discipline, to show that with all their mischiefs and risks, which are obvious, undeniable, and great, they can yet be wisely and nobly used, and that without them men would turn out weaker and more poorly furnished, when the shadows pass away and all that man was really made for is revealed,—this has been the purpose of these lectures in various separate departments of our modern social condition.

I have in my turn to speak to you of what is one of the most marked features of our modern life, the habits which have grown up in consequence of the vastly increased facilities in our times of movement and communication between different countries. I have to speak of " Foreign Travel." The series of subjects in which it has a place limits the way of considering it. I speak of foreign travel as it has become part of the customary manner of life with great classes of people, not as it is with the explorer, or the man of business, or the missionary, or the student in some particular department of inquiry, physical, political, moral—an enterprise having its definite and separate object—nor even as it used to be regarded, the complement and finish of a man's education ; but foreign travel as one of the advantages which the changes of time have made common and familiar to leisure and competence, one of the new openings of our day to knowledge, enjoyment, and recreation. Thousands travel now for one who travelled in our fathers' days ; regions and places are easily visited which were out of reach except to the adventurous and the patient ; we travel as a matter of course, as we take our holiday as a matter of course. Such a vast and signal addition to the resources and opportunities of life deserves more consideration than we always give to it.

The subject seems naturally to break itself into two parts : (1) What ought foreign travel to do for us, as part of our ordinary and customary manner of life ; and (2) What ought we to do, what ought we to watch against, that it may have its " perfect work," and that we may gain from it what it ought to yield.

1. What ought foreign travel to do for us ? The life of this great city, the life of English society which it reflects in its most energetic and concentrated form, presents the two salient aspects of toil and pleasure— toil, the most severe and unremitting ; pleasure, the most varied and absorbing. I speak not of the special character of either, how they are controlled by other influences and affected by aims and rules beyond themselves. But they are the two great facts which meet us all day long here. And what travel does is this—it interrupts both.

Of all breaks in the course and tenour of our lives, except the breaks of disaster and death, it is the

most abrupt and emphatic. We pass across our
own border, and all is new and different. Nothing
has such an unconscious yet powerful influence in
making us feel that we are living continually under
the same set of conditions, as hearing in every
one's mouth all day long the same familiar words
and speech. We start and look round us, if by
chance the spell is broken by hearing as we pass by
in the street a foreign language. And the sensation
of strangeness is of course much greater when, instead
of that we are accustomed to, we find every one round
us, in the smallest matters as well as the greatest,
taking for granted an entirely novel and perhaps
perplexing instrument of speech ; when we find ourselves, it may be, absolutely cut off from our fellow-
men in the commonest intercourse, by the snapping of
a link of which we were hardly conscious till it was
broken ; when, even if we are acquainted with the
language, it costs us distinct thought and effort to
frame our own words, to catch the unaccustomed
sound and phrase in reply ; when we hear a language
which we consider it an achievement of skill and
industry to have mastered, and which we pride
ourselves on as a peculiar possession and accomplishment of our scholarship, sounding all about us from
the mouths of the ignorant, the poor, the little
children. But this is not the chief break and
change. Our condition is changed. Here at 'home
we have our well-known place, our recognised relations to the persons and the system and the society
about us, our business, our subordination, our varied
ties and bonds with all we see, those whom we know,
and those who know us. All at once, we are

whirling about like unconnected atoms, in a system
as vast and organised as our own, but in which we
have nothing to bind us to it or assign our position,
neither part nor lot, nor function nor interest,
touching it and in it, but nowhere *of* it ; without
home of our own in it, without name or recognition,
without citizenship, aliens to the laws, the habits,
probably the traditional religion, of the community—kingdom, or republic, or empire—in which
we are wayfarers or sojourners.   Again, it is a
change in our social station ; some of course carry
this with them wherever they go, but for the most
part the distinctions which were sharp and marked at
home become confused abroad ; a new set of under-
standings arise ; whoever we are, great or small, we
are lost in the crowd, and, except occasionally or
accidentally, find ourselves all on a level.   And our
manner of life changes, perhaps is absolutely reversed :
we have, it may be, to rough it and put up with
rude invasions of our ordinary ways, with abandonment of habitual appliances of life ; our own artificial
habits have to give way to other artificial ones, fashions
are altered, and the rules of intercourse ; very often
a simpler manner of living, coarseness and personal
hardship, are the price and only condition of our travel.
And meanwhile, the whole external scene round us
changes.   All that outward look of things which had
become the accustomed frame of our life, and met
our eyes every day, has disappeared, the face of the
earth, the cities and homes of men, the outlines of
the landscape, the light and aspect of the sky ; and
·the change is all the more marked and impressive,
because we have not, as at home, the current affairs

and interests of life to fill the chief place in our
thoughts, and we are at leisure to notice and attend
to all that is strange and different about us, as
it passes, perhaps, in rapid succession, day after
day, and with every kind of variation, before our
eyes.

Now it seems to me that in this marked and
complete break in our way of life, marked and complete for the time, but not violent and painful, there
is a great opportunity.   In our life of work and
business, more so in the life of amusement and
pleasure-seeking, we get into grooves.   We get entangled and engrossed, and lose our power of
reviewing our position, and finding our true bearings,
and choosing freely our course.   Day after day
brings the same cares, the same motives, the same
rivalries and antipathies, the same habits, the same
aims.   We are unable to rise above them, to look at
them as it were from a distance : our perspective is
confused or lost.   In this unceasing toil, in this unceasing excitement, we know, we *feel*, that there are
enormous and formidable temptations — temptations
all the more grave, that the uniformity and constant
strong current of custom keeps them out of sight,
while they are acting upon us.   We do need, if we
are to maintain our moral health and power, a pause,
a rest, for collecting ourselves, for disengaging ourselves from the blind round of custom.   And such a
pause, so salutary, so full of profit, may be, if we will
use it, the entire reversal of occupation and custom
involved in foreign travel.   Change of objects and
of scenes is a potent remedy to the sick mind and
body : it may be as precious in bracing, elevating,

quickening our moral nature; in restoring the
balance and harmony between its elements ; in easing
and restoring the springs which have been strained
by some exclusive and over-constant pressure.

And the refreshment may be so great. Far
indeed be it from me to suppose, that without
passing outside our own borders, there may not be
found enough and to spare, in our English homes,
our English landscape, our English hills, to charm
and satisfy, not only with the sense of novelty, but
of beauty. Our own land, our own cities, our own
rivers, will well bear searching through, and will not
be exhausted when we have done. But the world is
wide and wonderful. "The earth is the Lord's, and
all that therein is : the compass of the world, and
they that dwell therein." It reflects the infinite mani-
foldness of His powers, His purposes, His thoughts ;
it is the spectacle, in each age of time, of the amazing
and overpowering variety of faculty, and gift, and
power, ever showing themselves in fresh and unexpected ways, in the race which He has made to
dwell here. It is a spectacle worth becoming
acquainted with. Noble and beautiful as is that
which we have at home, there is greatness which is
not ours, there is beauty which is denied to us, there
are endowments, there are achievements which we
must not pretend to. We may *make* them in a
measure our own, but we must go out of ourselves
to do so. Foreign travel is like the opening to
us of a new literature, in its unknown ideas, its
unimagined powers and aims. The poet has reversed the analogy ; he has used the explorer's
joy :—

. . . like stout Cortez when with eagle eyes
He stared at the Pacific . . .
Silent, upon a peak in Darien,[1]—

to express the image of his own awestruck gladness, when the great domains of poetry which Homer
ruled were first made known to him. But it is
as true to say that the varied trains of surprise
and interest excited by a first acquaintance with a
great work of genius, or a first introduction into the
truths of a new science, represent the effect of a
living and personal contact with scenes and manners
and men which are unlike ours. We become in a
fresh measure alive to the narrowness of our past
horizon, we find it widening and widening onwards,
with new disclosures, with hitherto unconceived
possibilities, with enlarged experience and quickened
curiosity and altered points of view. A man turns
a new page in his life, when he finds himself actually
face to face with that he has heard of and imagined,
and knows perhaps familiarly in books, but now for
the first time beholds in its completeness, with its real
surroundings, its real atmosphere, as one connected
whole. It may be things, it may be men ; but he
understands that he has that which, whether for
knowledge or for delight, nothing but presence could
have given him. He has gained a new possession ;
he has gained that which enables him to put in new
and authentic touches in his picture of the world ;
to strengthen, to correct, to amplify his thought of
its realities. He has gained new bonds of interest,
it may be of sympathy, with his kind, with this
earth, his dwelling-place ; he has formed new relations

---

[1] Keats' sonnet, On first looking into Chapman's *Homer*.

with human minds and characters ; he has formed
new ties with new places, and has come perhaps
to feel for them an affection akin to that of
home. He has gained that which he could
gain no other way, of a first-hand knowledge of the
magnificence, the scale, the lavish variety, the charm,
the strangeness of nature ; of the manifold ways in
which men who are alive with us now live their life,
and direct their course, and fashion their social order
and the portion of the world allotted to them, and
use their gifts, and mark their passage through time.
To have seen with our eyes the river of Egypt and
the remains of its mysterious civilisation ; to have
seen with our eyes the hills of Galilee, and the golden-
hued columns of the broken Parthenon, and the
splendour in decay of imperial cities, the Old and
the New Rome ; to have become acquainted with what
makes up the daily life of a strange community, its
peculiar customs, its common sights, the faces of its
people, the forms of nature, the inventions of art,
the governing passions, the fixed pursuits, the characteristic ideas, social, political, religious, which sway
the minds of millions ; or again, to have known what
nature can be, in her greatness and strength, in her
stability and vast calm, in her terrors which never
visit us here, in her luxuriance and glory which here
she austerely withholds from us, her floods and endless plains and her mountain peaks, her Atlantic
waves, her tropical storms, her perpetual ice-fields—
to have had our eyes rest on all these things in their
own homes, as part, natural and harmonious, of that
stage to which we for the moment were transferred
from our familiar places—this is to have passed into

a new level of life, to have the veil so far removed
which hangs between our limited sight and feeble
imagination, and the vast and wonderful facts of
the existing world.   Nor is it necessary, in order
to gain this sense of things beyond ourselves, that
we should be ever searching for unvisited fields of
travel.   The world is always new, to those who have
eyes to see and minds to think ; and the most
beaten track will never be vulgarised by the crowd,
will never lose whatever it has of intrinsic charm and
value, will furnish fresh and increasing interest at
each repeated visit, if only we bring with us the
sympathy and the alertness of observation without
which all travel is vain.   And there is this about
those days when we are allowed, perhaps, some new
and striking insight into the great things the world is
full of—that the charm and delight are not confined
to the moment.   They form for us a treasure of remembrance.   Nay, they come back to us, it may be,
in their force and meaning, when the present vision
has passed away.   Perhaps at the time we were not
able to compass and reduce to order the impressions pouring in upon us.   It is after-reflection which
drives them home, which makes them our own for
good, which makes us understand what we were
feeling, when we thought we were only gazing.   We
knew it not, perhaps, when we were going through
some new experience, or hearing some unaccustomed
voice, when some wonder of nature or genius was
shown to us—we were dull or weary or confused ;
but afterwards, it turns out to have been a turning-
point in our mental or spiritual history.   In these
things, as it has been said of higher things, " we feel

at the time "—feel without knowing all we do feel—
" we reason and recognise afterwards."

This, travel may do for us—for us, to whom it is
something secondary and incidental, not as to the
discoverer, the scope and work of his life.   It is a
break and interruption and temporary change ; an
interruption for us in that world, of which here it is
eminently true that

> Late and soon,
> Getting and spending, we lay waste our powers.[1]

It is a healthy interruption, it is a fruitful interruption,
which refreshes, and, if we will, purifies, by giving for
the time a fresh direction to interest and a fresh aim
to effort.   It opens to us the opportunity of turning to
simpler enjoyments, "to nobler loves and nobler cares."
Into the prosaic round of life, it brings in something
of the romantic, the adventurous, the impressive ; into
our monotony of comfort, it brings the discipline of
slight trials of patience and endurance, of slight surrenders of ease, of slight loss of importance.   And it
may furnish us not only with many pleasant hours as
they come, but with a store of delightful and precious
remembrances, which shall come back upon us in the
dust and heat of business to enlighten and cheer, in the
confusion and whirl of excitement to calm and warn.

2. I pass to the other part of my subject.   This is
what travel may do for us.   What ought we to do, that
its opportunities may not be thrown away ?   Three
things seem to me to impair and spoil the effect of
travel, both as a recreation and a discipline.   (1)
Frivolity and careless, aimless ignorance ; (2) The
opposite faults of unjust dislikes and unreal sympathies ;

---

[1] Wordsworth, Miscellaneous Sonnets, xxxiii.

and (3) The loosening of the bands of self-control, and the evil of forgetting, in the bustle and novelty round us, our recognised standard of duty and right.

1. There is the danger of frivolity ; and many who are not frivolous at home, think that they have nothing to do but to be frivolous abroad. And it is melancholy to see how, in the presence of the grandest and noblest spectacles, people may stand and gaze with eyes which cannot see, and minds unconscious of the interest before them. There may be good in the mere change of scene. But where there is so much more to be had of present and of permanent gain, it is a shame when for mere idleness and want of thought this gain is thrown away. Lazy, unintelligent travelling is like lazy reading : in reading, what we learn and what delights us is in proportion to what we bring of our own : " we receive but what we give " ; the page, which is flat and without meaning to the unprepared mind, or to the uncongenial or unawakened mood, comes out in light and power to the quickened thought which meets it half-way. And so among these new and unaccustomed scenes, in which we often feel ourselves so stupid and out of tune that we can notice nothing but the most contemptible trivialities, it is we, not they, that are in fault. We have come to them with listless and vacant minds, without having taken any trouble to fit ourselves for our new experience, without knowing what to look for, or what wealth of interest underlies the bare sights which meet our eye, or what other minds have seen and felt and thought in the presence of them. And we have no excuse. Books cannot take the place of travel, but they may help indefinitely the value and the oppor-

C.S.,P.   U

tunities of travel. Where formerly people saw nothing, or saw but vaguely and imperfectly, our generation may see, if it will. The great features of nature, the rocks and the mountains, the waters and the clouds, have been in a manner newly disclosed to us. The keen and discerning eyes of genius have studied them, and by painting and eloquent commentary our teachers have opened our eyes also. The masters of natural science, the historians, the poets, are all there to help us ; and they will tell us, too, that the man who goes abroad with his own special questions to pursue, and points of interest to watch, who under the outward pomp and grand irregularity of nature traces its hidden and constant laws or its mysterious affinities with human feeling, who passes beyond that he sees and admires to what men have done there—to the course of an eventful history, or the growth of a polity, or the characteristics of a social state—is as far above the crowd of his fellow-travellers in the noble-ness and keenness of his enjoyment as the understand-ing or discerning eye is above the eye which knows no meaning in what it sees. Unless we come with some-thing serious even in our play, unless we come with minds capable of being stirred, easily to be enlightened and widened, able to investigate and interpret and assimilate what is presented to our experience, the question must often be asked of us, when we find ourselves in famous cities or among the marvels of nature—" What are you doing here, idling, trifling, wasting time, where all is so out of proportion with your trifling, and rebukes it ?   Here you are come to see where men have been in earnest, have done or have suffered, where God has so displayed His glory and His awfulness,—why not have stayed at home, if you came only for vanity and aimless lounging ; if not to meet what you knew would meet you here, and honestly to do your best to recognise it ? "

2. We miss what we might gain, or we spoil it, by our want of equity or our ill-informed and hasty sympathy ; by our want of care and consideration in our comparisons and our judgments. We start with the natural illusion, but yet it is an illusion, that our standard is the standard for all the world. We find ourselves thrown among people whose whole experience of life, whose memories, whose associations, whose habitual thought on the deepest and gravest matters of human life, are widely different from our own. And we make one of two mistakes. The most common, naturally, is one of dislike and contempt. I know few things more painful than the way in which Englishmen sometimes forget in a foreign land the right to their own ways, their own customs—it may be their own fashions—of its inhabitants. We forget the great saying of the large-hearted Apostle— that God " hath made of one blood all nations of men for to dwell on all the face of the earth." We forget that they are at home in the land which God gave them as He gave us ours ; and that we are there simply for our own pleasure, and not because they want us. And so we miss what it might do us much good to learn, the special gifts, the special perfections, of power, of intellect, of moral quality, of character and temper, which God has bestowed on them in contrast to our own—some in which they leave us far behind and show a nobler ideal and more refined standard. And we forget further, very often, that

these foreigners, who are so unlike ourselves, belong,
as much as we do, to the brotherhood of Christian
people.   They are divided from us by ancient,
perhaps incurable, quarrels ; they have grown up
under a different tradition and discipline ; they worship in a way which we disapprove and shrink from ;
but if they are blind to the fact, yet *we* ought not to
be, that in that Creed, that Prayer, those Sacraments which make Christendom one, they with us
and we with them are together ; that they and we
go back to the same sacred and awful beginnings—to
Pentecost, to Calvary, to Bethlehem ; that they belong
to Christ our Lord as we do, that they die as we do
in the hope of His Resurrection.   But we are so
alive to our differences, broad and glaring doubtless
as many of them are, that we give scarcely a thought
to our agreement.   We pass through their churches
as if they were little better than idol fanes.   We
stand and look on with cold and almost insolent
unconcern on worship which embodies the devotion
of sincere and fervent hearts, and which they, however mistaken, mean and hope to be pleasing to
Christ.   We criticise with easy indifference, and
without troubling ourselves to understand them,
venerable rites which, with whatever accompanying
error or hurtful usage, have kept before the thoughts
and the hearts of men the memory of Christ's
Passion, through the lands of Europe and the
changeful centuries of its history.   Or we make
the opposite mistake,—more respectable, I think, in
its origin but as unreasonable and as injurious.
When we begin to understand their ways, their
meaning, their feelings, we think that we cannot do

better than at once to copy them. With the same
thoughtlessness, the same want of justice, with which
others impatiently condemn, we assert our superiority
to prejudice by indiscriminate admiration and unbalanced sympathy. We become partizans against
ourselves, against the assumptions, the ideas, the
feelings, the fashions, with which we were brought
up—partizans, with necessarily partial experience, a
shallow knowledge, and an essentially artificial and
false attitude of mind. It is not so, that contact
with foreign things and men must widen and enrich
our thoughts, whether on literature or manners or
religion : it is not by hasty fancies and self-willed
imitations that we are to correct the enormous fault
of self-complacency. To be true to ourselves, and
to what we have of good and noble, is not to be
confounded with prejudice. What we owe to those
among whom we are strangers is respect and justice :
respect, from a sense of the smallness of our knowledge and power of judging ; justice, because where
there is good, where there is superiority, we are bound
to recognise it. If deeper sympathies are to come,
let them come with larger and more cautious acquaintance, naturally, gradually, reasonably, not as
an unreasoning revolt against unreasoning dislikes.
But certainly it is not they who depreciate what is
their own—the familiar blessings and excellences
which they know and which have made them what
they are—who can justly set a value on the good
things of others.

3. And lastly, there is the danger accompanying
all intermission in the ordinary habits of life. We
are tempted to give ourselves the privilege of a

larger and unwonted liberty, and in the hurry and
bustle of novel ways we lose our bearings ; we let
ourselves be distracted and confused by the crowding
and changefulness of our impressions ; we allow our
vigilance over ourselves to be put to sleep ; we
accept as inevitable a dissipation and indolence of
mind of which we should be ashamed at home.
It is a perilous thing to most of us to feel ourselves out of the control of our accustomed restraints,
with all removed that insensibly reminded us of
law and duty and personal obligation ; to feel ourselves suddenly cast loose from the orderly system
of which we were part, having only ourselves to
please, with no ties to anything about us, with
nothing to shame us if we misuse our freedom.   And
further, in the break-up of habits, and the haste
of movement, and the rush of new objects, it is
difficult to keep that power over ourselves which
we need in relaxation as well as in work.   " Heaven
is as near us by sea as by land," was the intrepid
sailor's word in danger : heaven is as near us, amid
all that dazzles, or amazes, or repels us in a foreign
land, as in an English village ; as near us in its
claims, its citizenship, its holiness, its hopes.   And
woe to us if we forget it ; woe to any good or
delight of our travel if we allow anything new,
anything troublesome, to blot out, even for a time,
what we remember of it at home.   In whatever
way we find it most profitable to keep up that
remembrance, unless we make a law to ourselves,
in one manner or another to keep it up, to recall
the truths and the prayers by which we live in
England, we shall come back the worse for our

travelling, with our reverence for duty blunted and
enfeebled, with our standards of right deranged, with
our ideas of truth disturbed and shaken. And
surely, if we would only collect ourselves, if we
would only withdraw our minds for a time from
the importunate claims of visible novelty, there is
no place where we ought more keenly and deeply
to feel the presence of the Lord whom we worship
than in some famous spot where His hand has
passed in judgment, or is still open in magnificence and beauty ; no place more befitting the
seriousness of self-judgment and penitence than
when we are alone in the solitudes of the sea or
the desert ; no place where the mingled greatness
and littleness of man, and the love and righteousness
of God, prompt more naturally the great strains of
the *Te Deum* than in concert with the roar of
mighty torrents, or when morning breaks over the
silence of the everlasting hills.

And now the question may be asked, What has
all this to do with Christian preaching ? It has
this : that every real part of our life ought to be
part of our *Christian* life, and that Christian teaching
is within its sphere in dealing with anything that
is an important part of the discipline, the trial, the
opportunity of those with whom it has to do.
Here is a great department of the lives of thousands.
It may be an utter waste of time, or it may be
time spent to the greatest advantage. It has its
obvious openings and chances for good ; it has its
characteristic dangers and temptations. They are
things which exist in fact ; they do actually make
men better or worse, raise them in character or

corrupt them. It is not unsuitable to this place
to urge on Christians that what they do they should
do well, should do wisely and not unwisely. No
matter that the same thing is said by others in
other ways, and perhaps much better. If the sacredness of a place, or the solemnity of a holy hour,
could impress more strongly on men that for all
that makes life enjoyable and full of blessings, for
all that relieves its weariness and makes up here
for its disappointments and pain, for all leisure, and
ease, and light, and greatness, and beauty, all the
gifts of God, which the world seizes upon and turns
to evil—for all this they must give account ; that
in all this there is a real trial of character, and will,
and purpose ; a real training, not in phrase or fancy,
but by the very facts of life ; a real means, if they
will use it, of becoming more fit for service and usefulness, each in his vocation and ministry,—if lessons
which a moralist might give, may be driven more
home by being spoken under the shadow of the Cross
and amid the associations of the Lord's Resurrection
and triumph in heaven, the attempt may have been
worth making.

God has been very bountiful to us. " The earth
is the Lord's, and all that therein is : the compass
of the world, and they that dwell therein." Go
where we will, we find the tokens and reflections
of His perfection, the traces of His manifold gifts
and loving-kindness to man. It is but for a short
time, the time that we are as children here ; but
He grudges not the varied wonders which delight
us, and which ought to enlarge and refine our
souls. Can we not be wise enough, strong enough,

self-commanding enough, pure enough in intent and heart to use His great bounty without abusing it ; to use His gifts for the high ends for which they were placed within our reach ?—May they help us in our path to those good things past man's under-standing which He has prepared for them who here have learned to love Him. May they, like all His other benefits, prepare us for what we were meant for at last ; for what flesh and blood can never see—that end of all the changes and chances of this mortal life, of which it is written : " Thine eyes shall see the King in His beauty : they shall behold the land that is very far off."

RELIGIOUS DISAPPOINTMENTS[1]

"Art Thou He that should come, or do we look for another?"
ST. MATT. xi. 3.

WAS this message of the Baptist from his prison to our Lord for his own sake, or for the sake of his disciples? Was his own faith shaken, or did he only want to strengthen theirs? The question has been differently answered. The words at first sight seem to be those of disappointment and perplexity in him from whom they came. But on the other hand, it has seemed inconceivable that he whose life had been so wonderful, whose ministry so august and so powerful, who had seen signs and heard voices from heaven, and whose confession of Him who was to come had been so emphatic and so unwavering, could under any circumstances of adversity and trial become a doubter or a complainer,—could ever have been "offended" at Him to whom he had borne such witness. It has seemed incredible, according to the laws of human character; it has seemed irreverent to the memory of so great a saint, one whose greatness has been so signally attested by the Master

---

[1] Preached in Kentish Town Parish Church, 1874.

of Saints and Prophets.   How can we suppose such
a man's faith to have failed, or even to have been
disturbed ?

Yet the Bible is a record of the faith, even of
saints, failing in the hour of trial—failing, but yet
not lost for the failure.   John's great predecessor, he
whose word had shut up the heavens, and brought
down fire on the altar of Carmel, lost hope and
heart when, after all the tokens of God's presence,
he had to fly for his life to the wilderness of Mount
Sinai.   One greater than John in the Kingdom of
Heaven, the witness of his Master's power on the Lake
of Galilee and at the grave of Lazarus, the witness
of his Master's glory on the Holy Mount, he whom
not flesh and blood but the Father in Heaven had
taught to make that great confession which is the
rock on which the Church is built — Peter, fore-
warned, prayed for, strong in purpose, quailed
before the force of the meanest of his Master's foes,
and denied Him.   I do not see anything strange or
improbable in the supposition that John the Baptist
in his prison might have been for the time overcome
by disheartening thoughts, as Elijah was, as Peter
was.   To him the contrast was so immense between
the vastness of the prospects which he had announced
and the present realities of his condition ; between
the greatness of his beginnings, and what they had
seemed to end in.   At his birth were renewed the
miracles of the early days, the wonderful story of the
Forefather of his people, and his child of promise—
of Abraham and Sarah and Isaac.   At his birth, the
long dormant gift of prophecy revived : inspired lips
welcomed the child of miracle, as one who was to be the

Prophet of the Highest, "to go before the face of the
Lord to prepare His ways; to give knowledge of salvation unto His people, by the remission of their sins";
it was the first effect of that "tender mercy of our
God; whereby the day-spring from on high hath visited
us; to give light to them that sit in darkness and
in the shadow of death, to guide our feet into the
way of peace." Here was his call and mission; and
his life had answered to it. He had spent his youth
in solemn preparation and austere training for his
work. He had come, and his awful voice in the
desert had shaken all Judæa and Jerusalem and
drawn them to listen. Men of all classes, the
educated and the crowds, priests and teachers,
publicans and soldiers, had felt the edge of his stern
words, and had come to his baptism confessing their
sins. He had proclaimed the coming of the Kingdom
of Heaven; and he pointed out, standing among the
multitudes, the present King himself. Here were the
great beginnings and promise of his ministry. No
one for ages had seemed to take such hold on the
hearts of his people. The great restoration, of which
he was the herald and forerunner, seemed at the very
doors. He had seen, he had anointed, the mighty
promised Deliverer, whose fan is in His hand, who
should throughly purge His floor; he had been
allowed to bear record to the Son of God, whose shoe's
latchet he was not worthy to stoop down and unloose;
to announce the presence of the Lamb of God which
taketh away the sin of the world. Here was the
promise: what had been the fulfilment? What
.fruit had those opening days of enthusiastic hope
produced? Where was that Kingdom of Heaven

which he had ventured to proclaim as at hand?
Where was that Chosen One, whom he had so
confidently pointed out to his disciples, in whom he
recognised the Lamb of God, the Saviour of His
people and of the world? Those early days were
passed away. He himself, after stirring the hearts of
all men, after winning the confidence of the people,
after touching the conscience and gaining the ear of
Herod, had been stopped in his career, silenced by
the intrigues of a vindictive adulteress. And where
was the Kingdom of Heaven which he had announced?
To all human judgment, the Kingdom of Heaven had
not come. He whom his own faith had acknowledged so loyally, was wandering about, an obscure,
itinerant teacher, among the villages and wilds of
Galilee, scorned and hated as an ignorant pretender
by the wise and the pious of Jerusalem. What had
become of all these hopes? What had been
fulfilled of all these high and sublime assurances?
Had it all been but the dream of a heated and
hasty faith, wildly shattered by the hard certainties
of the real world? If Peter's faith failed him, with
his Lord at his side, does it seem strange that
John the Baptist in his prison, apparently forgotten,
unprotected, forsaken, should send to ask, in perplexity and distress—"*Art* Thou He that should
come, or do we look for another?"

I own that to me his doubt and perplexity seem
very real and very natural ; and not only so, but
very instructive, and that in his doubt we have a
most valuable lesson. For in his discouragement at
the outward prospect of things which met his eye,
and which he could not fathom, he did what he ought

to have done. If he was perplexed, if his faith was
shaken by it, yet he did not despair. He did not
sink as low as Peter did, or the rest of the Apostles.
In his distress, he appealed to Him whom he had
such good reason to trust. He appealed to Him
whose greatness he had once known, though now it
was no longer present to his eyes—the Master whom
he had recognised with such unselfish loyalty. And
his Master sent him back words of strength and comfort, which might well encourage him to wait patiently,
and through all darkness and suffering to abide the end.

It is, I say, a lesson—a lesson very parallel in
what it shows and teaches to what happens in all
times. We have in it an example of religious disappointment and discouragement, and how it was
dealt with. And as long as the world lasts, as long
as it is the time of faith and not of sight, the time
of beginnings of which we may not see the end, as
long as difficulty, failure, perplexity are part of our
discipline and probation, we shall have to lay our
account for meeting with disappointment about religion, and to deal wisely with its causes and impressions. John, I think we may say, was disappointed.
He had hoped, and reasonably hoped, great things,
great results from the ministry he was charged with,
and the cause in which he was engaged ; and his hopes
appeared to have come to nothing. Instead, he had
seemed to reap more than an ordinary measure of
ill-success. I suppose that such a feeling is the feeling of many—the feeling, at times, perhaps, of every
one who thinks at all—about the general result of religion in the world. Religion is so great in its ideas :
it is so partial and imperfect in fulfilling them. Its

words of promise are so magnificent and unstinted,—
promises of forgiveness, of cleansing, of victory, of
restoration, of improvement, of elevation, of joy, of
peace ; yet in the plain matter-of-fact realities of life
and character, they seem on a large scale to come on
the whole to so little.   Its pledges of grace and
strength are so boundless ; yet why are men still so
weak—why is goodness, not to say saintliness, so rare ?
Its rules of living, its standard of motive and action, are
pitched as high as they can be, and are exemplified
in the Holiest and most adorable of Lives ; but to
how few is the Sermon on the Mount and St. Paul's
description of charity the real law of conduct ?   And
then, again, consider the descriptions of religion in
the Bible, the prospects which prophecy holds up before us, the anticipations to which the language of
prophecy has always given rise, the loftier and more
spiritual interpretation put on them in the New
Testament : what might it not have seemed reasonable, in the days of the Apostles, to look forward to,
of the victories of religion ; what might they not have
hoped for, from the gifts of Pentecost, the labours of
preachers, the sufferings of saints and martyrs.

And yet, what has been achieved, how short of the
great ideal; how chequered and unlike its beginnings,
has been the history of the Church.   The Kingdom of
God was promised, it was said to have actually come
—come, in the hearts and souls of men—come, in its
empire in the world ; but we look about us, and instead of the Kingdom of God as portrayed by
Prophets and Apostles, we see the old familiar imperfect condition of mankind, swaying still between
good and evil, between improvement and corruption ;

still full of passions unsubdued, and suffering unabated
and uncomforted ; still inconsistent, unregenerate, unreformed ; still, "through fear of death, subject to
bondage"; as if no such things had happened as the
Incarnation and Passion of the Son of God, or the
presence in the world of the Eternal Spirit of holiness
and power. The wise still turn foolish, and the
brave show cowardice, and the trusted betray their
trust, and the good turn out weak and poor, and
character deteriorates, and each man seems to meet
his fatal temptation at last ; and we see old age, instead of being refined and purified by experience,
showing greater fretfulness and selfish attachment to
the world ; and parties and causes which once were
noble and lofty dwindle away into factions, and
pettiness, and ignoble failure. We expect to be disappointed in the world ; but to be disappointed in
what has come to heal and save the world, this is
bitterness indeed. Were we mistaken in our hopes ?
Is there any Divine Power really among men, such
as the Gospel assures us of ? Is the Kingdom of God
really come into the world ? Or must we look for
something better ?

To these misgivings and anxieties there is more
than one answer. But the words which our Lord
sent back to John the Baptist suggest one which
appeals to those very impressions, made by the facts
of life, from which our disappointment springs.
"Go and show John again those things which ye do
hear and see : the blind receive their sight, and the
lame walk, the lepers are cleansed, and the deaf
. hear, the dead are raised up, and the poor have the
Gospel preached to them. And blessed is he,

whosoever shall not be offended in Me." As if He had said—There is doubtless, in what men see in Me and in My ways, much at which they may be surprised, shocked, perplexed. I am not here, now, to explain all this. But if they will look, they will see something else too : they will see all round Me, in the train of the Son of Man, power, and love, and compassion, and grace, and consolation, for the very meanest and most hopeless, for men's suffering and their sins, such as never were seen in the world before. That is a sight to appeal to men's serious reason, to their affections, to their higher nature and nobler thoughts, infinitely more than My present humiliation, and what seems to them weakness and failure, ought to arouse their fears. You look at the one, look also at the other. When you are astonished and offended at not seeing in Me more which is great according to the world's measure, ask yourselves whether this world ever before saw anything so wonderful and so new on the side of goodness and blessing as what I have brought into it, or anything so worthy of One coming with a message from God of reconciliation and hope ?

And such is the answer to religious disappointment and discouragement still. Religion is still enveloped in those humiliations and contradictions of our mortal condition, which in the days of His flesh clouded the glory of the Son of God. As He was, so are we in the world. Flesh and blood could not discern through His veil of abasement and obscurity those Divine and unearthly features of unique and amazing perfection which the good and honest heart of patient faith caught at last

—caught, and welcomed, and adored. It is not wonderful that we, too, are perplexed and distressed at much that meets us at first sight—much that meets us even after deeper looking. But if sight, and experience, and history have anything at all to tell us, they have something more to show us than unachieved hopes and unfulfilled promises. When we are discouraged by not seeing all we should wish to see, let us consider all that we should not see— of blessing, of goodness, of hope, familiar to us as our daily bread—if the Kingdom of God were not with us. We have now behind us a history of more than eighteen centuries. Take the world—the moral world of man and human character—at the beginning, and then in the progress and end, of those centuries, and see whether, with every allowance for immense and oppressive failure, the grace of the Redeemer of mankind has not left its ineffaceable marks, and wrought profound and permanent changes, on all that concerns the motives and actions of men, on all the purposes and laws and aims of human life. Turn away from the near and immediate details, which look so large because they are close to us, and affect us so keenly because they are personal, and look at the course of things on a large scale. What would a man of the old world, standing on the threshold of Christian history, have said, if he could have foreseen the changes, the reformations of every kind of which Jesus Christ has been the source? Translate those words of our Lord about His acts of mercy and recovery to men's bodies, into a moral meaning, as pointing to what He has done for the souls, the minds, the moral energies of

men.   Apply them to the moral changes in societies,
the conversion of nations, the reclaiming to order
of hopeless barbarism, the amelioration of degraded
conditions and classes, the care of the poor, the
extinction of slavery.   Apply them to Christian
influences or individuals—the elevation of the ideal
of character, the purification of the affections, the
introduction into life of nobler aims, the reclaiming
of sinners, the power of moral change, that most
amazing of new things of the Gospel—the zeal for
seeking and saving the lost, the deep and increasing
and widening sympathy for every form of human
suffering—the new devotion, new first in Christianity,
to the service of the poor—the characteristic enthusiasm, born and cherished in Christianity, for the
spread of truth and light, for education, for building
up the souls and characters of the young.   Apply
them to the inner history of the spiritual life—to
what the grace of Christ has done in awakening
conscience, in breaking through the blinding self-
deceit of sin, in cleansing from the growths of moral
defilement, in strengthening moral feebleness, in restoring to life souls dead, as St. Paul calls it, in
trespasses and sins.   Apply them to facts of experience, which, whatever else has changed since He
was here, have not changed.   Still from Him comes
the purity and trust and joy of holy homes and holy
lives.   Still from Him comes the softening* and
subduing grace, which can break and then heal the
disobedient heart, which can restore it to sincerity
and peace.   Where, but to the loving sternness of
the Cross, where but to the outstretched arms of the
Crucified and His Ineffable Sacrifice, where but to

His awful fellowship with us in pain and death, does
the parting soul, whose day is over—do the eyes that
are closing on the world—turn with imploring hope,
in the wrench of separation and amid the horrors
of dying,[1] in presence of the undisclosed and impenetrable mysteries that lie behind the grave?
And may not our Lord still send the dispirited and
the despondent, as He sent His disheartened servant
of old, to the realities which He, and He alone, has
introduced into this provisional state of time and
incompleteness?   Since He has been here, blind men
see again, and lame men walk, lepers are cleansed,
and deaf hear, dead men are raised, and poor men
have the message of glad tidings told them.

Our days, we say, are unsettled and anxious, and
full of perplexity and alarm.   They are so ; but let
us remember this—there never was a time in the
history of Christendom and religion when the days
were not so.   Each generation has its trials, and if
we have ours, our fathers, we may be quite sure, had
theirs, which looked as formidable.   Meanwhile each
century as it passes brings new and accumulating
testimony to the power and the vitality of those
seeds of light and goodness which the Great Sower
has planted in His field, this world.   Again and
again they spring up afresh, in new blessing and
beauty ; again and again new and varied forms of
excellence and self-devotion appear ; again and
again, after languor and corruption, Christianity
asserts its inexhaustible energy of recovery, of improvement, and advance.   There have been days
when it seemed as if men might despair, as if it were

1 " Malheureusement, pour être mort, il faut mourir."—Henri Perreyve.

all over with the hopes of man and the cause of
truth and God. But the time has never yet been,
when the cure came not at last to rebuke despair.
It is natural, amid the confusions and troubles of
life—it is natural to be disquieted, it is natural to
fear. The saints of old felt the same perplexities as
we do, and were oppressed by the same misgivings.
The discipline of their Master had for its end, to teach
them patience, to teach them to wait, to teach them
that *here* they must not expect to see the end. But
it taught them, too, that though all things seemed
against them, God was surely with them. John
the Baptist seemed to have wasted his strength in
vain, to end his days in ignoble ruin. He knew
not that he was the first soldier in the mightiest
of conquering armies, and that what to men
seemed a miserable death was to God a glorious
martyrdom. In his story, in his perplexity, in the
message sent to him, we have the lesson, as old as
the world, of faith against sight—faith in what is
worth believing and worth waiting for, against the
importunity of present defeat and failure. " Art
Thou He that should come ? " is a question many a
time asked since John asked it—asked, as he probably asked it, in despondency and distress.—Judge
for yourselves, is the answer, where such power on
the side of good and blessing, where such unexampled love, where sources of mercy and help-
fulness so energetic, so efficacious, so persistent,
could come from. Is not St. Peter's the true, the
only conclusion—"Lord, to whom shall we go?
Thou hast the words of Eternal Life."

XIX

A PARTICULAR PROVIDENCE [1]

> " Lord, what is man, that Thou hast such respect unto him : or the son
> of man, that Thou so regardest him ? Man is like a thing of nought :
> his time passeth away like a shadow."—PSALM cxliv. 3, 4.

PASCAL describes, with his usual force and directness,
the feelings which sometimes come on a man, when,
releasing himself from his acquiescence in the commonplaces of life, he contemplates his place and
existence on the earth, and asks himself—Where am
I ? Who put me here ? Is there any one over me,
whom I cannot see, but yet with whom I have to
do ? " I know not," he says, representing this feeling,
" who brought me into the world, nor what the world
is, nor what I am myself. I am in a terrible ignorance about everything. I know not what my body
is, nor my senses, nor what my soul is, nor even this
very part of me which thinks that which I am saying,
which reflects on everything and on myself, and
yet which knows not itself any more than all the rest.
I behold these frightful spaces of the universe which
encompass me, and I find myself tied down to a
corner of this vast expanse, without knowing why I

[1] Preached in Lincoln's Inn Chapel, 1884.

am set in this place rather than in another, nor why
this little time, which is given me to live, is fixed to
this point rather than another, of all the eternity
which has been before me and which comes after
me.   I see nothing but what is boundless on all
sides—infinities which shut me in like an atom, and
like a shadow which lasts but a moment and never
comes back.   All that I know is that I must soon
die ; but what I know least about is that very death
which I cannot avoid." [1]

Something like this must, I think, come occasionally with a kind of surprise and shock over the mind
of any one who thinks—who holds it worth while to
think—about his place here, and lets himself do so.
The world is all about us early and late, and its
films of custom meet our eyes day after day unchanged ; but sometimes they break, and we seem
to see ourselves, standing all alone in existence,
beset with questions to which custom and experience
have no answer to give.   We absolutely lose ourselves in our beginnings and our end ; now in the

---

[1] Pascal, ii. p. 9 (Faugère).   Cf.: " There is no doubt that of all
earthly creatures Man is the most important to us, yet we know less
of him than any other.   His history is more interesting than natural
history ; but natural history, though obscure, is much more intelligible than man's history, which is a tale half told, and which,
even when this world's course is run, and when, as some think,
man may compare notes with other rational beings, will still be
a great mystery, of which the beginning and the end are all that
can be known to us while the intermediate parts are perpetually
filled up.   So now pray excuse me if I think that the more grovel-
ling and materialistic sciences of matter are not to be despised in
comparison with the lofty studies of Minds and Spirits.   Our own
and our neighbours' minds are known but very imperfectly, and no
new facts will be found till we come in contact with some minds other
than human to elicit them by counter-position."—J. Clerk Maxwell
(1851), *Life*, pp. 159, 160.

present, indeed, we see and feel and think and act ;
but even now, where is the spring of all this, and
whence comes it ?   How came we to be what we
are ?   What shall we be in the time to come ?
What a great part, growing vaster the more we think
of it, has what we call accident had in all that has
brought us hither—this point of *now*, which seems to
be the convergence and result of countless lines of
forces known and unknown ?   And the tremendous
thought emerges, with even sickening keenness, in
its challenge—Which is it ?   Am I taken care of by
One who knows me, and whose care of me is like my
care for my children ?   Or am I indeed alone and
left all to myself in the world ?

   To these dreary questionings religion is the
answer ; except as the answer, religion has no
meaning.   A creed, a theory of the origin and order
of the world is not necessarily religion ; but whatever the case with other men, no religious man ever
doubted that he had a direct and immediate relation
to God, that he was God's choice and handiwork
and care.   Religion, in its earliest and in its most
perfect form, rests on this faith, as the first axiom
and foundation for all that it feels and hopes and
speaks and does and endures.   From the earliest
Patriarchs to the latest Apostle, from the words
spoken to or spoken by Abraham and Jacob, to the
dauntless and amazing confidence of St. Paul, standing
alone against the world, the same certainty is taken
for granted, the same profound conviction breathes ;—
from the words of promise to Abraham, " Fear not,
Abram : I am thy shield, and thy exceeding great reward "—and " in thee shall all families of the earth

be blessed," to St. Paul, contemplating the purpose
of his life :—" Paul, a servant of Jesus Christ, called
to be an apostle, separated unto the Gospel of God"; or
looking back on it, through the tumults of its course
and the uncertainties of its apparent results—" I know
whom I have believed, and am persuaded that He is
able to keep that which I have committed unto Him
against that day." It is the same, we know, through
that varied history of religion which the Bible has
saved from the wrecks of the ages, never to let the
world again forget its witness, whether believed or
not, that He who called man into being cares for
him. And there is one marvellous and unique book,
in which religious faith has bloomed and flowered
into the most manifold and unlooked-for forms of
emotion and affection, which with strange completeness represents all that is truest and deepest in
the soul, every shade of its gloom and fear, every
flash of its joy and love, which gives back every
note through the whole scale of feeling, in its
stormiest and wildest and most dangerous moods,
as well as in its most serene and glad and happiest
—a book in which every man, at one time or another,
has found the words which he wanted as he could
find them nowhere else. In the Psalter, men do
not take for granted only or believe, they "*live* and
move and have their being," in the faith that God
is over them and with them, about their path and
about their bed, understanding their thoughts long
before. "Whom have I in heaven but Thee: and
there is none upon earth that I desire in comparison of
Thee." "Nevertheless I am alway by Thee : for Thou
hast holden me by my right hand." "O my soul,

thou hast said unto the Lord, Thou art my God, my
goods are nothing unto Thee. . . . I have set God
alway before me : for He is on my right hand,
therefore I shall not fall." Such words represent
the feeling of religion, in its natural expression in
the Psalms. No greater contrast can be imagined
between this assured confidence of being watched over
and cared for, and that sense of desolate solitariness,
like a child lost in the wilderness, described by Pascal.

And I need not say that this assumption, which
pervades every line of the Book of Psalms, is also
the assumption of the Sermon on the Mount, is also
the basis of the whole ministry among us of the
Son of God, of the action of the Holy Spirit on
human character, and of the whole faith of all
religious men in every prayer they utter,—the
assumption that God has not only done and
purposed great things for the race, for the Church,
for His chosen and elect ones, but that for every
individual soul His eye is ever on it, His hand is over
it, His care and sympathy are certain. The very
hairs of our head are numbered by Him without
whom a sparrow falls not to the ground. Great and
least make no difference with Him ; of " these little
ones " their angels always behold the face of the
Father in heaven ; the one wandering sheep is of as
much account as the ninety-nine ; the cup of cold
water given to the least is marked and remembered.
It is not the will of the Father that one of these
little ones, the unknown and neglected ones, should
perish : first and last here, may in His judgment
mean something very different. And in this confidence in His care, we pray our familiar daily prayer,

that He would defend us by His mighty power, and
grant that this day we fall into no sin, neither run
into any kind of danger ; but that all our doings may
be ordered by His governance to do always that is
righteous in His sight, through Jesus Christ our Lord.

We know, confessedly, so little and so partially,
that it is not astonishing that difficulties as to this
view of God's relations to men present themselves.
They arise from different considerations.   They arise
from our ideas of justice and fairness compared with
experience. They arise from our ideas of fixed and unchanging law, as the only real and intelligible order of
the world, which cannot bend or deviate to individual
needs.   But they arise also from a defective power in
the human mind of conceiving such an ever-active
presence—continual, vigilant, beneficent, judicial.   I
shall not say anything of the first two sources of
objection, because the difficulties raised in them
reach much farther than to God's care for individuals :
they reach to, and claim to bar, the whole religious
conception of God.   I assume that God is, whatever
appearances may threaten my belief, and however
the logic of our reasonings entangle themselves in
the counter - currents of will and necessity, of
personality and law.   I assume that God is, in the
most real sense, the God of righteousness and mercy
and loving-kindness to the world which He has made.
But the question for me is, Is He this *to me ?* Unless
He is, what is it to me that great things are done for
the world and the race, if I am left, a forgotten
waif, to take my chance, unnoticed and unthought
of, on the vast " sea of being "?   But if this is
not so—if I am not forgotten—then I am, as

much as anything else in the world, remembered
by Him, taken care of. This is the doctrine,
as it is called, of a particular providence. And
what an overwhelming—to many, what an inconceivable—thought! To minds formed and trained
like ours, accustomed to make distinctions and
comparisons between great and small, important
and insignificant, that God should care for our earth
in any way is difficult to our sense and idea of
proportion. In the Book of Psalms we find the
earliest expression of this sense of the tremendous
contrast;—man and the immensity of the heavens
—" I will consider Thy heavens—the work of
Thy fingers : the moon and the stars, which Thou
hast ordained. What is man, that Thou art
mindful of him ? "—God and the nothingness of
man's life—" Lord, what is man, that Thou hast
such respect unto him . . . man is like a thing
of nought : his time passeth away like a shadow."
It seems impossible that God should occupy Himself
seriously and deeply—so seriously and deeply as our
needs require and as our Creed represents—with one
so infinitely small portion of His creation, a portion
which our senses, our severest science, our most precise
calculations assure us is but like a grain of sand to
the wilderness, or a drop of water to the sea. It
was a difficulty in the olden days, when this earth
was the centre of the universe, and was thought to
be in reality, as it seems to human experience, the
one scene and object of the care of heaven. But the
difficulty is now much enhanced, as our knowledge
has expanded the idea of the universe, and expanded
also to thought and imagination the idea of God.

From even the conception, magnificent as it is, of the Psalm—" In His hand are all the corners of the earth: and the strength of the hills is His also.   The sea is His, and He made it: and His hands prepared the dry land "—what an interval to the new worlds and new suns of modern astronomy!   God's Infinity, the mind pursues it in vain beyond space which has no end, the *flammantia mœnia* of the universe.

> Worlds,
> To which the heaven of heavens is but a veil.[1]

God's Eternity must have seen, and must be yet to see, countless *œons* vaster and more wonderful than ours. God's Omniscience knows all and always, both Himself and all that is not Himself, ranging to what we call the utmost extent of His kingdom, and down to its lowest depths and most infinitesimal divisions.   God's Almighty Power and Absolute Wisdom must find far greater and more amazing scope than things connected with our little transient world, to which we in our thoughts so exclusively confine them.   That He in any way should have busied Himself about " us men and our salvation," is a faith to which our measurements here, and familiarity with what is real and actual, find it not easy to accommodate themselves. But that He who is beyond the sun, beyond the first morning, is *here, to-day, with me,* this very moment watching me, guarding me, guiding me, judging me, loving me—the mind reels under the tremendous juxtaposition of the necessity of His immensity and my nothingness.

This   is   a   difficulty   which   often   impresses

---

[1] Wordsworth, Preface to *The Excursion.*

men, when their minds disengage themselves from the traditional and the verbal, affecting them in various ways—harassing, tempting, or paralysing them. But it seems to me to resolve itself, as many difficulties do, into a difficulty not of the reason but of the imagination. It is none the less serious for that, in beings like ourselves, who are swayed so much by that strange power of the mind—so keen, so fickle, often so uncontrollable, so unaccountable. But it is a difficulty of the same kind as that which made it so hard to think that the earth moved, that the heavens stood still. It is a difficulty not of the reason, but of the imagination, which gives to so many mathematical certainties the air of paradox.

Imagination stands for very different things. It is common to think of it as only something wild, lawless, extravagant. Of course it may be this ; but it is also really a most prosaic and business-like faculty. " That forward, delusive faculty," says Bishop Butler, "ever obtruding beyond its sphere " ; yet nowhere has it been more called upon to widen men's thoughts than in the reasonings of his great argument.[1] Nothing is more common than to say that men are cruel, or unjust, or stupid, because they have not enough imagination to see things as they are—to see what the abuses which they tolerate involve, or to open their eyes to the absurd, or to anticipate the inevitable. " What he had previously

---

[1] Cf. Pascal, ii. pp. 47, 48 (Faugère)—" C'est cette partie décevante dans l'homme, cette maîtresse d'erreur et de fausseté, et d'autant plus fourbe qu'elle ne l'est pas toujours. . . .

" Cette superbe puissance ennemie de la raison, qui se plaît à la controler et à la dominer pour montrer combien elle peut en toutes choses, a établi dans l'homme une seconde nature."

only *known*," says the historian, speaking of a great
disaster fully breaking on a man's mind,[1] " he now
both knew and imagined." Imagination is at once
the most misleading and the most truth-bringing of
mental powers. It amuses us with dreams ; and it
brings before us the realities for which words are
imperfect or feeble equivalents. It is that which
gives the power of holding together in thought a vast
and intricate system, or the composition of forces and
their reciprocal play, or the balancings and counter-
poises and compensations of a subtle argument. It
deludes, no doubt, the enthusiast and the theoriser;
it inveigles the story-teller ; it plays tricks with the
average careless thinkers among men ; but it serves,
as nothing else can, the mathematician, the discoverer,
the man of science, the statesman, as much as it serves
the poet and the artist. It translates formulas into
that which the mind sees and holds fast. It raises a
name or a symbol or an abstraction to a new and
higher power, to a real and substantial thing, to a
living whole. Give it a substantial basis, and the
idea of it almost coincides with the Apostolic definition
of faith, as the faculty by which we behold the future
and the invisible, " the substance of things hoped for,
the evidence of things not seen."

It is a failure of imagination which in this case
makes the difficulty. We do not bring to the
mastery of the great question the completed equipment of our complex mental organisation : we leave
out that strange and powerful inward faculty, which
sees when the eye-sees not, and hears when the ear
hears not, and feels and touches when nothing material

---

[1] Kinglake's *Invasion of the Crimea*, vol. vi. p. 291.

sends its signals to the brain ; which fills our ab-
stractions with reality and life.   It is a dull and short-
sighted imagination, carrying our familiar comparisons
of great and small into the Infinite and the Eternal,
which makes us think it disproportionate to God's
majesty that He, being so high, should have " respect
unto the lowly."   It is our power of imagination
which is at fault, when it shocks us to bring Him
from the Throne of the universe, from the farthest
bounds of His Empire, to be the Father of the father-
less and Guide of the wanderer, to the pauper's sick-
bed and the petty troubles of the school-boy.   It is
not reason.   Why should He, who made and sees
and upholds all things, *not* care for the least thing
that His love and wisdom thought good to make ?
Would not dry reason say that if He made, He was
not only *capable* of caring, He *must* care ?   How
could it be otherwise if God is what is meant by
the name of God, and not a formula or a blind force
or mechanism ?   What is it to reason, in a matter
like this—the difference between small and great,
between the multitude and the few ?   What is the
difference, before the mysterious Creator of both, between the smallest atom and the vastest system ?   The
absurdity, in the eye of reason, is that He who was
able to call the countless multitudes of beings out
of nothing, should ever lose sight of one of them.
You say that you cannot take it in.   Your imagination, confined to the experience of this present state,
fails in the effort.   But have you called on your
imagination to exert its powers in the presence of
so tremendous and stimulating an idea as this idea
of the Living God ?   Because neither we, nor any

intelligence that you can conceive of, could attend
at once to the myriad purposes of His universe at
infinitely distant points, cannot you imagine the
possibility of *His* doing so, who is above all created
and all conceivable intelligence? Because it is not
wholesome for you to care for trifles, and lose yourself in attempting to follow what is beyond your
ken, is He so limited of whom we say in words, that
" His wisdom is infinite "? Let us put meaning and
reality into our words, and, though many problems
remain unsolved, many questions remain unanswered
and unanswerable, this, at least, disappears, that our
insignificance is any reason why God should not
care for us. Yes, let us open our eyes and see.
Does God *not* care for things because they are small
and perish? Does He, in fact, show His hand less
in the flower and insect than in the vast law of life
which binds together all living things, than in those
laws of force and order and measure upon which the
visible world depends? *Is* He really more wonderful
in the sun, in the light, in the stars, than in the
infinities of littleness, which escape our eye ; in the
microscopic shell, so perfect and beautiful in its
countless patterns ; or in the primitive animal or
vegetable cell, pregnant with all the future powers
and qualities of life; in the intangible but scientifically
necessary molecule ; in the imponderable agents of
nature ; in the unreached springs of human thought,
—by which He builds up all we are, and lays the
ground for all we do? If present everywhere, why
not present to each soul on its course ;—present in
His moral attributes, in His mercy, in His love, in
His righteousness, in His patience ;—present in His

care and discipline, nurturing the heathen, teaching
man knowledge, we know not how, according to
each man's case ?   He who is Lord of all these worlds,
of all these souls, why should it be thought a thing incredible that He should know them all by name ; that
He should, since *He is able*, guard, direct, help them ?
What is their *number* to Him to whom magnitude
is nothing, and who dwells in His own immensity ?
To reason, to believe that He cares for the least is
as easy as to believe that He cares for the greatest.
It is not reason, it is poverty and feebleness of
imagination, which is afraid to give Him the government of the creatures He has cared to make, which
shrinks from the instinct which leads us in hours of
trouble to put ourselves in His hands, and raises the
misgiving that it cannot be that He regards and
sympathises with us.

It is not reason but imagination—imagination
narrowed and dulled by the unresisted influences
of what we daily see and hear.   But imagination
may remedy what imagination has maimed and
injured.   Imagination may, if we will, put us on a
fair level with reason ; it may help us, if we will give it
fair play, to raise and widen our thoughts to spheres
worthy of the subject—help us to realise possibilities
and likelihoods against which sight and sense and
the experience growing out of them pronounce.
We are not talking of common things, of things as
they are on the ordinary level of this world, when
we talk of the ways of God.   We are talking of
One who surely must be as infinitely wonderful in
His dealings with souls as He is visibly seen to be
in the universe of nature.   Nothing in nature that

our knowledge has discovered, putting aside the
mere element of magnitude, is more wonderful
than the soul and spirit of man ;[1] and not according
to the limitations of our material life, not by the
laws of time and place and magnitude, can we
suppose God, who is the Father of Spirits, to visit
and order the souls that He has made.   We cannot
see Him.   We cannot follow Him.   We cannot say
for certain, that *here* or *there* His hand has shown
itself.   Our age has rightly learned to be more
reserved and cautious than ever, in definitely inter-
preting God's judgments ; we are more sensible than
our fathers always were of the mystery that en-
velops them, of the difference between God's knowledge and ours, of the danger and the mischief of
mistakes.   In one case only, in our own, we may
venture to think that we can sometimes almost
discern the nearness of His hand :—in strange dim
ways, indeed, which to no one could mean anything
but to ourselves—to ourselves only, in that mysterious
assurance that tells us that a presence is near us,
even in the dark.   We cannot tell to others, we
cannot prove it to them, or expect them to accept
it ; but we may *feel* ourselves, how God's eye has
been upon our life and history, ruling it in mercy
and in judgment ; how He has been there, in saving
us from ourselves and doing us good that we did not

[1] Not Chaos, not
The darkest pit of lowest Erebus,
Nor aught of blinder vacancy, scooped out
By help of dreams—can breed such fear and awe
As fall upon us often when we look
Into our Minds, into the Mind of Man.
                    Preface to *The Excursion.*

want, in adjusting, with strange and awful equity, just the deserved retribution to our mistakes and sins. We do not know enough to trace His providence in the lives of others ; but in our own, many *do* know enough to recognise His wisdom, His kindness, His justice, in the prayer refused to be more than compensated, in the stern blow turned into blessings, in the unexpected help at critical times of need—it may be in the fulfilment of the weird saying of the Psalmist, " He gave them their desire, and sent leanness withal into their souls." What is it that has, perhaps, so obstinately accompanied us in our temptations to do wrong? What is it that has so inexplicably baffled and resisted and balked us, time after time, on the very edge of sin ? Whence have come those persistent warnings, more impressive than conscience, at the most unexpected times, from the most unlikely quarters, startling us as if they came from some one who knew our thoughts, unveiling ourselves to ourselves, showing us the precise self-deception which was beguiling us ? Is the Psalmist unreasonable when he cries out, " My times are in Thy hand"? Is the promise an unmeaning one, " I will guide thee with Mine eye "? Is the augury groundless, " It is He that teacheth man knowledge, shall not He punish"? Is his hope idle and vain when he says, " Into Thy hands I commend my spirit : for Thou hast redeemed me, O Lord, Thou God of truth"?

The vicissitudes of life, its anxiety, its depression, its pains, await us all. And when they come, then, to thinking men, there are but the two great alternatives. Is all a blank, incomprehensible, horrible, far more strange to reason than even the greatest perplexities which surround the moral government of God ; or is it, as the Book of Psalms represents the world and life—God in the midst of us, God with us, taking part though we see Him not, in all that concerns and interests men, in the strife and fate of kingdoms, in the joys and praises of the saints, in the fears and troubles of the poor and the sinner? It will be well for us, before our trial comes, that we have made up our minds by which to stand ; whether, in this world, at once so bright and so dark—bright with beauty and genius and affection, dark with ignorance and sin and death—we can find no guidance but our own, or whether we can take refuge in the care and providence of God, and rest under the shadow of His wings ; whether we are " strangers in a strange land," or whether we are here for our appointed time, in our appointed and guarded home, among the many homes of God. May our lot be that of the Psalmist, to rest, in our trouble or success, in joy and pain, in life and in death, on that great conviction, than which there is no other stay and foundation for the soul—" Whom have I in heaven but Thee : and there is none upon earth that I desire in comparison of Thee. My flesh and my heart faileth : but God is the strength of my heart, and my portion for ever."

THE GREAT RESTORATION [1]

" For, behold, I create new heavens and a new earth : and the former shall not be remembered, nor come into mind."—ISAIAH lxv. 17.

THE Bible and human experience agree in this : that they regard the condition of the world as one of great disorder, with constant tendencies to degeneration and decay, but also as a condition in which disorder and decay are kept in continual check, by remedies, improvement, renewal. " The earth our habitation," says Bishop Butler, " has the appearance of being a ruin." But it is not a ruin consigned to despair and hopeless wreck. It is a ruin where the work of the rebuilder more than overtakes the work of the destroyer. There are no doubt ruins which no effort can now repair, fixed and irretrievable. But we look at them with awe, and are thankfully conscious that we are not concerned in those terrible played-out scenes of human history. However much we may have to correct and amend, the way of amendment is still one of our unforfeited possessions. This among the many

[1] Preached at the reopening of St. George's Church, Botolph Lane, 1884.

contradictions of our mortal state is one of the
lessons of experience ; and it is a lesson which
suggests and justifies hope.   It opens before us the
reasonable prospect of real and solid progress : of
an indefinite strengthening of the healing and restoring processes, of a restraining and weakening of
the tendencies which injure society, perhaps of the
extinction of some.   But the Bible goes beyond this.
It holds up before us indeed, as history does, these
two great points of our state here—the actual fact,
the sustaining hope.   It sets before us decay on one
side, repair and new life on the other.   It sets before
us ruin, no doubt, vast and terrible and recurring ;
but also remedies for it, unexpected and amazing,
influences of healing which evil cannot tire out and
which can cope with its mischief.   Experience and
Scripture unite in putting before us this picture ;
but the Bible holds up to us, what history and
experience cannot—what nothing in the appearances
of this world can warrant even to the most
sanguine—the promise of something final and complete.   Imperfection is now at the best the law of
all that is done on this earth ; and, at last, a final
passing away, through dreary steps of pain and
weakness, is the appointed course of all existence on
it, the highest and the lowest.   But the Bible, in
addition to the support which it gives to our belief
in the mighty powers of recovery in the world that
now is, tells us, in the name of God, of something
beyond all we can know or even see here, which
shall " repair the wastes of time," and accomplish the
destiny of God's creation.   The great forces of
restoration which we see at work under all the dis-

advantages of our confused and crippled condition, are to have their victory at last. "The creature itself also, shall be delivered from the bondage of corruption into the glorious liberty of the children of God."

In this great restoration which the Bible expresses in so many ways, there are two distinct things involved: the process itself by which God is preparing for it ; and the end and result of it. The one belongs to this world ; the other to the world to come.

1. The steps to what St. Peter calls "the restitution of all things," are made here. We are still in the midst of those ruins of God's work, that anarchy, that contradictory and confused world, which has grown out of the revolt of free and responsible wills against the Divine law of right. Darkness and ignorance and self-will and passion have made havoc of man's moral nature. The gulf of separation between man and the Unseen and Most Holy appears at every turn. But all the while, amid all that is strange and dreadful in the aspect of the world, a counter movement is at work. There is life among us, purpose, effort. Physical life may be said to be the continual struggle every moment against surrounding and imminent death : the resistance of that undiscoverable principle within us which makes us what we are—against unceasing forces, attacking, exhausting, consuming it ; and it holds its own and lasts, by replacing waste, by repairing injuries, by counteracting and repelling poisons. Just so, in the dispensation by which God, with a patience which has lasted throughout all the ages, seeks to bring back our race to Himself ; *so* is that

spiritual life maintained among mankind, which seems to hang on such slender threads, and to be threatened by such formidable dangers, and yet survives, and is the only road to the perfection for which we were made. We see the ceaseless tendency downwards, but we see too the unceasing recoil from it. The disheartening spectacle is before our eyes of good wearing out—of good men tiring of what made them good—of noblest things becoming base in the using—of power wasted on self-destruction—of truth and height of character swerving from its road and dwindling into unreality and mean-ness. But this is not the whole of our experience. It is a balance of forces, between the powers of mis-chief and decay and the antagonist powers of repair. Side by side with miserable failure rise up new enter-prises of improvement. The good which foolish or bad men brought to nought to-day is replaced to-morrow by another form of it, from the inexhaustible store of Him from whom all good things do come. All seems at one moment drifting to confusion—we say it is vain to fight against the current ; we think that all has been lost—when, the next, the tide comes back in its strength to save us, and behold, more than we had lost is recovered. Decay eats into what is strong, saps the sources of life, consumes and lays waste what is beautiful and glorious ; then comes the bold eager hope, and the zeal of the restorer, calling things back to what they should be.

> Say not the struggle nought availeth,
>   The labour and the wounds are vain,
> The enemy faints not, nor faileth,
>   And as things have been they remain.

If hopes were dupes, fears may be liars ;
    It may be, in yon smoke concealed,
Your comrades chase e'en now the fliers,
    And, but for you, possess the field.

For while the tired waves, vainly breaking,
    Seem here no painful inch to gain,
Far back, through creeks and inlets making,
    Comes silent, flooding in, the main ;

And not by eastern windows only,
    When daylight comes, comes in the light,
In front, the sun climbs slow, how slowly,
    But westward, look, the land is bright.[1]

And thus, silently, slowly, painfully, almost insensibly, is built up out of human souls and lives the spiritual house of God amid the conflicts and fluctuations of time ; its fortunes vary, it bears many a blow and mark from disaster and change and human folly ; yet it rises. The threatening forces of destruction seem to justify the fears or the presages, which confound it with those mortal things that are doomed sooner or later to perish. But the gracious powers which heal and renew and replace and rebuild are as subtle and quick and manifold and untiring as those of ruin. They do their work often out of human sight, often not as human thought would look for ; but through the alternations of wasting and restoration, through the uncertainties and vicissitudes, the apparent progress and apparent reverses of what passes in the world, they prepare for the fulfilment of God's purposes ; they are the sure pledge that those purposes will be fulfilled.

So it is :—so are things kept wholesome and hope-

[1] Clough's *Poems* (ed. 1888), p. 452.

ful ; so is evil kept at bay, in ways which tell us at
once of our own weakness, and of a strength which
will never be allowed to fail us.   Like most things
here, they bring with them both pain and joy.   The
forms in which *here* we mostly know good, are those
of healing, remedy, repair, restoration; the compassion
and mercy and pitying love of God, and what man
can do to copy it in charity and sacrifice.   They
run through all our language about the history of
souls—the new birth, repentance, a renewed life,
the image of God regained.   We live, as I said
before, in the midst of ruins—ruins of nature, ruins
of fashion and opinions gone by, ruins of human
works, and pride, and success, ruins of human
generations and all their passions and interests, the
ruins of our former lives and former selves ; but
ruins, out of which fresh life is ever springing, which
are ever becoming new, and the materials of better
things, and more beautiful and perfect.   Yes, it is
" truth "

> That men may rise on stepping stones
> Of their dead selves to higher things.[1]

But still it is, to eyes *here*, a chequered prospect.
If we live long enough, we may see things change
for the better, in ways which, when we were young,
we never dared to dream of or hope for.   But if
we live long enough, we shall, also, certainly see ideas,
prospects, achievements, memories, which we set
most store by, passing out of date and a new world
coming in, of blended good and evil, but which is
not ours—which is leaving us fast behind in its
sympathies and aims—which it is one of the pains

[1] *In Memoriam*, i.

of advancing years not to be able to keep up with or understand. No doubt, what we are improving and renewing will one day be judged, perhaps be found fault with, be undone, just as we have tried to better what was left to us imperfect. But when a pang shoots through us at such thoughts, let us remember that this unceasing destiny of change, this memorial of our " bondage to decay," also carries with it all the hopes and possibilities of improvement to the world, and points onward to their accomplishment at last. The perfect work which needs no mercy, which asks no forgiveness, which requires no correction, which calls for and admits of no repair— *that* is for the state which is to come.

2. For—to come to the second point, the end of all these wonderful processes—as there is *one* decay and *one* overthrow, for which there is no restoration here, the overthrow of death, so there *is* a restoration beyond it, on which no further change can pass. Here, we rebuild, we renew, we remould and refashion our institutions, our lives, our dwelling-houses, our household thoughts : we try, if we are wise, to bring them nearer and nearer to that excellence, unattainable as it is, which God has made us long for ; we hold in our hands wonderful powers of self-correction, remedy, compensation. But at last we meet with that for which here there is no repair, no renewing. There is a break and pause in that familiar order of continual change. Hopes, and fears, and ignorance, and success, and failure give place to the fixity, the certainties of death. But then begins the *other* order—the order of the unchangeable, the order of the perfect and the final. In that order, the in-

corruptible takes the place of the decaying and the perishing, and life triumphs without the companionship of death. The goal is reached : the preparation, the slow discipline of improvement, the painful and dangerous trial, are left behind. That is what is reserved for us after all our changes—for us, if at last, by God's all-pitying, all-forgiving grace, we are counted worthy ; for us, if at last we find mercy—we, to whom it is so hard to correct what is amiss in us, and who with all our trying do so little. The shattered tabernacle is to pass into a house not made with hands, eternal in the heavens ; the bones which God had broken, the humbled and dishonoured form of the dead, shall once more be restored—once and for all. Once more, and then for ever, " the eyes of the blind shall be opened, and the ears of the deaf be unstopped . . . and the tongue of the dumb sing " ; for One is coming, " who shall change our vile body, that it may be fashioned like unto His glorious body." In place of what we have *here* of *best*, will be the inheritance of the saints in light, the victory over sin and pain and death, the Vision of God. And in place of what we have here of *worst*, there will be that which will make up for all losses, and recompense all toil, and obliterate all sufferings, and efface the memory of even shame—the voice of acceptance from our Master, the Holy One and the True—" Well done, thou good and faithful servant " ; the rest that never shall be broken; the benediction which shall wipe away for ever all tears from all eyes.

Thoughts like these come naturally into our minds amid the satisfactions —the rightful satisfactions—of

a day like this. You do well to keep festival over the
completion of your work. You have been distressed
at the waste made by time and neglect, and your
hearts have kindled in you to repair it. You have
understood something of the mingled shame and indignation and joy and hope which filled the children
of the returning captivity of Judah, and burst forth
in those Psalms of Degrees which add such deep and
pathetic interest to the histories of Ezra and Nehe-
miah. You have stirred yourselves up to do your
part in your time against the ceaseless encroachments
of indifference and careless selfishness, and now you
have good reason to rejoice to see what has come of
your efforts. You will not think that I want to
throw a shade on your rejoicing, if I remind you
that there is no building, no renewing here for
eternity ; that what you make new must again grow
old, what you build, those after you may pull down.
What is all restoring here, but making fresh and
vigorous for our time and according to our duty, that
which must grow obsolete when we are gone ? Tastes
change and work wears out, and what one age
admires another throws aside. " For the fashion of
this world passeth away." But there is that beyond
it, which does *not* pass away. There is that which,
when once it is made new, never grows old. There
is a restoration of what is decayed, a recovery of
lost beauty and majesty, which, when once it has
been revealed, shall never more be out of date. See,
in what you are doing and celebrating to-day, the
presage and figure of that eternal consummation.
See, in the share which you take in the ever-continu-
ing necessities of repair and improvement, the pledge

and sign, that the crooked shall at last be made
straight, and the ruins built again ; that that magnificent promise which echoes once and again throughout Isaiah's prophecy shall be in truth fulfilled—
" They shall build the old wastes, they shall raise
up the former desolations"; "Thou shalt raise up
the foundations of many generations ; and thou shalt
be called, The repairer of the breach, The restorer of
paths to dwell in."   Look on your work to-day, not
in its earthly perishableness, but as your offering in
the sight of the Lord of all the ages, to attest your
confidence in His Eternal Word. Go forward in your
thoughts to that great time, when God, " who has so
wonderfully created man and more wonderfully redeemed him,"[1] shall at length own for ever the work
of His own hands : " when the world shall know and
see the restoring of the things that have been cast
down, the renewing of the things that have grown old,
the return of all things once more to their perfection,
through Him in whom they took their beginning—
Jesus Christ the Lord."[1]

[1] Cf. Collects in Roman Missal (mixture of the chalice), and Office
for Easter Eve.

XXI

THE TIMES AND SEASONS OF GOD'S WORKING[1]

"And He said unto them, It is not for you to know the times or the seasons, which the Father hath put in His own power. But ye shall receive power, after that the Holy Ghost has come upon you: and ye shall be witnesses unto Me both in Jerusalem, and in all Judæa, and in Samaria, and unto the uttermost part of the earth."
—ACTS i. 7, 8.

THE Apostles felt themselves standing on the threshold of a new world when they asked the question to which these words were the answer. Dimly, indeed, and vaguely, for they knew as yet but little of the realities amid which they stood, and of the momentous changes which had passed over the prospects of mankind. They were as men suddenly transported to a new sphere where all proportions and perspectives were strange and different, and defied their measurements. Still, they felt that a new age had come; and the form in which Jewish imagination and Jewish hopes had shaped it out of the visions and promises of prophecy at once presented itself to their minds—"Wilt Thou at this

[1] Preached at the opening of the Chapel of St. Oswald's School, Ellesmere, 1884.

time restore—art Thou at this time restoring—the kingdom to Israel?" *Any* reversal of present things might be thought of; for one thing was certain: the old fundamental conditions of life and death were altered before them; their Teacher and Master, whom they had seen die, was alive again from the dead, was with them once more as of old, and though, as was inevitable after such a change, in new and unaccustomed relations to them, could still be seen with their eyes and handled with their hands. What was this overwhelming, unexampled fact the beginning of? What unthought-of, unhoped-for, inconceivable changes did it announce and bring in? Plainly they were on the eve of a revolution such as the world had not yet seen. What more natural than that they should wish to look down the ages that were coming—to descry something of what was to follow, of what must be close at hand, for themselves and for all that they loved and cared about?

It was a natural question, but in itself a hopeless one. To understand the answer to a question, there must be not only the truth and fulness of the information given, but the prepared and experienced and illuminated mind. And at that period of their training, the answer to their question, if it had been put before them, would have come with all the perplexities of an enigma, would have found them incapable of the faintest approach to comprehending it. For it would have been the history of the Christian Church. Imagine the vision of the actual history of the Christian Church, as it has been in fact, as it was known in God's foresight, unrolled before them at that moment. What could they have made

of it?   How could they have taken it in?   What a
scene of confusion, what an inconceivable series of
contradictions and surprises, of perplexing mixtures
of good and evil, of unheard-of triumphs and shocks
of failure, would it have looked to men with only
their experience.   Even that early part of it which
was to fall within the limit of their lives, even that
part of it told in the Book of the Acts, would have
been to them then as the interests of statesmen, or
the debates of a Parliament, or the controversies of
science in the schools, are to the minds of children:
different from all their assumptions, not to be
adjusted to their common ways of thinking.   Their
question was not only a premature one: it was one
which till they were changed, in spirit and level of
thought, it would have been useless to answer, for
the answer could not have been understood.

And so it was answered, as untimely and unpro-
fitable questions were so often answered by Jesus
Christ.   He brought back the questioners to a sense
of their true position, and its true proportions, in that
immense scene of God's purposes and action of which
the greater part is veiled from mortal knowledge.
And on the other hand, in place of an idle longing
to know what man cannot know, He set before them
the definite duty and business which they *could* do,
and which He had called them to do, and the gifts
with which they were to be equipped for their special
service at that special time.   " Times and seasons
are for Him whose wisdom and whose will, from the
beginning to the end, orders all things ; leave them
alone ; they are not for you ; you could make no
use of the knowledge, if it was possible for you to

have it.   But in the fulfilment of God's order, you have, indeed, your own—a unique and indispensable —place. God wants you. God has called you. God has not forgotten you, nor the helps and powers necessary for that work on which the whole history of the future turns.   The Holy Ghost shall come on you, and with Him power for that work in which you succeed to Me. *You* have seen *Me*. You have heard Me. You have handled Me. You knew Me before the cross. You knew Me after. On you are the generations to come to depend for that witness of the reality of My Presence, of the meaning of My victory. That is your calling ; is it not enough for you ? Leave 'times and seasons' to Him in whose hands they are." Yes, that company were to shape the new world that was coming ; but they were not to know it, nor the wonders of what they themselves were doing.

Does not this scene represent and shadow forth what has often happened in the history of the Church ? How often have men, more or less consciously, asked the question analogous to that of the Apostles—Is not the time now come at length for the restoration and settlement of the Kingdom of God, for the full accomplishment of the prophecies ? Have they not been led, as the Apostles were, by some signal evidence of God's delivering and quickening power, to surmise, whether this is not at last the glorious close, the end of the long waiting, the dawn of the new day ? The Edict of Milan stops the persecution : the judgment of Nicæa clears and declares for good the faith of Christendom :—What is there for the Church now but to enter on her inheritance and do

her work in peace ?   Augustine is raised up to meet
the questions and difficulties of theology, a match for
every debate, profoundly sympathetic with the whole
range of human thought and human affection :—Was
not here the very master and teacher the Church
needed to make the path of Christian wisdom and
knowledge safe and certain ?   Might it not be hoped
that the appearance of such a teacher meant that the
times of controversy and dissension should now be
over ?   And so, when some superhuman efforts had
wrought their results, when some decisive victory had
been gained over abuses or error, when some great
outburst of zeal and charity had moved society and
won men's hearts—it seemed as if all now was going
to be settled in final obedience to Christ—this or
that one great obstacle overcome, and the Church
will be in harbour.   The barbarians were converted
to the purity and earnestness of saints ; power was
concentrated in the hands of great kings and pontiffs ;
great armies of Christian champions rose as it were
out of the ground, out of the masses of the poor and
lowly, to witness practically to the Sermon on the
Mount, to faith in an unseen but ever-present Christ ;
the great Christian schools reigned over the intellect
of the world.   Is not this at length the restoration
of the Kingdom ?   Is not the Church now going to
blossom and be at rest ?   When great abuses became
intolerable they were attacked and partly swept away
by a great reform ; now then, so was the hope and
assurance, we shall see an end to what corrupted and
disgraced Christendom.   Or a great religious movement stirs the Church.   The Spirit of God moves on
the waters—renews the face of the earth.   Where

there was coldness there is zeal ; where there was
luxury and selfishness there is sacrifice ; where there
was the dulness of a routine religion there is the joy
and light of the converted, the peace of the faithful
and true.   Is not the meaning of this that at last a
great change is indeed at hand in men's ideas of
religion ; that at last the day is come for its purity,
its simplicity, its honesty, its manliness, its depth, its
perseverance ?—

> Dies venit, dies tua,
> In qua reflorent omnia.

We wistfully ask—Are we standing where that day
is breaking ?

Ah ! my brethren, it is not for men on earth " to
know the times or the seasons, which the Father hath
put in His own power "—to forecast the ways of His
Providence, to venture into the secret of His counsels,
to assume to know enough to say how He will shape
His work, what He will create and what destroy,
what He will bring to pass, what He will permit and
tolerate in the time to come.   Former generations
thought that they knew, and were mistaken.   Beyond
Nicæa, and beyond St. Augustine, and beyond the
reforms of the eleventh century, or the thirteenth, or
the sixteenth, the fortunes of the Church were to go
through vicissitudes that no one then counted on ;
her trials and her activity and her influence ,were
still to take ever unthought-of shapes.   Beyond the
hopes of the most sanguine and beyond the alarms
of the most anxious, new achievements were to
follow, new mischiefs to threaten.   Things have gone,
in fact, better and worse than men beforehand could

possibly imagine.   Even the fourth century could not
have imagined the varied, the amazing history of the
saints who were to come ; it could not have imagined
the inconceivable perversity and folly and depths of
corruption which the world was to see in Christians
and in the government of the Church ; it could not
have conceived possible the coexistence of great
evil with unsuspected forces of recovery, with the
power to retrieve and to compensate.   What would
the fourth century have said if it could have looked
forward to the relaxation of that stern penitential
discipline on which it relied, of which it was so
jealous ?   What would it have said if it could have
foreseen the great shattering of the unity of Christendom, the break up of East and West, and then the
break up of the West ?   Could they have conceived
the faith surviving the shock ?   Could men have conceived, with whatever losses and drawbacks, the main-
tenance of serious and vigorous morality, the love, still
strong and loyal, of righteousness and purity and truth?
In each generation a state of things which they could
not foresee or understand was to follow them.   But
to each was assigned what was the necessary duty of
their time ; and to each were given gifts of light and
power from their Master.   It was not for them to
know ; but to each generation was given all that was
needful to fulfil the responsibilities imposed upon it,
to prepare the way for that triumph which was to
be seen *at last ;* but *not now.*

An occasion like this, which brings us together to
mark another step in one of the greatest religious
enterprises of our time, naturally prompts thoughts
which measure the present and go out to the future.

It seems to me just now to be a remarkable moment.
I do not know that I recollect any one precisely
like it in the fifty years which have made the religious
history of this century so eventful. It is a pause—
not of defeat, nor of weariness, nor of fear, nor of
exhaustion ; but after long conflicts, of quiet; after
long controversies, of rest from the strife of tongues ;
after long striving, of recognition of a higher level
and worthier standard in important things; after
violent explosions of exasperation and suspicion, a
welcoming of the wisdom and the beauty of a larger
patience and a nobler tolerance ; after extravagant
acts and unmeasured words, of soberness and
recollection. I say, a pause, for none of us know
enough to say how long it may last, and how far it
is the sign and precursor of a permanent state of
things. But I think it is true to say that there has
been for some time lately a remarkable interval—
a "peace of the Church"—a time when sympathy
and the realising of the truths of Christian fellowship,
and a sense of the awful needs and dangers of society,
and a generous acknowledgment of self-devoted
efforts to meet them, have overborne the old forces
of repulsion and estrangement, strong as they were,
and for a while have commanded and forced the
fighters to stay their fighting. A pause, a breathing
time, a stillness and calm, taking its rise in the
solemnities and peace of death-beds, and consecrated
by their memories. And when in this moment—
it may be a mere passing one—of pause and calm,
our minds go back over the past, what a wonderful,
overpowering sense of change comes over them—
change which, with all drawbacks—and they are

many and very serious—has been for the advantage of the cause of Christ and His Church. It has robbed us of much that was ours : we think of what the Church had *then*, and has *now*, at the great seats and centres of English education ; but if it has impaired our machinery, it has quickened and stimulated men. Fifty years ago, I can remember it, a young man was ashamed to kneel down in church : he would have thought it unfashionable ; he would have thought it affectation. Fifty years ago, for a young man to stay for Holy Communion would have seemed even to good people eccentric and unreal, a profession beyond his years. Fifty years ago there were churches which hardly saw the Eucharist from year's end to year's end. Fifty years ago, except in the Prayer Book, except in the ideas and perhaps the shy practice of a few obscure students or devout observers of ancient usage, that which is the foremost and indispensable part of Christian worship was looked upon as something meant exclusively for the stricter and more devout few, or as the rare and occasional incentive to a flagging faith. Fifty years ago, there was scarcely the pretence of any special training, at least in the Church, for the Christian ministry, and except in special instances, the poorest preparation either for confirmation or orders. Fifty years ago, who dreamed of attempting to rally the masses, or even the middle class, despaired of and despised as they were, to an intelligent loyalty to the Church ? Who recognised adequately the tremendous obligation of providing for those masses an education which they could not give themselves, or realised the terrible penalty of not doing so in time? Who thought then that by the end of fifty years a vast and energetic Episcopate, a new ecclesiastical world in America and the Colonies, would have come into existence, "to redress," as it was said on another occasion, "the balance of the old Latin world"? Who thought of anything beyond the kind of beneficence, genuine and gracious as it was, of women like Elizabeth Fry? Who thought of men and women, gently nurtured and refined, with the choice of an easy life before them, choosing in numbers and with cheerful hearts to give up everything in order to nurse the sick, to live *with* the poor and *as* the poor, to be the daily companions of the sinners and the miserable? Who thought then of crowded churches, except to hear the eloquence of the favourite preacher of the hour? Who would have thought of seeing working men, in their guilds and societies, gathering in numbers to early Communion at a cathedral altar? God forbid that we should forget how much serious and active goodness there was in those days, how much earnest and persevering devotion, how much purity and faith, and manly force and unostentatious self-control, how much humble simplicity of life,—the days of Joshua Watson, and William Stevens, and Norris of Hackney, the days of Henry Martyn, and Wilberforce, and Simeon. Things would have gone very differently if there had not been the reality of religion deep in the heart of the Church. But men living can remember how its outward and public aspect, as it looked to spectators in a stirring and almost revolutionary time, was at best one of apathy, and respectable routine, and timid caution ; and how

an incapacity for originality, a dread of enthusiasm and enterprise, marked an institution which
represented that Divine Society, which had dared to
undertake the conquest of the world. Whatever these
changes mean, whatever they are worth, there they
are; and surely they are not for nought. It is not
of evil, that there has come the deeper and more
energetic love of the brethren, the keener conscience
of duty and sin, the more awful sense of God's
greatness and goodness, the more eager desire to
exalt and proclaim His Name. There were those
who in those days asked in despair—in unwise,
unwarrantable, but not unnatural, despair—but they
asked, " Can these bones live ? " Our eyes, the
world, have seen what is the answer.

What is this, then—a lull, a gleam of sunshine in
the progress of the storm ? or the first step in a new
and more blessed order, long prayed for, now granted?
Ah ! my brethren, our thoughts go back to the lessons
of the eve of the Ascension. Times and seasons
are out of our hands, out of our forecasting. Anticipation is seldom more than idle work. No stranger
collection of mistakes and surprises could be made
than a list of the falsified predictions of the wisest
men. History is full of them. We know not what
awaits us ; and with all that makes us glad, no one
can be blind to changes, to presages, of a very
different kind. We see in our day energy, daring,
confidence, force of character, even self-devotion,
given, as I don't think they were ever given before,
to the overthrow, the suppression, the extinction of
what we believe to be the hopes of mankind. I am
not speaking of our own case alone ; Christendom,

after all, is one, and all are interested in the fortunes
of every part ; and all over Christendom there is the
same awful shadow.   *Apparent diræ facies.*   Not
doubtfully visible in the darkness of

> The appalling future as it nearer draws,[1]

there are the new enemies with which Christian faith,
and all that it involves and protects, will have to
reckon.   To the old spirit of mockery, coarse or
refined, to the old wrangle of argument, also coarse
or refined, has succeeded the spirit of grave, measured,
determined negation—no longer raising questions
and urging objections, but starting from the assumption that everything is decisively and finally ruled
against us, that all intelligence and all honesty, it
may be reluctantly, views our claims as hopeless.
It is in the air, this implacable foe.   It fears not to
speak out ; it imposes its axioms and its principles
on society and legislation ; but, in still more subtle
and impalpable ways, it meets us at every turn, in
literature, in the press, in what furnishes nine-tenths
of the reading and thinking of the thousands who
read.   I do not forget how very bad, how very un-
believing the old days often were, when religion
seemed to rule unquestioned.   I do not forget that
in the very heart of the Middle Ages—the ages, as
they are called, of faith—there lurked a spirit of
audacious revolt, of a fierce, bitter, aggressive unbelief.
But never, I think, has unbelief appealed so widely,
so boldly, and with so much fatal effect, to the
masses.   And never were the sources of public
thought so charged with deliberate unbelief ; never

---

[1] *The Christian Year*, Advent Sunday.

had so many of the minds which led their generation
in speculation, in culture, in judgment on the past,
in laying down the political and social lines of the
future, accepted, though perhaps with courteous and
even sympathetic respect for religion, yet with settled
and calm decision, some one or other of those deadly
philosophies which make serious religion impossible.

Thus there is before us a future of great hope,
and with it, also, a future of ghastliest menace.
Which is most likely?   We cannot tell.

> If hopes were dupes, fears may be liars ; [1]

and the Divine Word comes back—" It is not for you
to know the times or the seasons."   But what we do
know is that the promise is to us as much as to the
Twelve—" Lo, I am with you alway—all the days—
even unto the end of the world."   What we do know
is our office and charge and duty, to be witnesses, as
they were, to Christ crucified and risen—to be
witnesses, as they could not be, to all that has been
done for that City of God which carries in its bosom
the hopes of men.   Ask not how the world is to go
on.   Be content with knowing that you are called to
act upon it—to act upon it, if you have the heart, if
you have the wisdom, with power of which you know
not the limit.   In that faith began, with such sure
foresight, in that faith has been carried on, with such
undecaying conviction, that great Institution [2] which

---

[1] Clough's *Poems*, p. 452.

[2] The Institution to which allusion is made is St. Nicolas College,
founded at Shoreham by Canon Woodard, whose aim was to bring
Public School Education on definite Church principles within the reach
of all classes above those for which elementary education is provided.
Ellesmere College is intended for the lower middle class, and is one of
schools belonging to the Midland Branch of Canon Woodard's Society.

has brought us here to-day, and which has sought on so noble a scale to retrieve the unfaithfulness and to overtake the shortcomings of past times ; which has sought, in such varied and skilful ways, to recover and establish for the Church and for Church religion its due influence on the education of the middle classes. It was one of the strange oversights of former times that the absence or weakness of this influence on the middle classes was hardly noticed and heeded by Churchmen. They thought of the poor ; not of the tradesmen and farmers. Forty years ago an individual clergyman, deeply impressed with the want and the danger, devoted his life to a great and systematic effort to regain what was lost. What the success has been there is no need to tell ; look at the banners which led your procession. But what is worth observing is this, that education is one of those forces by which the course of things cannot but be affected, and the future controlled and shaped ; and education is eminently one of those things which it *is* in our power, in the power of each generation to set in action or to neglect. It depends on us, as many other things do not depend, what we will do with our children—whether and how we teach and train them. Will we take the trouble ? will we be at the expense ? will we choose fit instruments ? will we inspire those instruments with our own convictions and purpose? Practically there is no limit to its working, but the interest and the means of those who promote it. If there is anything certain, it is that where there is a good education, men will seek it for their children. And a good education is a thing which we can supply, if we will go about it.

We need not, it is a most important point to re-member—we need not let education on a great scale slip out of our hands. If we do, I do not say that God will not find other means to recruit, perhaps to reinvigorate, His Church; but we shall have a heavy account to give, if from negligence, or want of courage, or want of public spirit, or fear of spending, we throw away that natural and immense power over the future which God has placed in our hands.

We have lost much. Let us be honest, and say that we deserved to lose it. We certainly did not turn to due account the immense privileges which had come down to us. There was a time when boldness, and earnestness, and faithfulness on the part of the Church and its leaders might have so far got hold of the education of the country, that it would have been almost impossible without violence to have deprived us of it.[1] That time is gone by; we find ourselves with formidable rivals, and the spirit of the day against us. Part of the offered chance is withdrawn and will not be repeated; but part of it still remains, and is still offered to us, on its strict conditions. Here in England at least we may still count in the long run on fair play. If we choose to accept all that is involved in a serious effort—trouble, expense, opposition, worry, occasional mistakes and disappointment — there is a vast province still open to us to occupy. God grant us the will. To have recovered for Christ and His Church so important a part of the education of the

. [1] Cf. a letter from Dean Hook to Mr. Gladstone, 1843: *Life of Dean Hook* (abridged edition), p. 346.

country, by patience and sacrifice and the enthusiasm
of honest work, may console us for much that is
dark and threatening in the future.   It is a token
that the power of Christ is still with us.   My
brethren, let us take courage from all that He has
done for us and shown us, from our wonderful
history.   Let us arise and go forward, in the words
of your motto, and like your hero-saint, King
Oswald—" *Pro patria dimicantes* "[1]—fighting against
sin and sloth and ignorance; fighting for our true
home and country, the Church of God ; fighting like
men for this dear and beautiful England.

[1] " *Pro patria dimicans*," the motto of King Oswald (Bede, iii. 9),
taken as the motto of the school.

THE END

Printed by R. & R. Clark, Limited, *Edinburgh.*

By R. W. CHURCH, D.C.L.,

Late Dean of St. Paul's.

THE GIFTS OF CIVILISATION, and other Sermons and Lectures delivered at Oxford and in St. Paul's Cathedral. Second Edition. Crown 8vo. 7s. 6d.

GUARDIAN.—"A suggestive and fascinating volume, which, if we mistake not, will make its way in quarters where ordinary sermons are but little read, and tell upon the world by its singular adaptation to the more serious of modern thought."

ADVENT SERMONS. 1885. Crown 8vo. 4s. 6d.

GUARDIAN.—"They are worthy of the preacher, and therefore worthy to rank among the great sermons of our Church; and not only so, but they will be found full of strengthening and consoling power for simple and devout Christians, whose minds are cast down and oppressed by the thought of the unknown future that lies before them."

HUMAN LIFE AND ITS CONDITIONS. Sermons preached before the University of Oxford in 1876-1878, with Three Ordination Sermons. Second Edition. Crown 8vo. 6s.

ACADEMY.—"They never aim at oratorical display, nor attain any high flight of passionate utterance, yet we are sensible throughout of an earnest though controlled enthusiasm."

CATHEDRAL AND UNIVERSITY SERMONS. Crown 8vo. 6s.

VILLAGE SERMONS. Preached at Whatley. Crown 8vo. 6s.

SCOTSMAN.—"The thinking is clear as crystal, and the language simplicity itself. . . . The discourses are of a very practical kind, and enforce duty with a mingled fidelity and kindliness which is altogether admirable."

VILLAGE SERMONS. Second Series. Crown 8vo. 6s.

THE SACRED POETRY OF EARLY RELIGIONS. Two Lectures in St. Paul's Cathedral. Second Edition. Pott 8vo. 1s.

LITERARY WORLD.—"There are some choice and suggestive thoughts in this little volume, which we commend to all theological students."

MACMILLAN AND CO., LONDON.

WORKS BY J. B. LIGHTFOOT, D.D.,

Late Bishop of Durham.

NOTES ON EPISTLES OF ST. PAUL FROM UNPUBLISHED COMMENTARIES. 8vo. 12s.

ST. PAUL'S EPISTLE TO THE GALATIANS. A Revised Text, with Introduction, Notes, and Dissertations. 20th Thousand. 8vo. 12s.

ST. PAUL'S EPISTLE TO THE PHILIPPIANS. A Revised Text, with Introduction, etc. 19th Thousand. 8vo. 12s.

ST. PAUL'S EPISTLES TO THE COLOSSIANS AND TO PHILEMON. A Revised Text, with Introductions, Notes, and Dissertations. 14th Thousand. 8vo. 12s.

DISSERTATIONS ON THE APOSTOLIC AGE. *Reprinted* from the editions of St. Paul's Epistles. Second Edition. 8vo. Cloth. 14s.

THE APOSTOLIC FATHERS. PART I. ST. CLEMENT OF ROME. A Revised Text, with Introductions, Notes, Dissertations, and Translations. Second Edition. 2 vols. 8vo. 32s.

THE APOSTOLIC FATHERS. PART II. ST. IGNATIUS. ST. POLYCARP. Revised Texts, with Introductions, Notes, Dissertations, and Translations. 2nd Thousand. 3 vols. 8vo. 48s.

THE APOSTOLIC FATHERS. Abridged Edition. With short Introductions, Greek Text, and English Translations. 3rd Thousand. 8vo. 16s.

ESSAYS ON THE WORK ENTITLED "SUPERNATURAL RELIGION." Second Edition. 8vo. 10s. 6d.

ON A FRESH REVISION OF THE ENGLISH NEW TESTAMENT. Third Edition. Crown 8vo. 7s. 6d.

LEADERS IN THE NORTHERN CHURCH. Durham Sermons. 5th Thousand. Crown 8vo. 6s.

ORDINATION ADDRESSES AND COUNSELS TO CLERGY. Third Thousand. Crown 8vo. 6s.

CAMBRIDGE SERMONS. 3rd Thousand. Crown 8vo. 6s.

SERMONS PREACHED IN ST. PAUL'S. 3rd Thousand. Crown 8vo. 6s.

SERMONS ON SPECIAL OCCASIONS. 2nd Thousand. Crown 8vo. 6s.

BIBLICAL ESSAYS. 2nd Thousand. 8vo. 12s.

MACMILLAN AND CO., LONDON.

WORKS BY B. F. WESTCOTT, D.D.,

Bishop of Durham.

THE INCARNATION AND COMMON LIFE. Crown 8vo. 9s.

THE GOSPEL OF LIFE: Thoughts Introductory to the Study of Christian Doctrine. Second Edition. 6s.

ESSAYS—THE HISTORY OF RELIGIOUS THOUGHT IN THE WEST. 4th Thousand. 5s.

A GENERAL SURVEY OF THE HISTORY OF THE CANON OF THE NEW TESTAMENT DURING THE FIRST FOUR CENTURIES. Sixth Edition, revised. 10s. 6d.

THE BIBLE IN THE CHURCH: A popular account of the Collection and Reception of the Holy Scriptures in the Christian Churches. 15th Thousand. Pott 8vo. 4s. 6d.

INTRODUCTION TO THE STUDY OF THE FOUR GOSPELS. Eighth Edition. 10s. 6d.

THE GOSPEL OF THE RESURRECTION. Thoughts on its Relation to Reason and History. Seventh Edition. Crown 8vo. 6s.

THE REVELATION OF THE RISEN LORD. Fifth Edition. Crown 8vo. 6s.

THE HISTORIC FAITH. Short Lectures on the Apostles' Creed. Fifth Edition. Crown 8vo. 6s.

THE REVELATION OF THE FATHER. Short Lectures on the Titles of the Lord in the Gospel of St. John. Second Edition. Crown 8vo. 6s.

CHRISTUS CONSUMMATOR, and other Sermons. Third Edition. Crown 8vo. 6s.

SOME THOUGHTS FROM THE ORDINAL. Crown 8vo. 1s. 6d.

SOCIAL ASPECTS OF CHRISTIANITY. Second Edition. Crown 8vo. 6s.

THE VICTORY OF THE CROSS. Second Edition. 3s. 6d.

GIFTS FOR MINISTRY. Addresses to Candidates for Ordination. Crown 8vo. 1s. 6d.

THE EPISTLE TO THE HEBREWS. The Greek Text, with Notes and Essays. Second Edition. 8vo. 14s.

THE EPISTLES OF ST. JOHN. The Greek Text, with Notes and Essays. Third Edition. 8vo. 12s. 6d.

THOUGHTS ON REVELATION AND LIFE. Being Selections from the Writings of Bishop WESTCOTT. Arranged and Edited by Rev. STEPHEN PHILLIPS. 2nd Thousand. Crown 8vo. 6s.

THE NEW TESTAMENT IN THE ORIGINAL GREEK. The Text revised by BROOKE FOSS WESTCOTT, D.D., and FENTON JOHN ANTHONY HORT, D.D., Vol. I. Text. Vol. II. Introduction and Appendix. Crown 8vo. 10s. 6d. each.

MACMILLAN AND CO., LONDON.